FUR NATION

'*Fur Nation* is a fascinating romp through a   ... of texts and historical moments, from Jules Verne to Isaac Mizrahi, from Gene Tierney to Brigitte Bardot. Witty and often naughty, Nadeau is also deadly serious and profound, making important discoveries and connections, and reasserting the importance of gender, sexuality and materiality in all historical constructions of nations and cultures.'

Professor Thomas Waugh, *Concordia University*

Fur Nation traces the interwoven relationships between sexuality, national identity, and colonialism. Chantal Nadeau shows how Canada, a white settler colony, bases i-   ~conomy based on wo

Nadeau t   udies, including H   Bardot and her whi

Nadeau b   aring, exploiting (ture's master buil   ilized around fem   iomic developmei   elf is conceived a   ly are the fabric o

Chantal N;   ordia University,

WRITING CORPOREALITIES
Series Editor: Elspeth Probyn

This series seeks to encourage innovative writing about corporealities. It takes as a leading premise the fact that writing and studying embodied forms of sociality are intricately mutually informing. The type of work presented under the rubric of this series is therefore engaged and engaging, as it understands that writing itself is an embodied and social activity. The range of theoretical perspectives privileged may be wide but the common point of departure is a certain *parti pris* to study the materiality of contemporary processes and realities. Beyond discrete description, through different forms of writing, bodies, discourses, forms of power, histories and stories are put in play order to inform other relations, other corporeal realities.

AIDS AND THE BODY POLITIC
Biomedicine and Sexual Difference
Catherine Waldby

WILD SCIENCE
Reading Feminism, Medicine and the Media
Edited by Janine Marchessault and Kim Sawchuk

Forthcoming:
THE SPECTACLE OF VIOLENCE
Homophobia, Gender and Knowledge
Gail Mason

FUR NATION

From the Beaver to Brigitte Bardot

Chantal Nadeau

London & New York

First published 2001
by Routledge
11 New Fetter Lane, London EC4P 4EE

Simultaneously published in the USA and Canada
by Routledge
29 West 35th Street, New York, NY 10001

Routledge is an imprint of the Taylor & Francis Group

© 2001 Chantal Nadeau

Typeset in Garamond 3 by
Keystroke, Jacaranda Lodge, Wolverhampton
Printed and bound in Great Britain by
Biddles Ltd, Guildford and King's Lynn

British Library Cataloguing in Publication Data
A catalogue record for this book is available from the British Library

Library of Congress Cataloging in Publication Data
Nadeau, Chantal, 1963–
Fur nation: from the beaver to Brigitte Bardot / Chantal Nadeau.
p. cm.
Includes bibliographical references and index.
1. Fur garments. 2. Fur trade—Canada. I. Title.
TT525 .N33 2001
391′.2—dc21
00–065295

ISBN 0–415–15873–7 (hbk)
ISBN 0–415–15874–5 (pbk)

CONTENTS

ILLUSTRATIONS

ACKNOWLEDGMENTS

This book would have never existed without the chorus of fur ladies, real and fake, who constantly gave me their support, relentlessly indulging my own crazy quest for the beaver. First, my thanks to two wonderful research assistants, Caroline Martel and Tamara H. Vukov without whom I could not have gathered all the kooky and rich information necessary for this project. Their priceless contribution to the shaping of this book has been a constant liberatory intellectual adventure. "Fur is fun," was the motto and we certainly did explore fur in all its playful potential. Big hugs and purry thanks to two buddies in furs who have helped me to find my trail at the end of the manuscript. To Kevin Crombie, for copy editing, again to Tamara, for her textual shearings, stylistic revisions, and incommensurable complicity in my fur hallucinations.

This research encompasses tremendous primary material, and my gratitude goes to the fur ladies in the archives for being so resourceful and excited about this book. Specifically, I wish to thank Eva Major-Mahorty, Jennifer Devine and Jean McPherson from the National Archives of Canada; Debra Moore and Anne Morton from the Hudson's Bay Company Archives; Suzanne Morin and Stéphanie Poisson from the McCord Museum; as well as honorary fur lady Gordon Burr from the McGill Archives. A special nod to Philip Preville for scouting the Winnipeg's Hudson's Bay Company Archives. For sharing fur patches and fur passion so genuinely, I thank the ladies from the trade: Caroline Labelle, splendid in her fur parlour; Mariouche Gagné, as generous and funny lady as any one; Lorie Blondeau, wacky and dashing in her faux beaver fur bikini. My gratitude to those who generously gave permission to reproduce the illustrations: Serge Chapleau, Alan Hercovisci for the FCC, Lorie Blondeau, the McGill Archives, the McCord Museum Archives, the National Archives of Canada, the Hudson's Bay Company Archives, Sogides, and June Sauer. June . . . I confess a tenderness of its own for fur lady June Sauer. Her generosity and warmth have certainly constituted the highlight of this research. At the glittering and respectable age of oh! hush! June drives the most fabulous 1970s metallic blue Mustang one could dream of, while being a member of the so well-groomed Anglophone socialite wedding scene. Beyond our ethnic, political and class solitudes, we did construct an encounter of a third kind. June, dearest, *vive le poil!*

My thanks go also to the colleagues, colleagues of colleagues, students, students of students, relatives and relatives of relatives, friends, and friends of friends who kept bringing me Brigitte Bardot memorabilia and fur patches of all origins to enrich my own private beaver fur collection. Please know that your furry potlucks brought wonderful sparkling moments.

I feel so lucky that so many lovely fur ladies have believed in my fur delirium, and some of them have been the best fur trappers ever, true physical, spiritual adventurers on the beaver trail. My deepest thanks to my two favorite bear boys: Serge Boucher and Paul-André Perron for venturing freely into the unknown of beaver-land with me. Between runs in the park and strolls between bars, they have listened with elegance and coy smiles to my beaver tales, offering refreshing thoughts and bright touches to this journey. Paul-André, thanks as well for mastering the index. Thanks to all the misses Skeene and misses Furr, brilliant, witty comrades in arms in this project with whom I share horror stories and joyful conversations over beaver taxonomies and allegories: Lisa Cohen, Ann Cvetkovich, Siobhan Somerville, Marie-Louise Nadeau, Patricia White, Catherine Mavrikakis, Marcie Frank, Kim Sawchuk, Jackie Stacey, Eric Clarke, Thomas Waugh, and my parents Jacques and Gabrielle.

My genuine thanks to the editor of this series and dearest friend, Elspeth Probyn, who from the very beginning, gave me the most enthusiastic, warm, affectionate and inspiring intellectual support. Her insightful and talented suggestions and comments at the revision stage allowed me to polish some fussy, furry thoughts, and her eagerness to see me complete my beaver journey was not only theoretically motivating, but extremely valuable for my own sanity. My thanks also to my editor Rebecca Barden and her assistant Alistair Daniel – so efficient as the fur sentinels and true believers in the power of the little muncher.

Besides an uncanny beaver fever, the accumulation of capital carried me through this fur research. My thanks to the goddess of them all, the Social Sciences and Humanities Research Council of Canada for her generous funding and for being there – still. Despite her policy mood swings, she remains one of the best and most respectful research grant agencies in Canada. Cultural capital was mandatory to explore the various trails. My hearty thanks to the Women's Studies Programme at Lancaster University, Jackie Stacey, once again, Sara Ahmed, and Maureen McNeil for kindly inviting me in May 1998 to present beaver stitches in their speakers series, *Skin*. My thanks also to Rebecca Schneider and the Women and Theater Performance Group for extending an invitation to present the fur project at the 1999 colloquium in Toronto. The generosity and thoroughness of the comments that were addressed at these two events contributed to the refinement of my conceptual and analytical schemes when I felt I had reached a dead end.

Finally, "*merci*" to Venus par excellence, Joy V. Fuqua. Dearest toi, I cannot tell you enough how emotionally, intellectually, and physically inspiring you have been during this furried hunt. As on any trail, there were many ambushes.

ACKNOWLEDGMENTS

Like the most reckless of voyageurs we managed for quite a while to conquer them to reach our posts, crossing the Québec, Pennsylvania and Louisiana bridges, rivers and forests on our feverish fur adventures. 3,000 kilometers apart, 100,000 words later this travelogue has found its blessed end. This book is unarguably a sweet patch of you.

PROLOGUE

A fur journey

If history is in the details then there can be no history because who could ever know these details unless he was actually there? But it *is* possible to grasp the whole, which must be the way the poet works, I should think, being a lawyer myself.

Vidal (1998)

Fur Nation explores the liminalities of the conceptualization of nation, as well as its marketability within and beyond theories of sexuality, within and beyond the containment of the national. The ways that nations are sexualized, are touched and secured historically and politically, evoke a "culture of nations" (Williams 1983). Crucially, this reasserts the importance of material and economic culture in the construction of the national. In other words, the business of the transnational and the intranational is a business of sex and sexuality. This fur journey is my call for a better understanding of nationalist politics as intimately implicated with that of sexuality. What national imagery tells us, and how it speaks to us, transforms the commodified and political value of the female body as a sexualized and ethnic locus carrying a specific resonance and peculiar representation within the transethnic and transsexual dimensions of the national. The concept of the fur nation does not so much respond to an Andersonian 'imagined community' as to a careful regime of circulation and commodification of female skin as a national resource and desireable subjectivity.

The fantastic journey that the many crossings between fur and skin brings allows me to move away from the dominance of the imaginary in the constitution of nations, so as to further investigate the sexual economies that delimit, and often disrupt, the narrative of the nation. Somewhere, somehow, between the contingencies of capital and the seduction of the imaginary, there emerge the sensational and sexual edges of the seamless ties and tales that unite women, fur, sexuality and nation. This holds whether we are encountering such traditional tales of fur ladies as those of the Native country wives in the seventeenth and eighteenth centuries, the European and Canadian ladies of

1

the fur business in the eighteenth and nineteenth centuries, the fictional Lady Barbara in the twentieth-century Hollywood film *Hudson's Bay* (I. Pichel, 1940); or more recent fur lady figures such as the anti-fur animal rights activists led by Brigitte Bardot; and even the new generation of fur designers in Québec active in the recycling and vintage fur scene. *My* fur ladies, through their bodies and practices, consolidate and challenge the natural resources of the once colony, now postcolonial space.

Fur Nation: from the beaver to Brigitte Bardot thereby offers a close look at how the long-neglected question of the beaver, as an exchange value for female sex/uality, is indissociable from a national history so infatuated with colonial and postcolonial beaver fever. From the outset, my interest has been shaped by two intertwined sets of questions: how the contours and textures of sexuality are linked to national formations, and how fur constitutes a perfect expression of the symbiotic, almost biological relation between the female body and the Canadian postcolonial fur enterprise. For all the countless studies of the fur trade produced over the last century in this country, none have actually satisfactorily considered or pinpointed how it is that the sensuality of female skin and the raw materiality of fur have actually mingled to create the fabric of a nation.

My research began with a repentant fur lady and powerful symbol of the woman-made-nation: Brigitte Bardot. Though French-from-France, Bardot was also the perfect ambassadress of French colonial remainders in the post-colonial-turned-wannabe-nation space of Canada and Québec. Sex symbol, man hunter, right-wing nationalist, and anti-fur advocate, Bardot embodies all the contradictions and possibilities emergent from the manifold articulations between female body, sexuality, economy and nation. Following the re-enactment of the 1977 baby seal outrage in 1995, a runway of fur ladies have paraded before my eyes, eventually giving shape to this book. If, in the beginning, my eyes focussed on fur coats, it soon became clear that my interests lay first and foremost with the fur ladies. In a sense, one might say that I am not at all interested in fur. This book is less about fur, fur fashion, fur design, or fur money, than it is about the ladies who have contributed through their skin, whether directly or indirectly, to the commodification not only of their bodies, but also of their labour. On the other hand, looking at women in fur not only constitutes a way to question female agency in national formations, but it also offers a clear way to consider how the nation is sexualized. Skin and fur are at the very basis of the sexual economy of the nation, and women represent powerful agents and producers of this sexual economy. Confronted with the fact that women and the Canadian nation have for centuries shared a longing for beaver, my use of 'beaver tales' became the best way to encapsulate my own narratives about fur, women and the nation. 'Beaver' quickly became the term I relied on to capture the value of skin and fur as national/natural resources.

In a sort of Joan of Arc-style response to all the beaver clubs and other corporate national gentlemen's clubs that have aggressively kept the beaver out, I wanted to recreate my own version of the abundant fur lady tales that have significantly marked the national landscape, and who have sensually punctuated my own discovery of beaver land. I have organized my fantastic reveries like a map to guide readers through my fur journey, a voyage that seldom ventures from the sceneries of the twentieth century. Pro or anti-fur is not my primary dilemma, nor the main question to preoccupy me. What matters to me most is their shared indulgence in the rich encounter between fur and skin. Very few historians have allocated space or time to understand the uncanny way in which these women have placed themselves at the forefront of the national economy through their encounter with fur over the last centuries. This led to my desire to intermingle official historical accounts with fictional tales and desirable encounters as part of my examination of the Fur Nation and the land of fur ladies.

In what follows, three fur trails are drawn: fur nation, beavers, and Bardots. Each trail constitutes a tale of its own, yet nicely points towards the others. Each trail is enriched by two fur posts that together form six little rest areas from which to consider specific features of the fur ladies. In the most genuine sense, the fur ladies in this study constitute sights/sites of infinite pleasure and delight for the brain and the body. This book is my fantasy of a fur nation.

Part I

FUR NATION

1

MY FUR LADIES
The fabric of a nation

A fur garment is like a beauty salon. The lady who goes in comes out different. She not only looks different, she *feels it*.[1]

Am I an accomplice to murder by stroking the softness of animal fur with the tips of my fingers? I have no remorse and I refuse to renounce the shiver of a body wrapped in fur, the emotion of the moment, when the evening closes with promises of night.
Konopnicki (1995)[2]

Feeling fur

I was originally seduced into researching fur ladies by the extraordinary possibility of reaching for the timeless quality of fur, the sensational tactile value of fur in the evolving links between women, sexuality and nation. In this book, I propose the following: that fur exposes the relationship between women and nation like a touch, like a contact, a contract that goes beyond the natural property of skin. Thinking fur and skin as touches calls for a critical understanding of how the nation is both a tactile and a visual experience.

In his essay, *Le toucher, Jean-Luc Nancy* (2000) Derrida suggests that the very act of touching calls not only for the sensation of reaching, of knowing, but also of representing and imagining the relationship between two bodies, two textures, two moments. For Derrida, *toucher* goes beyond the visible appearance of an encounter, or the physicality of skins as static matter. *Toucher* is to *expause*, an expression that compresses the word *peau* (skin) and the verb expose. To *expause* the contacts between fur and women brings out a new set of points of contact that are rendered when one fabric strokes against the other; in other words, touch-ing as *expause* is to reach beneath the skin. Touch-ing is then a conceptualization of a network of relational effects and affects, a way to capture a sensation, to describe an encounter at once. There is a sensual dimension to this, a sensual dimension that also crosses that of experience. And because touch-ing is about reaching, it is very much about encounters. And this is what this book is about: encounters between skin and skins, between the female body, the beaver and the nation.

According to Derrida, touch-ing is as much visual as tactile: to touch is also to see. Fur too is as much about visual as tactile formations. When I look at fur, I cannot help but seeing the feeling of the fur at the tips of my fingers, I cannot help but feeling the skin that is wearing the fur; when I touch the fur ladies, I cannot help but uncover the many tangents that have made the fur nation possible as a sexual economy. In this sense, this project examines the representation of fur ladies as an encounter, an experience between skin and furs. In the word 'toucher,' touch and touching, there is necessarily a reflexive moment, an intimacy with the subject. When we say that we have been touched by something, by someone, there is a carnal, sensual and pleasurable quality to touch. There is the moment when the subject encounters the other, but also when the subject confronts her own boundaries. Henceforth, to be touched can also mean to be reached in a self-critical space. In his essay, Derrida uses "le toucher" (touch-ing and touch) to invite the readers to an encounter between two lives, two worlds: his and the philosopher Jean-Luc Nancy's, author of numerous phenomenological essays on "le toucher." As a way to talk about my encounter with the fur ladies, allow me to steal from Derrida his unique encounter with Nancy, and to reappropriate it to my own use – is it, in fact, what Derrida urges the reader to do when he argues that in the touch one takes over and makes her own what originally was 'external' to her?

Fur Nation is about the encounter between skins – human and animal, yes – but also between an array of representations. The very gesture of touch-ing and *touch in* the context of this book serves a double function: a conceptual and heuristic dimension, and a methodological and analytical one. When fur pelts and the women's skin touch in their whimsicality or opposition, it is an an encounter, a contact (*un "tact"*, a tip, as Derrida describes it) that is established. From this interplay between the tactile and the visual, a vivid conceptualization of the ways the skin and fur feed each other to construct another space, another materiality, emerged: and it is this other texture, this third skin that is referred to as *Fur Nation*. In a similar fashion to Konopnicki's description cited at the opening of the chapter, a feeling (touch) of fur and women extends that of the softness of animal fur to reach that of a woman's skin. This is the moment where fur and skin becomes fur ladies and fur nation, where the sexual and the national are interwoven. In this economy of touch-ing – defined here as sexual economy – fur is not only the most pristine woman's second skin; fur reinvented in the fur ladies *is* the fabric of a nation. Skin, flesh, fur all act as interfaces of the female body, and in these material proximities lie the fundamentals of the national as a necessarily sexualized ensemble of geographies. In refusing to dissociate the sensuality of skin from the raw materiality/physicality of fur, I seek instead to articulate some of the cultural, political and historical interactions between women and fur. In this sense, this book unveils the sexual economy of a nation in which the ties between fur and skin are central. In other words, in the social and historical encounter between skin and pelts, fur lies at the very foundations of the sexual economy of the nation.

As part of a strategy of touch-ing, of skinning, central to my analysis is the notion of *fur ladies*, a term that fleshes out the multiple crossings between sexuality and nationalism in Canada, blurring the boundaries between the political, economic and sexual value of the beaver in the establishment of Canadian identity.[3] The notion of *fur ladies* thereby condenses sexualized national narratives and encounters – tales and tails – in which the beaver appears as something more than a trading commodity, a token of value for the fur business, or a symbol of the French and British colonial enterprises. It also highlights the crucial yet shadowy role women have played as producers of the national economy. Hence, the gesture of (dis)articulating the boundaries between women, fur and nation relies on a very simple assertion: without skin there is no fur. And without 'the beaver' there is no trade, there is no movement of capital, there is no crossing of national borders, there is no memory, no nation. The beaver economy, drawing on the interfaces of skin, flesh, and fur, is what keeps the business of the nation going, wonderfully echoing the Hudson's Bay Company's motto *Pro Pelle Cutem*, a skin for a skin's worth. Fur in and of itself holds no interest in *Fur Nation*; the many ties and tangents that exist between skin and fur do. It is through this constant exchange, trading between sexual reference and gender that the fur ladies gain all their magnificence as national commodity. The interplay and simultaneity between the sensuality of skin and the raw materiality/physicality of fur provokes a critical reconsideration of the cultural and political formations that mark the 'authentic Canadian beaver' as both an emblem of national unity and a marker of national sexual economy.

In this context, the notion of fur ladies not only marks the encounter between women and fur, but also encapsulates the contractual proximities that exist between skin and fur in the construction of national spaces. The contract here is not only economic, it is also sexual. It is a touch, a contact ("tact") that consumes and seals the nation, that sketches its representational circulation through a close bond. This double articulation between economy and sexuality begs a series of questions regarding the ways that nation, sex/uality and identity intersect: how profitable has "the beaver" – in its animal and human/female embodiment – been for the nation? How busy have the fur ladies/beavers been in the construction of a national economy? How is the representation of women as agents negotiated in a culture and a market where the expressive value of fur involves overshadowing the traces of skin? The notion of fur ladies represents a specific embodiment of the intersections of nationalism and sexuality, illustrating the connections between representations of a homosocial nation and representations of skin as more than skin. The troubling articulations between women, fur and nation embrace a broader context of signification than the one limited to the materiality and the visibility of the fabric in its most obvious form.

9

References to fur in the cultural economy of Canada go beyond the colonial – animal and human – imagery of the beaver to include the sexual and racial commodification and subjection of women in the more popularized mani- festations of national discourses. In addition, the fact that the fur economy is necessarily transnational – after all, the fur trade is one of the many beauties of the French and British colonial legacies – accentuates its national trait. In a context of increasing transnational movement and transnational geographies, the value of fur is still shaped by the ways that gender, race and sexuality are localized and embodied within women's practices and proximities with fur and skin as production and commodity forms. At the core of my analysis on nation/women/sexuality and fur/ladies is the importance of thinking the nation through skin, and the ways that the production of the trans/national stems from a bewildering interplay between identities and performances, between the national and sexual boundaries that are constantly drawn and redrawn. As the nexus of skin and nation, fur speaks to the complex and contradictory participation of women in the shaping and mapping of the national – including the various textures of female agency in relation to the fur business. Like the process of skinning the beaver pelt to gather felt in the production of beaver hats,[4] the role of women in the cultural fur enter- prise in Canada is encapsulated in the very act of skinning the fur to get to the skin.

The way that sexuality unfolds to reconfigure national issues is key to my argument that without skin there is no fur. Along the same lines, the close encounter between fur and ladies seeks a reconciliation of the contradictions between the ubiquity of women *in* furs in the production of national imagery and popular display on the one hand, and with women's marginalization from political and economic formations of the nation on the other. If a sexual edge transpires in popular modes of representation and the consumption of popular events such as tourist campaigns, fashion trade, official commemorative imagery, and anti-fur rhetoric, the sexualization of these events within the nation and postcolonial space has yet to be explored on a theoretical level. While most feminist work addresses the centrality of gender and its bodily expressions in the process of defining the conditions of subalternity and agency for women in the national/postcolonial moment, very little attention is given to sexuality as central to the organization and development of the colonial and postcolonial enterprises. By sexuality I mean not only sexual identity and the various technologies at work in the constitution of national bodies, but also the specifics that intervene in the sexualization of the nation.

The critical gesture of dislodging sexuality from the liminalities of the body places sexuality outside of the body, or at least in its excessive and eccentric manifestations. This "distance" is not fortuitous, when one considers that the most readily available popular image associated with women and fur in Canada – and still today with the revival of the fur industry – has been that of an animal: the beaver – sex, race and class confused. Modes of production of fur imagery, even contemporary ones, consistently feature and position women – both as subject and material (skin) – as the real fur, because beaver and women in their economical reciprocity constitute the perfect marriage.

Even if the perfect match between woman and beaver originated from the outset of the fur trade, countless political events and cultural representations since then have reinforced this symbiotic encounter between skin and fur. Interrogating the obviousness between beaver and woman as surfaces uncovers the sexual value of skin in the fur economy. The trading (or contract) of proximities between women and fur is strongly entrenched in the production and representation of postcolonial ties as promiscuous ones. Promiscuity here refers to an analytical double entendre: i.e., in *skinning* and *re-dressing* the fur ladies, I question how women participate in the process of circulation of commodities, goods and the culture of national production, and how sexuality maps the development of a nation. While historically, the fur trade has been presented as an exclusively male homosocial controlled activity (Innis 1956; Newman 1985 and 1989; Mackay 1948), the production of fur as the *national skin* forces to reconsider the relations of intimacies that produce the national as a sexualized environment. For instance, in one of the founding texts of contemporary national history, Innis declares that "The history of Canada has been profoundly influenced by the habits of an animal which very fittingly occupies a prominent place on her coat of arms" (Innis 1956: 3). Beyond the fact that Innis's story discards a fundamental dimension of the politics of the fur trade and national formation, that of the trading of women, it does offer a close look at the origins of Canada – most notably a fascinating erotic taxonomy of fur geography where the richness of beaver (fur) is a question of northerly attitudes and exposure.[5] Innis's fascination with the beaver, and the fact that his book *The Fur Trade in Canada: An Introduction to Canadian Economic History* starts with a chapter appropriately entitled here 'The Beaver' 'resonates' in a peculiar way here. The beaver that Innis is describing is an ethnographic matter, but also an intimate one.

Innis's beaver is compelling because it is at once a beast, a pelt, a national symbol, and captures in one word a very intimate relation to the land. It speaks to the unspeakable: the sexualization of the nation. While Innis cannot find room for women as women in his study, he clearly hints at the sensuous quality of the relations between the beaver, the nation, and its so-called habits, habits that are motherly transgendered, as was recently discovered (see chapter 2). While Innis cannot possibly talk about gender, and the troubling sexuality of the Canadensis Beaver, he does make the association between an animal – and a female intimate anatomy – and the nation the centrality of his analysis of the national development. The normative relation of the fur ladies to the nation is all the more remarkable for a critique of sexuality and nation given that Canada, as the land of the beaver, owes its foundation to the penetration of the beaver trade/trail by European traders. I cannot take credit for such an insight; Harold Innis made it in his landmark study of fur.

11

This detour via Innis helps us to revisit the tradition of seeing fur ladies as a sort of picturesque equivalent to the national landscape. The question of visibility is reflected in the publicness of women in furs as an accessible resource of the nation. In his study of homoerotic venues, *Virtuous Vice*, Eric Clarke stresses the importance of dislodging visibility as solely a matter of quantity, to actually reinscribe this visibility as a matter of normative quality; in other words, as a normative relation to publicity or publicness (Clarke 2000). What I take, and likely deconstruct from Clarke's insightful critique of representation as visibility is that, in the case of the fur ladies, the so-called 'absence' of women from studies of fur and the genealogy of the nation is as much a matter of sexual becoming as it is of commercial value, no matter how much the desire for representational equivalence may pose a temptation for legitimacy in constructing accounts of women's so-called involvement in the trade.

In terms of this research, the notion of 'quality' is intended to bring sexuality to the center of the analysis of fur – a sexuality sometimes normative, sometimes homoerotic and homosocial, and often, simply queer. *Fur Nation* is about reappropriating traditional ways of naturalizing the origins of the nation and deconstructing the sensual and sexual potential of the nation (the fur nation). The fur nation that is proposed here is then "bi" and "trans" by virtue: economically and sexually. It is in this sense that the conceptualization of fur ladies as the quality of *toucher*, touch-ing reveals all its potential: first because it moves fur from the dead fabric – an economy of death – to *expause* the skin – the living matter, within and outside regulatory and recognizable (i.e., "visible") references; and second, because it avoids quantifying women in furs, instead looking at gender and nation as a nexus of tactile experiences.

Beaver tales

Il n'y a pas des faits de répétition de l'histoire, mais la répétition est la condition historique sous laquelle quelque chose de nouveau est effectivement produit.

Deleuze (1968)

For the *Beaver Tales* exhibition sponsored by the Oakville Gallery in July 2000, in a suburb of Toronto, Wendy Coburn made her own erotic and trans-species interpretation of the contact between beaver and women. For this collective thematic exhibition, Coburn chose to present the encounter between two beavers as an erotic one. A bronze figurine with the punning title, "The Spirit of Canada Eating Beaver," Coburn's piece shows a beaver performing cunnilingus, a close (sheared?) reference to artist Joyce Weiland's cast bronze "The Spirit of Canada Suckles the French and English Beavers," which thirty years earlier displayed a woman breast-feeding two beavers. The two bronzes provide an ironic yet stellar way to demonstrate not only the sexual quality of the

12

national symbol, but also to capture in a raw sexual performance the historical reproductive bounds between the the two beavers: the beast and the beauty reunite in one single embrace, in one single body: that of the ultimate fabric of the nation.

My thinking about women and fur is informed by a multitude of images, including Coburn's and Weiland's beaver sex performances, and narratives of fur and snow, that I have come to affectionately and intellectually designate as "beaver tales." These beaver tales, that simultaneously speak to geographic, economic, sexual, historical and racial ways of deliberately troubling fur and skin, are recoded in a series of anecdotes, bio-tales, novels, films and popular memories. Each of them unfold critical cultural and social accounts that have shaped the intimate contact between women and the transformation of the land into a commercial beaver fair. Travel accounts, diaries, memoirs and official biographical compilations constitute prolific and popular genres that give face to the "pioneers" and "beavers" of the nation. Whether visual or literary, fictional or historical, tall tales about the princes and princesses of the beaver trade intertwine with more official representations of the agents of the fur economy. The nature and origins of these texts share a mainly homosocial representation of the pretty beavers of the trade. As I argue in chapter 2 regarding the Beaver Club, the fur trade was and still is an exclusive gentlemen's club. Even though certain boys have railed against the beaver boys' culture, as I discuss in relation to Falardeau's documentary *Le Temps des Bouffons* (chapter 2), these recoded tales nicely finesse and perpetuate a white, male construction of the nation where the scope of critique still espouses an obsession with historical memory and the national imaginary, rarely on issues that address the sexualization and racialization of these sensational accounts of the trade.

For decades, countless commercial and national tales have exposed (and *expause*) the circulation of tensions between sensuality and sexuality, domesticity and globalization. The 1950s, for instance, represent a particularly prolific moment both for the fur retail trade and Canadian nationalism and have provided rich narratives of the intimacies between skin and fur. Fur advertising campaigns mapped a range of strategies used by the fur trade and the corporate nation to expose and display the close ties between women, beasts and the land. For instance, this 1950s advertisement (Figure 1.1) promoting the new beaver collection of Montréal fur manufacturer Arpin-Gendron Limited glitters among dozens of other ads highlighting the fiftieth anniversary issue of the Canadian Fur Review. Sensually entitled "Natural Beaver: Choisy," the advertisement features a brunette model, a femme fatale yet definitely classy. Glamorously gazing at the camera, the model is all fur, as much as the beaver coat she is wearing is all skin. One cannot help but see two Canadian beavers in this image, reunited in a troubling yet vivid representation of the intimate association between women and fur for the vitality of the national trade market. Model and coat hit the catwalk of the 1950s Canadian fur industry fashion show, introduced to the buyers in the following blurb:

Figure 1.1 Choisy – the Natural Beaver (model C. Lister). *Canadian Fur Review*, vol. IV, 1950.

Full-length coat of Canadian beaver. The luxurious beauty of Canadian beaver, lavishly styled into a magnificent coat! The flared back falls in four deep folds, emphasizing the markings of the skins. The club collar can be worn straight up – or turned down in a casual manner. The deep sleeves are cut in the new spiral pattern.[6]

As the image powerfully evokes, this 1950s fur advertisement celebrates how women – white women in particular – have been traditionally presented as quaint cultural vignettes for the colonial and national fur trade. The advertisement appeared in the fiftieth anniversary of the Canadian Fur Council album at a time when the postwar fur industry was in total economic and cultural transition. No matter how "modern" the trade fancied itself, its foundations were still embedded in the inescapable display of the fur coat as a natural extension of female skin; in other words, as a national trademark, where skin and fur barely touch each other.

Fur as erotic imagery. For anyone familiar with popular representations of fur and erotic experience, the reference that comes immediately to mind is Leopold von Sacher Masoch's *Venus in Furs*. As a primary condition of the contract between the masochist Severin and his mistress Wanda, the fur coat becomes an object of exchange and consumption. Not only is the Venus in Furs the ancestor of Xena the leather lady, through fur Venus is invested with an extraordinary sexual power that not a human soul could resist. It is the combination of Venus and furs, the interface of skin and fur that creates the conditions of sexual gratification/exchange between Wanda and Leopold. Sensual, fascinating, and perceived to be the embodiment of desire by the enslaved, the Venus in furs crystallizes the coldness of authentic feminine purity and beauty. It is Wanda/Venus with her furs that allows the materialization and concretization of the contract. Fur has no magic by itself, nor does Wanda. The carnal and intimate contact between Wanda's skin and the fur creates a unique and complete entity – the Venus in Furs. It is this new materiality embodied by the Venus in Furs – and not the coat per se – that has the power to tame Severin-the-beast, promising him infinite pleasure in exchange for his devotion and adoration. For Severin/Sacher-Masoch, fur is the Venus's privileged skin, that which allows the pleasure, the trading, to materialize. And if, on some occasions, the tactile act of petting the fur suffices to fulfil Severin's sexual fantasies, he never forgets that the fur of lust that arouses his desire belongs to Venus (Sacher-Masoch 1967: 119–248).

By historical detour, behind Sacher-Masoch's *Venus in Furs*, I see Brigitte Bardot. From her film-within-a-film role as the Leopard Goddess in *Boulevard du Rhum/Rum Runner* (Robert Enrico, 1971),[7] her participation in the early 1970s in the Blackglama "What Becomes a Legend most?" campaign as the ultimate Venus, to her tearful performance over the baby seal massacre, furs have been definitively associated with a Bardot characterized by Simone de Beauvoir as "the sex hunter" (de Beauvoir 1972). Described by media and critics

15

as wild and racy in her love relationships, Bardot's popular public story resembles a tapestry of fur patches and hunting trophies, in which BB herself is exposed and displayed as the quintessential bird of prey. Beyond the sex kitten celebrated by the media and male directors, de Beauvoir was keen to recognize in Bardot's ingenuity a fierce predator. In fact, Bardot has been a hunter both inside and outside the cinematic apparatus, as her frequent interventions in politics and her peculiar conception of national culture and national diasporic/colonial practices have shown. Outspoken, rebellious but politically conservative, a suddenly mature activist Bardot would naturally embody the perfect marriage between economy, nature and survival in a postcolonial culture. Her public outrage about the seal hunt is clearly informed by a humanist tradition *à la* Renan (1882), where Europeans – even confronted at the ends of the colonial world – would maintain their self-construction as the civilized world, while the barbarians still needed to be educated.

In this sense, Bardot's minimal, if not primitive knowledge of Canadian and Québec political and economic histories is totally reinforced by a colonial representation of the relations of power between Québec/Canada and France. Carried away by a sense of the mother country's duty to intervene for the sake of her daughters, Bardot would even board a helicopter and literally restage some of the epic rescues that filled the imaginary of colonization. However, Bardot was not a nun, so it was the mistress BB who came to discipline the hunters, using her animal rights activist rhetoric as a whip to tame the true beasts, the hunters and politicians supporting the commercial seal hunt. Bardot is the other side of Venus: she trades her skin for babies, transforming her sexuality into a gesture of reaching for survival.

Can we say subalternity and agency?

The complex ways that fur and skin are forged within the nation raises issues of agency, resistance, reproduction, sexuality and race in the materiality of fur and beaver. How do women negotiate their multiple positionalities within this context? As national wombs, skin bearers, or anti-fur movement advocates, how do women impinge on the culture of the nation? In most recent studies on women, sexuality and nation conducted by Western feminist scholars,[8] the locus of analysis is too often reduced to visual representations and texts in which the *national* is gendered through the imagery and commodification of women's bodies. In other words, women and fur are understood as fetishes, hardly as subjects.

In relation to fur history, recent critiques have further condoned the separation perpetuated by traditional histories of fur between the material production of fur and its symbolic production. For example, Julia Emberley in her new study on fur as cultural artifact, *The Cultural Politics of Fur* (1998), argues that codes of exchange are principally tied to a network of "textual libidinal economies," with little consideration of the existing distinctions between text, image, politics and the libidinal exchanges that define the material girl. As instructive and as remarkable as Emberley's work is at the aesthetic level, it does not allow for an adequate response to questions concerning how sexuality, women and fur mingle to constitute the very center of a national stock exchange within which skin and fur together are valued. In reclaiming symbolic production as an essential dimension of a feminist analysis of fur, we risk reproducing the traditional exclusion of women from material production, by emphasizing women as bearers of symbolic production and material signifiers par excellence ". . . in the traditional discourses of political and libidinal exchange" (Emberley 1998: 4). While Emberley's work offers a revised history of fur qua fur, it does not sufficiently consider how sexuality, women and fur constitute in their very intersection a natural resource for the nation. Countering such "flatness," I argue that fur per se has no value without the raw materiality of skin, and the constant rearticulation and sexualized negotiation between skin and pelts, between the apparent mobility of the body and the aberrant stillness of fur, creates the sexual economy of the nation.

Against interpretations that construct the female body as static, I wish to introduce movement and displacement as an essential dimension of the understanding of the female subject as "national agent." Without a context of representation, production, and consumption of the skin as a material "good," there is little room for analyzing the body beyond its surface. A critical approach to women as both surface and interface allows us to frame women as both bearers and producers of the nation. The gesture of apprehending the fur ladies beyond the frozen glimpse of the fur coat speaks to a tactic that embraces a more productive, yet sensitive – tactile – approach to the cultural economy of fur and nation. It implies, for example, a consideration of agency in its multiple articulations to power: as a means of resistance to the postcolonial/ national order, as strategies of reproduction and consolidation of national enterprise, but also as an intimate contact with the economic. Too often the use of the term subalternity provides a critical framework that maintains: first, that national identity is a male homosocial practice; and second that sexuality opens up to a marginal space from which to confront the culture of economies involved in national identity and postcolonial subject formation.

Traditionally, women have been framed as bearers, guardians and even cultural producers of the resources of the colony and the nation (Lewis 1996). However, an approach that positions women not only as agents but also as economic producers of the fur ladies allows us to understand how specific cultural events and economic activities coalesce within a sexualized, gendered and racialized organization of domestic space. From this perspective, the nation is not only a commodity spectacle, as McClintock argues (1995), but also a sexual stock exchange within which femininity and fur act as the prime trading values. By analyzing the fur trade as a sexual economy, we confront the antagonistic yet complementary dimensions of female agency and production.

The status of the subject in the colonial space, more specifically in relation to a traditional history of Canada and Québec, intersects with the conditions of subalternity under which gender and sexuality come to be formed in the sexual economy of the nation. More importantly, conditions of subalternity cannot be generalized to all women and daughters of the colonies, nor to all women who are nationally subjected. Nevertheless, I believe that women – not regardless of but due to their class, ethnic and social belongings – have lived through their skin in unique ways as objects and subjects of the colonial enterprise and the fur trade. I want to use two specific examples of this 'transracial' and 'transethnic' subalternity, where the mobility of the subject is foremost a matter of transaction, of sexualization within hegemonic trading rules.

My first example addresses the beaver tales of "country wives." Very often common-law partners, second spouse after the White European "legitimate beloved," their position was officially that of the native informants for white and company traders. However, in their global subalternity they were *skins*, and their traces become akin to the listing of goods conditional to a fair deal, a sort of list of "essentials" to maintain the wealth of the corporate nation. Documented at length by the officers of fur trade companies – including the Hudson's Bay Company – over three hundred years, the culture of country wives was depicted as central to the process of negotiation and exchange of goods between white retailers, traders and native trappers. In this economy of human and animal skins, the native woman is a trading matter, because she literally injects the national and domestic space with a sexual exchange value. Her skin was as banal as the traded pots and pans in the materialization of the deal between white traders and Indian hunters. The country wives represent the interracial, gendered, class nature of the trade, and the commodification of fur is subordinated to this tension between native women as "native informants," as agents of microeconomies, and their skin as fabric, matter of cultural and economic exchange. All the fur trade is constructed on the extension of the boundaries of the female skin: a site of numerous contacts – touches – and contract where the fabric-ation of the nation is recoded as a sexual, intimate economy.

Country marriages and country wives were then part of an economy of sexual intimacies. As Sylvia Van Kirk argues in *Many Tender Ties: Women in Fur-Trade Society* (1980),[9] "country marriages" and "country wives" were common terms for the interracial "intimate arrangements" between Hudson's Bay Company or North West Company men and their native mistresses. The country marriages were a lucrative system in which commerce, trade and exchange intertwined to maximize the value of skin. Without diminishing the power relations at play in the corporate imperial bodily trademark, these two sexual economies question the means through which sexuality informed the feminine *professionalization* of the fur market. And that those who traded their skin, and those whose skin was traded, overshadowed the racial and sexual flavor of the colonial enterprise expanded through the fur trade. Using their bodies, knowledge, expertise and social skills as part of their investment in the production of the fur economy, women such as *Les Filles du roy* and the country wives recoded the relations between development, survival of national space and renewal of fur geographies as a sexualized contact.

My second example concerns the market of *Les Filles du roy*, the King's girls. Unsuitable for the mother country, and unfit to the kingdom, these women, or should I say, girls – as some of them were reportedly barely teenagers[10] – were sent by royal proclamation to the new colony for marriage, in other words, for the procreation of the white race. Knowing that the future of the new colony as well as its economic structure was totally dependent on the fur trade, *les Filles du roy* played a crucial role in the consolidation of French dominance in the New World. Their very presence secured the participation of French *engagés* (so-called associates, but in reality hired men) to the commerce of fur, forcing them to swear allegiance to the King for the duration of their contract with the fur companies. In an analogical way, each *Fille du roy* was worth a beaver pelt.

Traditionally, both the country wives and *Les Filles du roy* have been analyzed in terms of domestic partnership and imperial domination, while very few allusions have been made to the contractual/commercial nature of these bonds of love, nor to the desirability of female skin in the development of the colony. For instance, the presence of *Les Filles du roy* was not only a means to secure French control over the fur trade, but also to deploy the ethnic sanitation of the new colony as white French land. As most of *Les Filles du roy* were white – though some Christianized native girls who were brought to the King of France's court as entertainment and exotic evidence also ended up as unfit subjects of the kingdom – their very value as objects of exchange also renders the ways that the value of skin was part of a system of economic/racial purity. White girls would marry white boys, providing in this sense a pure lineage for the fur business.

With regard to these examples, how are we to reconcile the traditional representation of the subaltern subject as presented by postcolonial theorists with the imperative to challenge a monolithic racial and ethnic understanding of subaltern conditions within the postcolonial process of national becoming? Is subalternity only a matter of race or ethnicity? Or, on the contrary, does subalternity call for a complex and sometimes contradictory set of relations with the cultural economy of the female body in relation to the colonial enterprise and national formation? Here I will use subalternity as a way of reevaluating the national as an intra- and inter-ethnic and sexual space. In this sense, subalternity is not only materialized and performed in a context of cultural and racial power dynamics between the colonized and the colonizer, it also impinges upon the ways that sexuality and femininity are configured under specific imperatives and regulations imposed on both the colonizer and the colonized. Subalternity is a set of economic, cultural, social and sexual positionings that converge in expressions of power that necessarily bring relations of antagonism, dominance, subordination and resistance to operate in the same place. In other words, subalternity is also informed by hegemonic ties.

In this context of conflicted hegemonies and power subordination, how can we make "use" of Spivak's analysis of widow sacrifice, or sati, from and within specific modalities of agency (Spivak 1988) in order to understand the mixed agencies at work within the sexual economy of the fur trade?[11]

Let me first describe very sketchily Spivak's reading of sati. In her analysis of sati, Spivak questions the role of the organic intellectual as much as the conceptual consuming of the widow sacrifice in the context of postcolonial and feminist studies. Outside and within cultural, racial, class, gender and intellectual boundaries, Spivak analyzes the transactions of violence at work in the sacrifice, but also the impossibility of the postcolonial critique reaching for the intimacies of subalternity as *death*. What is conceptually compelling is how Spivak redirects her concerns about "speaking" as act ("Can the Subaltern Speak?"), into death as subjectivity. In other words, Spivak questions how death becomes a moment of translation that bears marks on the body of the widow. Half-rhetorical, half-reflexive, the sati commends awareness, reflexivity and in Derridian terms "nonknowledge", explains Spivak. "We act out of certain kinds of reflexes that come through, by layering something through learning habits of mind, rather than by merely knowing something. This is the way in which her action was inscribed in her body" (Spivak 1996: 289). For Spivak the condition of the widow is translated through issues of representation, wherein the regulative presuppositions of historiography erase the agency of the subaltern – the subaltern cannot speak. But more, the question of the subaltern goes beyond the matter of the burnt flesh. What I see here is a critical and conceptual problem: i.e., how to understand burnt flesh like a moment of contact, of touching, a moment where the subaltern through the burning flesh will not only talk and speak, but also reach for.

One could always argue that sati is the widow's burning flesh. But as Spivak demonstrates, it is the reverberations that the burning flesh produces: the sexualized and economic ritual that makes the subaltern woman (the Hindu woman) the support of dominant modes of producing domestic continuity and national resources (Spivak 1999: 68), which I will say skin is part of. Then, what links the burning flesh and skin as fur? Just as the burning of the flesh provides a way to capture a specific set of intimacies that intervene in the national and the postcolonial, so the interplay between fur and skin at work in the fur ladies also reaches and exposes the articulation between the national, the postcolonial and the sexual. What links the burning flesh and the skin as fur is this moment where from the skin and the flesh a sexualization of the relations between gender, race and nationhood is deployed. By analogy – and not by equivalence, I must insist – what makes fur speak is the ways that female sexuality is enshrined into the encounter between the dead matter (fur as dead animal skins) and the female skin as an alive fabric.

20

The theoretical and political understandings of subalternity cannot be dissociated from that of agency, or that of women as cultural agents.[12] In this sense, the strategies and practices initiated and collaborated on by women as cultural agents and economic producers within and outside a situation of exclusive domination intertwine with the specifics of a sexual economy that can be either corporate or institutional. As Floya Anthias and Nira Yuval-Davis state "The relationship between the state, women and ethnic and national processes does not take a necessary form" (Yuval-Davis and Anthias 1992: 114). The links between women, nation and sexuality are all informed and embedded in an economy of life – through various manifestations of production and reproduction, such as biological reproduction, reproduction of national boundaries, production of symbolic order, etc. – and an economy of death, what Yuval-Davis and Anthias frame for instance, as participation in military efforts (Yuval-Davis and Anthias 1992: 115).[13] This is precisely what I see every time a woman is "wearing fur": the spectacular display and circulation of fur and fur ladies as both agents of an economy of death and an economy of life, a dynamic configuration of female productiveness within and outside the national borders.

On the other hand, if it is true, as Anthias and Yuval-Davis argue, that "at the level of agency, women act as participants in national struggles and as members of dominant ethnic groups or classes, as exploiters and oppressors particularly of subordinate-position women," (Yuval-Davis and Anthias 1992: 115) does it mean that the subaltern subject cannot be a producer of her own story? Benita Parry strongly claims that the voice of the subaltern can be recovered in anticolonial nationalist struggles, where "women [have] inscribed themselves as healers, ascetics, singers of sacred songs, artisans and artists" (Parry 1987). Interestingly enough, the female subaltern subject's resistance and participation is framed in relation to a cultural authenticity, assuming that colonial rule has not altered, affected or mediated so-called native cultures in any way. Native women who were country wives, for instance, who were subjected to trading bonds, and white European women who came as emissaries either of Britannia or Mother France had to embrace the colonial order and later nation-state regulation in the most vivid of ways, though their relations with the circulation and distribution of national ties were often positioned differently. In the refusal to acknowledge that the terms "native" or "white" are also defined from within by specific regimes of class, caste and all sorts of cultural, sexual and ethnic hierarchies, a theory of subalternity has no choice but to claim the homogeneous subaltern subject in order to fulfill the process of representation and the act of "speaking for" in one voice.

Hence the following concern: Who is a subaltern? If one brings the notion of class as well as ethnic identity in relation to the colonial space, what do we say about white women who were not part of the elite, who never went to their motherlands, and whose contact with the Empire was constantly mediated by commodities, narratives or tales of the old world? In the specific conjuncture of Québec, how do we negotiate subalternity beyond the predictable antagonistic relations between French and English people? Within this ethnocentric and reductive geography that poses the nation as the creation of two settling peoples, what is the place of native communities, and also the Jewish, Lebanese, Greek and Italian immigrants at the turn of the twentieth century who have since contributed significantly to the development of the contemporary fur industry? The ethnic configuration is all the more fundamental because it provides a framework for understanding the transformation of the demographics of the fur trade in Montréal, as I discuss in chapters 5 and 6. Even if sexual and racial divisions were constantly re-activated by economic and political rules as well as cultural exclusions, it seems to me that the category of the subaltern is not constituted by only one marker, but by a series of qualities, situations and events that shape subalternity. As Loomba points out, while "individual and collective subjects can be thought of in multiple ways at any given time, we must keep open the very meanings of subalternity and domination." In other words, "situating the subaltern within a multiplicity of hierarchies is not enough: we must also think about the crucial relation between these hierarchies, between different forces and discourses" (Loomba 1998: 240).

Herein lies the importance of understanding the centrality of fur in Canada in terms of a sexual economy. In so doing, I do not pretend to avoid all generalizations, nor do I claim to avoid reproducing any gaps in my own reconstruction of fur narratives. However, what I want to challenge in traditional tales of the fur nation is their very narrow way of understanding the positionalities of women in the materialization, reproduction and circulation of fur as the landmark of national representation. In framing the role of women in terms of the antagonistic and controversial links between subalternity and dominance, I am seeking to effect a movement between the different fur posts and fur tales that unpack the exchange value of the female body for fur economies. Moving through this motif of skin and fur, one question necessarily haunts this book: do women act as agents when it comes to fur? On one hand, it is tempting to argue that the only way that women have to a certain extent resisted the colonial legacy is through their participation in anti-fur movements, highly publicized in the case of Québec by Brigitte Bardot (chapter 5). There are also numerous examples of native women who have opposed commercial animal trapping, arguing for a better respect of mother nature. Probably one of the most famous and mythical examples is that of Anahareo/Pony, an Iroquois woman and widow of the legendary Grey Owl (alias Archibald Stansfield Belaney, 1888–1938), the white-wannabe-Indian-beaver-protector, whose life has recently been retold Hollywood style. Freely adapted from Grey Owl's writings, the film *Grey Owl* (Richard Attenborough, 1999) features the pro-animal rights advocate couple, portrayed by Mr. Bond himself, Pierce Brosnan, and French-Québecois actress Annie Galipeau, raising little beavers as pet couples in this romanticized portrait of Owl's struggle for ecological preservation. With such inspiring lines as "too many trappers and not enough beavers" and "I'm speaking for the beaver now," this beaver tale mostly focuses on Owl's impressive personae, over-shadowing the role that Anahareo played in Owl's conversion from hunter to preservationist.[14]

On the other hand, if subalternity is understood only in relation to ethnicity, what are the implications for white bourgeois women who are animal rights activists? And yet again, what are the implications for the next fur generation of native designers who have reappropriated native and Inuuk traditions in their fashion collections (chapter 6)? In order to be consonant with the subaltern debate, would I exclude native designers, and retain only the native women who have acted according to the dictates of animal rights discourses and strategies? But then, what does it mean to consider the experiences of white pro-animal advocates as part of a subaltern position?

Part of the answer to these questions is embedded in a repositioning of subalternity as a series of touches, of critical intimacies. Subalternity is less a status, an identity, than a complex nexus of relationships that make women simultaneously and alternatively symbolic commodity, economic makers, and sexual traders. Through the series of points of contact between fur and skin, subalternity evokes an extension. If for Spivak, subalternity has a definite geographic quality, let's stretch this quality through its transversality/ transnationality to reach that of the female tissue. When Spivak says that the burning of the widow's flesh constitutes an exemplary moment where the subaltern is silenced – within the national space AND in its transnational reverberations – she means that most critics cannot go beyond the flesh and interrogate the representations at work in sati. What is exposed and represented goes beyond the burning flesh, because as Derrida puts it, skin is as much to be seen as to be touched, in other words skin is *expaused*. But while for Spivak, the subaltern cannot escape a certain fetishization in the postcolonial world, I suggest that with the contact to skin, fur undergoes a de-fetishization of the obvious, i.e. fur as the sole fabric of the nation. Resisting a simple analogy that will reduce at once skin, flesh and fur to a fetish, the touch-ings between skin and flesh, skins (animal) and skin (human) contribute to reinvent the tensions between the consciousness and agency of women.

In order to inscribe the subjects in a broader economic and cultural frame-work, we must take into account the following: animal rights discourses today constitute a huge business, with budgets that in some instances are higher than the budget of the Fur Council of Canada (FCC) for the promotion of the Canadian beaver (chapter 5). The International Fund for Animal Welfare (IFAW), one of the most aggressive anti-fur advocacy groups, is controlled by white English-Canadians and North Americans, with a total budget of $3 million expended to fight the fur trade in 1997. On the other side of the fence, the FCC looks almost ridiculous with its yearly $700,000 budget for its pro-fur campaign (although this rather meager figure does not include the indirect "free publicity" that fur displays around the city gather). This troubling situation begs an essential question: Where does IFAW fit in a subaltern analysis? Because IFAW is not outside the transnational capitalization of the animal business, and because IFAW publicity campaigns employ romanticized narratives of nature and native women in the protection of the wilderness while claiming to represent and speak for communities – animal and human – a paradoxical representation necessarily emerges between the different hierarchies and discourses that are produced by specific agents and groups that are too dependent on the animal market, as well as the different positioning created for them.

Native women are represented in anti-fur advocacy discourses in a double dimension: as members and activists, but also as the human face affected by the bloody war of trapping. This creates an objectification of "the" native woman that in my opinion is not so far from the postcard imagery frequently shown in tourist stands featuring the true Inuit woman of the authentic North. Displayed as such, do they speak? Or do they talk? Meaning that they are visible, but outside the realm of representation? (Spivak 1996: 289). Are their subjectivities fully addressed and deployed through networks of political, social and cultural ties that weave the circulation of women in furs? And what about the women who reconstitute a different memory of fur trapping as a means to rethink the tensions between traditional and contemporary economic practices? In other words: how much subalternity needs be embodied in the subaltern female body in order to be considered as an agent? How much does the presupposition of an authentic, "true" subaltern group get in the way of a critique of the conditions of subalternity as an "ever-receding horizon of possibility?" (Landry and MacLean in Spivak 1996: 292).

There is no clear positioning, nor is there a commonsensical nature to such debates. In Spivak's terms "For the (gender-unspecified) 'true' subaltern group, whose identity is its difference, there is no unrepresentable subaltern subject that can know and speak itself: (. . .)" (Spivak 1999: 272). In this sense, maybe against Spivak, one way to answer these questions lies in our critical ability to revisit contingent instances of women as agents and subjects that are not necessarily defined by the contingencies of an economic scenario of exploitation and differences, but rather to a sexualized correspondence between the conditions of production of the nation and that of identity. Fur ladies are positioned in a contradictory if not antagonistic manner as agents, yet some of their actions, practices and politics might lead us to move away from a transformative definition of agency as clearly defined by political consciousness, and closer to a conception of subjectivity as contractual proximity and economic intimacy. Within the tradition of feminist theory, the concept of agency necessarily carries a sense of change, of opposition to domination, a struggle against the established order, the development of strategies to open up a closed space, a desire to be seen not only as a consumer, or a re-producer, but also a mediator, a territory of transit. This is why, contrary to theorists such as Hannah Arendt who argue that "nobody is the author or producer of his own life story . . . In other words, the stories, the results of action and speech, reveal an agent, but this agent is not an author or a producer" (Arendt 1958: 184). I battle to reveal a female subject – here the fur lady – as a producer and reproducer. Through these two apparently inseparable dimensions of subjectivity and experience, the female agency is shaped by a form of "transnational literacy" to echo Spivak, "a sense of the political, economic, and cultural position of the various national origin places in the financialization of the globe" (Spivak 1996: 295).

With regard to the specificities of popular and fantastic stories of the fur trade, this re-productive mediation is necessarily reenacted within the contours and conditions of the colony and the nation. This challenges a dominant silence on the role of women in the colonial enterprise and in national formation in terms of economy, as if *l'argent sale* (filthy lucre) could not inform identity construction. As I have argued, fur per se has no value without the materiality of female skin, i.e., the sexual economy of the female body. Most Western feminist studies on women, sexuality and the nation (including McClintock in *Imperial Leather*, 1995) reproduce this narrow locus of analysis of texts in which the nation is sexualized through imagery of women. Framed as a text or as an iconographic encounter, the female body remains a static fabric with no sense of mobility, or touching, that for me is essential to the recognition of the subject as *national agent*.

Under such arguments, the politics of fur are either reduced to a history of development of the country or limited to an aestheticized politics where conflicts are cast in terms of anti- and pro-fur advocates, between the "goodies" and the "baddies." Rarely is the simultaneity of the symbolic, erotic and material nature of fur addressed. To do so necessarily leads to questions of the construction of the subject as an economic producer and cultural and political agent. As much as questions of representation and its discursive correlations have been crucial to the critique of gendered subalternity, very rarely are these same issues of representation and discourse also mediated by questions of value and exchange. Insisting on sexuality as pivotal to national formation becomes a way to reappropriate the paradoxical texture, the burning touch of fur ladies. The fur trade translates the sexual economy of the nation as a sexual stock exchange in which femininity (skin) and fur are crucial tokens of value.

As I discuss in more detail in chapter 4, women have historically understood this. For instance, Lady Aberdeen, socialite entertainer and wife of the Governor General of Canada at the end of the nineteenth century, understood and encapsulated the ultimate richness of women as (re)producers of the new nation. For one of her many Victorian fancy dress ball extravaganzas held in Toronto in 1887, Lady Aberdeen organized a series of *tableaux vivants* featuring women masqueraded as different natural resources that have defined Canada as a promising commercial and economic land. What strikes me about Lady Aberdeen's delirious *mise en scène* is how fur and other natural resources were staged not only as cosmetic displays but were necessarily embodied through the materiality, and the political and economic potential of the female body. As the official mediator, Lady Aberdeen's vision of the role of the daughters of the empire totally embraced the white male colonizer's position in constructing and displaying the female body as a token of trading value on the colonial/ dominion market. As a female agent, Aberdeen insisted that female skin was as precious as fur in the political production of the nation. In fact, in enticing women to personify natural resources, Lady Aberdeen insisted that the very act of embodying nature belonged to the domain of women's engagement with a celebratory national project.

Lady Aberdeen's *frou frou* extravaganza raises insightful issues regarding questions of access to national resources, and their differing inscriptions in the exchange market for white women, immigrant and native women. If it is right to quote Anthias, that "no post-colonial state anywhere has granted women and men the same access to the rights and resources of the nation-state," (Anthias 1992: 92) the challenge of this book is to dislodge the very factuality of access and rights to capital in the definition of resources, to explore the fantastic – vs. solely "historically accurate" – manifestations of skin value as a national resource for reproduction, and to disrupt the sexual economy that is at the origins of the "national." While it is true that very few women have legally had access to capital, and more specifically to fur trade stock, politically speaking this does not mean that indirect channels have not existed through which women have mediated their participation and intervention in the development of the fur trade, and what it has come to signify for the nation. This is why, "any instance of agency, or act of rebellion, can be truthfully assessed in many different ways" (Loomba 1998: 239), including, I would add, through power relations and discourses of transformation. In most of the fur posts and beaver tales reconstituted and recreated in this book, it is difficult to draw a clear line between commodity, producer and agent. Without going so far as to make such generalizations as stating that all women acted as agents or producers in the fur adventure, my understanding of national formations calls for a reinscription of the materiality of skin in the sexual economy. This is why, as part of a self-critical position, I argue for fur culture and the national sexual economy in terms of beaver tales in order to both situate agency as an uncanny subjectivity, and to force a reinterpretation of official archives as fantastic narratives.

In relation to fur, women have not only served as emissaries for the empire and promotional muses for the nation[15] – notably as fur babes – but they have embodied the sexualized nation in a very unique way, disrupting binary standards of activity and passivity as a means of evaluating one's affective intervention in the national corporate enterprise. Moving away from the cursory split between active and passive that still dominates many feminist analyses of women's participation in national politics and agendas, I also want to ask what we mean when we say that women are "active" in the colonial and national project? I propose that by "active" we understand the simultaneous roles and discourses that women have come to produce as makers, users and mediators of national and colonial economies. Such a framework seeks to broach the conditions – economic, political and cultural – that inform the participation of women in national agency, national production and national consumption of the sexual economy of fur.

Regarding the delicate question of resistance to domination that necessarily plays differently for certain groups of women – the famous question of who is the true subaltern – my response, as I show in chapter 5 on anti-fur advocacy culture, is quite contradictory and necessitates a recognition that "whoever our subalterns are, they are positioned simultaneously within several different discourses of power and resistance" (Loomba 1998: 239). Women's participation in imperial, colonial or anticolonial campaigns has been strongly informed by gendered and racial ambiguities vis-à-vis their own interventions, and each of the chapters in this book engages with these gendered and racial paradoxes. It is often through a close participation and refinement of transnational and transracial ties that women underpin the economic structure of the fur trade. This is why fur is not a sign, but a substance, a trait that marks the skin in visible and palpable ways. Every time I see women wearing fur, I see seamless relations and tensions that route a representation of sexuality, body and nation as one fabric. Every time I touch fur *as* women, I reach for an horizon of possibilities of thinking and knowing the nation through skin(s).

2

PRINCES, BEAR BOYS AND BEAVER MEN

Tales from the Beaver Clubs

The beaver is a monogamist.

(Innis 1956: 4)

The symbolism is inescapable. Just south of the nation's capital, in South Nation River, Canada's national animal – the beaver – lives in profusion. And sexual confusion. Two professors were looking for something specific and they found it in 100 percent of the males – a uterus. The finding may someday officially tag the North American beaver, *Castor canadensis*, as a pseudo-hermaphrodite – an animal that has sex organs from both genders.[1]

Jacobs (1999)

The deployment of the fur nation is inseparable from the political and economic legacy of colonial development sealed by the Hudson's Bay Company (HBC), a trading corporation created in 1670 to conduct the exploration and expansion of British colonial interests in America. The association between Canada and the HBC is mythical to say the least. Its movement from coast to coast reverberates through a myriad of national sites, commercial and official . . . found in the remainders of fur posts and fur houses, in the creation of shopping centers like the three hundred year old company's retail store The Bay, or in the incorporation of the HBC archival collection into the Manitoba Provincial Archives in 1977. The HBC's ubiquitous presence in the cultural, economic and political landscape of the nation has been abundantly told and romanticized by historians, columnists and novelists over centuries, generating a fascinating collection of tales of the country, mainly featuring impetuous men in furs.[2] According to these HBC tales, Canada was made by princes, bear boys, and beaver men, a buoyant gallery of voyageurs,[3] traders, merchant princes and gentlemen who conquered the wilderness driven by one imperious goal: the beaver hunt.

Figure 2.1 Men in furs: the Earl of Dunraven and Mr Campbell, Montréal 1875. Print
courtesy of NPA.

While abundant and eclectic, most traditional sources overlook the sensual nature of the economic development of the fur trade. I suggest that the links between the fur business and male homosocial and homoerotic culture are inextricably configured in one of the most popular and popularized tales of origin of the Canadian nation: the founding of the Hudson's Bay Company. In this chapter, I reconfigure the making of this story of origins as a sensual enterprise, in which the obviously male homosocial quality of the trade is sealed in the corporate skin/fabric. As the Company's motto *a skin for a skin's worth* illustrates, the close bonds between skins propel a series of trading movements in which bodies, masculinity and nationhood are sexualized.

Conversely, I suggest that the sexual politics of the nation are established through a form of dynastic entertainment marriage between such gentlemen's clubs as the HBC, beaver clubs, Hollywood, and ultimately, the fur nation. This chapter offers a close look at how the construction of masculinity for the homosocial nation is intertwined with the construction of the corporate beaver, an exchange token for female sexuality and femininity for the fur market. Using the Hollywood production *Hudson's Bay* (I. Pichel, 1940–1), a film that maps the origins of a nation onto stories of male bonding and beaver hunts, this chapter seeks to uncover the fascination – cultural and political – with return to the wilderness as the epitome of national unity and triumphant colonialism. "Displacing" such idyllic visions, I show how the double articulation between the homosocial wilderness and the commodification of the beaver constitutes a critical space in which the ties between geography, sexuality, and bodies incite a sexualization of the grand narrative . . .

The displacement of the borders between "the intimate" and "the official" gains resonance in a transnational context. Instead of containing the homosocial grand narrative within the limits of the domestic market and processes of domestication, I propose to tie its national value to a process of transnational production. This collaborative initiative between Hollywood representations of Canada as the romantic other and the HBC's own invention of its roots marks an alternative retelling of the national story as an interplay between men and nature, rather than women and nature. The naturalism of the intimate bonds between men in the wilderness is an economic and conceptual necessity to this corporate mapping, in which the physical and metaphorical encounters between bodies, beasts and the land inform the ultimate naturalization of sexuality.

Popular narratives and tales about the trade are numerous in hinting at a sexualization of the nation through the fur trade, while many film documentaries have revealed the more modern side of the fur nation and the gendered culture of empire. From the HBC corporate movies[4] to the National Film Board documentaries on the trade,[5] to the lavish Hollywood film productions, also known as the "snow movies," the beaver tales have been photographed countless times, yet always with a renewed taste for the monumental male body and the celebration of the white explorer. Still today one of the best examples of the male homosocial corporate encounter with the wilderness is *Nanook of the North*.

A powerful example of a corporate production funded by the Révillon Brothers, another fur business, Robert F. Flaherty's quintessential representation of the links between fur, race and homosociality shines in a way that Hollywood would soon follow with the Canadian snow flicks.

It is in the context of this "Hollywood does Canada" movie circuit that *Hudson's Bay* stands as a salient expression of the paradoxes of the sexual economy and the male homosocial history of fur. As I demonstrate in the following pages, while pivotal to the fur market and the Company's commercial activities, the association between fur ladies and the HBC has been a marriage at odds. Indeed, such misfit associations are visible though the marginalized traces left by the fur ladies throughout the fur economy: from the crucial role played by native women in the culture of trading from the beginning of the fur trade exchanges, or the ambiguous agency of the daughters of the empire who crossed the ocean to become the diplomatic wives of the company in the nineteenth century, and in a less romantic fashion, the contribution of female fur entrepreneurs and trappers in the development of the fur trade regional economies.

There is female skin behind the fur economy, and the sexual dimension of the trade is tightly attached to the buddy-buddy narration of Canada as Hudson's Bay country. In contrast, the fur ladies who haunt the tales of the company are seen first as natural resources and trading commodities – as national Venuses – right next to the blankets and other goodies used by the company men in their commerce with native communities. The sexual and gender tensions that necessarily impinge on the fur nation lie in this paradox: that the very value of the national fabric and its circulation is contingent on the double construction of the fur market as a feminine one, and the fur trade as masculine one. In these ways, women were inserted into the fur exchange, both as exchange tokens themselves (in the case of country wives and indirectly *les Filles du roy*) and sometimes as agents of negotiation (for native women, given the importance of country marriages in the trade). For instance, one of the wildest moments of the history of north American colonization surrounds the restitution of Nouvelle-France by the British authorities in 1632. Maguelonne Toussaint-Samat, in her *Histoire technique et morale du vêtement* (1990) writes that la Nouvelle-France – mostly the northeast coast of North America – after three years of British regency, was restored to the king of France in exchange for the guarantee of payment of the balance of the debt of Madame Henriette, sister to King Louis XIII of France and wife of the King of England (Toussaint-Samat 1990: 90). The restoration of beaver land under French colonial control was made possible through the trading of a bale of pelts for one blue blood skin. Given that the activities of the fur trade in North America occurred on the shores of St Laurent, this is clearly one of the very first legal cases based on the value of female skin in relation to the fur trade: the princess' skin for more beaver skins.

This is why, rather than seeking to uncover women's traces on the beaver trail in a form of historical revisionism, my analysis of the making of the HBC as a sensational tale/story (Cvetkovich 1993)[6] inscribes the de-centering of female sexuality (de Lauretis 1990) in relation to the production and articulation of the monumental male body and homosocial fur bonds. In this context, the supposed evanescence of the female body in histories of fur and the genealogy of the nation is revisited outside the materiality and the physicality of gender as evidence, reappearing in the process of sexualization of the nation. A film like *Hudson's Bay* becomes a site from which one can seek out and reconstitute the crossings between skin and pelts in their gender, racial and sexual transversality, and not only in their specific gendering. In other words, the absence of female characters in the film does not get in the way of thinking of the homosocial constructions of nationhood as a key strategy of narrating the nation.

For instance, Jane Jenson rightly observes that Innis, in his founding study *The Fur Trade in Canada*, showed very little interest in thinking of the nation as a gendered and sexualized financial center, focussing his interest on the beaver. Jenson argues that:

> Harold Innis was stonily silent about matters of women and gender relations. Like most of his generation, he never wondered about women's place in political economy. Nor did his life-long assault on oppressive social institutions extend to examining the ways in which the inequalities of gender power shape and reinforce markets, trade, development, or communication (. . .). Whereas *The Fur Trade in Canada* . . . devotes full attention to the beavers' mating habits (monogamous), family structure (multi-generational cohabitation), and rearing of the young (weaned at two weeks; independent of mother at a year), this classic work is virtually silent on the same issues for the Europeans and Indians whose contact was essential in the development of the fur trade.
>
> (Jenson 1999: 177)

While Jenson interestingly critiques the non-gendered treatment of such foundational texts as Innis's *The Fur Trade in Canada*, she misses an important element: that the absence of ladies from the text is rearticulated in the queering of the overexposed beaver. In other words, Jenson neglects any transversality – even at the symbolic level – between the beaver and women, European and Native. Yet this is what makes the tales of the beaver so evocative in the intersections between sexuality and nation: the simultaneity of the graphic asexual descriptions of beaver and the erasure of gendered critique maintains the economy of fur in a prudish instrumentalization.

Most studies on the Hudson's Bay Company advocate a purely mercantilist and racially sanitized approach to the colonial excursions into Canada and North America. Such accounts frame the Company interests as strictly a matter of the colonial economy, and later on the nascent capitalization of exploration. In the HBC world, there is no room for religious conversions, priests, "slaves," or financial deeds with the Church, and no room for missions, wives, and contentious interracial marriages: just a bunch of adventurers in the wilderness and the bliss of fur pelts. The world depicted is mainly that of a gentlemen's club.[7] It is only later, during the second part of the nineteenth century, that British ladies were sent to fur country as diplomatic wives, led by Dame Simpson. Frances Simpson, wife of all-star HBC governor George Simpson and prominent Daughter of Britannia, was the first of the HBC governor's wives to leave mother England to settle in Canada, troubling the country wife economy established by the company's employees, and the homosocial ruling of the trade. As Newman recounts:

> Country wives were common, and increasingly tolerated by the Company, right into the nineteenth century, although mixed-race women later became the preferred brides. What finally ended the custom was the arrival at Red River [Manitoba] in 1830 of George Simpson's English bride Frances. Overnight she created a fashion for white, church-wed wives.
>
> (Newman 1995: 161)

But before Frances Simpson came to disturb the surfaces of the country of beavers, the prince merchants and the bear boys were the true kings and queens of the land.

Prince Rupert: man-made fur

"On May 2, 1670, Charles II signed the charter granting sweeping imperial powers to the Company of Adventurers of England trading into Hudson's Bay" (Mackay 1948: 26). Prince Rupert, cousin of the King, was nominated as the first "beloved" Governor of the Company.

Is the fact that the fur nation is so homosocially masculine based on the fear of beaver? What has kept the beaver from being read as a man? While such eminent voices as Harold Innis or Douglas MacKay have discussed the strong collusion between the fur trade and mercantilist policy in the development of New France and Western Canada, none have paid attention to the mediated intimacies at work in the development of the trade. I want to stress that the culture of camaraderie so often evoked by historians as a genuine trait of trade was very much a homosocial adventure. The company, led by the beloved Governor, provides a powerful mean of thinking through the intersections between masculinity, nationhood and the commercialization of fur.

The more I researched this project, the more I came to believe that Prince Rupert was the first fur lady to be discursively translated in an asexual history of the fur trade. After all, Prince Rupert has inspired such flaming dandies as Oscar Wilde to cross-dress and perform as the notorious prince at a London fancy dress ball in 1878. In his famous biography of Wilde, Ellman reports that:

> On 1 May 1878 he [Wilde] dazzled an all-night fancy-dress ball, given by Mr and Mrs Herbert Morrel at Headington Hill Hall for three hundred guests, by wearing a Prince Rupert costume with plum-colored breeches and silk stockings. This finery pleased him so well that he bought it from the hiring firm and wore it playfully in his rooms.
>
> (Ellman 1988: 87)

Without conferring the status of "historian" to the flamboyant author, Wilde's vivid impersonation of the Prince speaks to the suggestive homosocial resonance of "the sad young man" (Dyer 1993).[8] Wilde's embodiment of the Prince displaces the traditional asexual portrait of the Prince as a fierce bachelor and respectable "recluse" of the royal family.

My favorite Princely tales come from Peter C. Newman, journalist at the Toronto-based magazine *MacLean's* and author of many popular accounts of the fur country and its merchant princes.[9] As a kind of contemporary Prince by proxy, Newman's public love for the company and the queen of England are immortalized in the fairy-tale tone that imbues his romantic explorations of the company of adventurers.[10] Newman lavishly mythologizes the homosocial fabric of the corporate nation. He infuses his HBC tales with extravagant descriptions of boys in the wilderness, detailing with tenderness the male bonding experience of the trade, the exploits performed over the course of 400 years by the bear boy culture. A wonderful storyteller, with a distinctly queeny and gossipy flavor, Newman's narratives navigate between intimacies and publicness with the same fervor.

It is through Newman that my attention was first titillated by the sexualized dimension of the skin market and the fur trade. The flourish of Newman's narratives prompted me to consider the germinal impact that Rupert and his cousin Charles II (the king of England) had on the sexual economy of the trade. In a documentary produced for the CBC North cable network on the fur trade, Newman suggests that Charles II's hasty approval of the financing of the "first" official expedition of the HBC's ancestor Company of Adventurers in 1667 was largely motivated by questions of a sexual economic nature.[11] According to an ecstatic Newman, his majesty had thirty-nine mistresses who each expressed a fondness for fur and furry reverie. Surrounded by this gallery of fur Venuses, it appears that the King had no other option than to pursue the colonial exploration necessary to fill their fur wardrobes. Along with Charles and his fur ladies, another member of the beaver club played a central role in the deployment of this global skin/pelt trade: Prince Rupert.

Rupert bears the kind of dream persona and public stature that provokes consideration of the homosociality of the fur adventure. While Rupert never crossed the sea to embrace beaver land and to encounter the beastly Canadian muncher, his association with the company has always been a source of pride and honor, a moment of capitalized affect. Described as a discreet yet fierce commander, an eminent spirit and independent intellectual, Prince Rupert became the first governor of the Company and stayed on as the grand commander until his death in 1682. Unlike his cousin Charles, Prince Rupert did not have thirty-nine fur lady mistresses; he did not even have one. A famous figure of the late seventeenth century in the Canadiana market, Rupert still enjoys star treatment in the HBC memorabilia hall of fame. Official colonial pin-up of the developing British American colony,[12] Rupert's private life has been the object of much speculation as to the exact number of beavers captured during the glorious HBC expeditions. Depicted as secretive and "lonely," Rupert's interest in fur seems to have been motivated mainly by his business skills and his negotiating qualities.

This rather "sad young man" is an icon of the power of the fur trade. British historian Hugh Trevor-Roper sketches the following portrait of Rupert:

> [Rupert was] a man of intense loyalties, but few friends, proud, reserved and morose, uncompromising, unpolitical, and undiplomatic, single-minded in his chosen craft of war, which he saw as a personal adventure. (. . .) For the rest, he lived to himself, in a private world, with his blackamoors and his poodles, his books, his laboratory and his instruments of art.
>
> (Newman 1995: 33)

The poignant yet cryptic image of Rupert in such a queer political and private environment evokes my fancy that perhaps the Prince, alongside King Charles, was the Queen of the Company of Adventurers. After all, the Prince's devotion to the business of the state was not so different from Radisson's physical bonds to the beaver land, as I will soon discuss. Two issues that participate in the sexualization of the trade are intertwined here in a troubling fashion: male intimacies as part of the sexual economy of the trade; and homosociality through membership in the bear boy family. These intertwined qualities might explain why, in the context of the seventeenth century, Rupert's queer behavior seems to have "passed." He was known and feared as a fierce politician and a skillful officer as well as a remarkable business man.

Second, Rupert has to be seen and understood as a member of the fur trade gentlemen's club, where manhood and kinship longings for fur were paramount. In this context, Rupert's quasi-monkish devotion to the Company and his private value for the fur economy point to the public sexualization of the colonial enterprise: Prince Rupert's legacy is that of a historical agent who sealed the future of the corporate nation. The trade was born from a queer alliance between the Prince and the King, and the sexualization of the fur economy might be fancied as the outcome of their contingent yet complementary tastes for skin and pelts: Charles II's virile fascination for beaver geographies; and Prince

Rupert's extravagant tastes for trimmed fur coats and muffs, along with his butch mastery of the beaver economy.

Prince Rupert's eccentric life and fancy taste for skin/fur raises an important question concerning the cultural and social particularities of the fur market in Europe in the seventeenth and eighteenth centuries. Histories of fashion have documented at length the fact that until the mid-nineteenth century, fur ladies were both male and female. Toussaint-Samat makes clear that fur was in high demand among the blue-blooded men who competed to commission the fur extravaganzas and discoveries.[13] The association of fur and power (and powder) also has strong historical ties to the religious wars and the European and Asian conquest expeditions (notably what would become known as the Seven Years' War, 1756–63). Already in Europe, from Russia to France, the grandeur of armies was proudly displayed in the numbers of pelts worn by soldiers and officers (Emberley 1998). Fur acted not only as a coquetry and coterie, but as a political marker of imperialist domination over defeated armies and populations. Long before bear hats become a symbol of the British army in the nineteenth century, Napoleon's army was known as the dandiest military fur catwalk of all, officers and soldiers modeling fur like no other army (Ewing 1981: chapter 8). In this manly fur environment, fur fashion in the golden age of the transcolonial fur trade was as much a matter of imperial/national corporeality as social and ethnic class, as the frenzy for beaver hats that swamped Europe during the second half of the eighteenth century would show. This gendered crossover taste for beaver and bear hats might explain the romanticization of the fur trade in the eyes of Hollywood and eminent fans such as Newman, who emphatically suggests that the HBC was born out of a sort of romance – "the passionate union of the Castor Canadensis and European fashion" (Newman 1995: 14). . . .[14] Newman's romantic prose speaks of intimate encounters: on the one hand, Charles II and his thirty-nine mistresses, and on the other, Prince Rupert with his poodle dolls and fur slippers. Using the film *Hudson's Bay* as a point of contrast, I want to examine how the interplay between homosocial representations of national masculinity and the circulation and reproduction of femininity for the fur economy critically dislodges a sexualized account of the nation.

Hollywood goes to Canada: the HBC fairy tale

Hudson's Bay, the glossy 20th Century Fox production, recounts the famous and anecdotal adventures of two French renegades and the success story of their enterprise that led to the creation of the Company of Adventurers, the glorious ancestor of the now famous Hudson's Bay Company. In 1667, Médart Chouart des Groseillers (Laird Cregar)[15] and Pierre Esprit Radisson (Paul Muni) leave the rich beaver coasts of the Canadian colony to go to England with the vested interest of convincing Prince Rupert (Nigel Bruce), cousin of Charles II (Vincent Price), to finance an extraordinary and unprecedented British fur expedition to Hudson's Bay. The film, which also features Gene Tierney as the fur lady Barbara, stands as a romantic illustration of the origins of the fur trade, in which daredevils, pelts, wigs and panting royal court ladies constitute the best elements of a so-called historical epic staged in the snowy mountain (see Figure 2.2).

How did Hollywood ever become interested in this rather remote and dull local story of beaver fever? Hollywood's fascination for the North and the snow led to the production of hundreds of films by the major studios, all claiming to depict real life in the North. According to Pierre Berton, in Hollywood alone the frenzy of fascination for the snow country has generated over 500 movies in a sixty-year period (Berton 1975). While it is beyond the scope of this book to consider the question of why Hollywood produced so many movies about Canada, we can still speculate on the attraction that impressive snowswept forests, sexy mounties and snow white ladies might carry in the New Mexico and Nevada deserts, as well as other quaint American landscapes. Primarily melodramatic, with a twist of desperation and racial villainy – French Canadians being the stand-in for Mexicans – likely to draw the most resistant of spectators, the movies are known to be notoriously bad, B movies with limited audience reception. Nevertheless its "sameness out there," to quote Berton, in addition to the low cost of production and export of formulaic Hollywood scripts from the desert into snow country, made the snow movie a strong vehicle for cheap costume-drama production. While an offended Berton understands the "Hollywood does Canada" economy as a powerful ideological and exploitative system misrepresenting a *true* depiction of Canadian history and Canadians, for my part, I adopt a more ironic approach to the culture of snow movies. Snow movies are not vehicles for knowledge of the authentic other, but instead constitute an inefficient yet fascinating and perverse tactic to reappropriate historical moments for an audience that was fundamentally clueless about what a Canadian beaver looked like in any case.

While the ethnographic tradition of films à la *Nanook* stand as the classic reference points for northern exposure, Hollywood has had its shares of icy jewels. All things considered, it is not surprising that among the Mounties and other beauties of the nation, fur became the great exotic and romantic teaser for representing all things above the 49th parallel. Romantic accounts of such marriages between Hollywood and the new fur country are commonly informed by a homoerotic and macho tone. The Mounted Police, northern alter ego of the American cavalry, were popular heroes of these snow tales, always getting their men, even if it meant losing their gals. Less lucky than the intrepid, buff-looking Mounties, the HBC factors were often represented as crooked rascals exploiting everything alive in the North, beast or human. Over the years, several of these icy jewels have attained the status of Canadian anthology classics, such as *Northwest Passage* (K. Vidor, 1941), *North West Mounted Police* (C. B. DeMille, 1940), and the all-time favorite of the 1990s fake-fur renaissance designer Isaac Mizrahi (see chapter 6) *Call of the Wild* (W. Wellman, 1935).

Figure 2.2 Scenes from the Beaver Club banquet. Prince Rupert, Charles II, Radisson, Lord Crewe, Lady Barbara. From the 20th Century Fox film *Hudson's Bay*, taken from *The Beaver* magazine, December 1940. Print courtesy of *The Beaver*, Canada's National History Society, HBCA/PAM.

Initiated in 1937, the proposal to do a film on the origins of the HBC fur merchants *en Canada* quickly received the approval of the Company, which at the time was also busy creating multiple venues to increase its control over the retail fur business, threatened by the penetration and growing influence of the French fur house, Révillon Brothers. No wonder that when Paramount Pictures, through General Manager George Bagnall, approached HBC General Manager Philip Chester in Winnipeg to obtain permission and copyright clearances to make a film "celebrating" the great entrepreneurial spirit of the company, the governor's response was enthusiastic, though it would eventually prove to be naively misguided. The making of *Hudson's Bay* represented an important moment for the Hudson's Bay Company, as the abundant corporate correspondence documenting this event shows. The official company papers on the film are catalogued in eight files, ranging from the years of pre-production, to discussions about the marketable value of the film, to the historical contribution of the film to Canadian history, notably as an educational text.[16] While the film addresses the circumstances of the birth of the company in the seventeenth century and the necessary male bonding that arises from months of tracking beaver in the wilderness, its production and marketing was much more indebted to a call for economic nationalism (disguised as patriotism) and political colonial allegiance, two dimensions that are not estranged from one another in the context of the 1940s wartime period and the call for comrades in arms. Although directed by and infused with the Hollywood *art de faire*, the movie was clearly marketed as a Canadian "product", hence the impressive means deployed by the company to ensure that *Hudson's Bay* would fulfill its historic epic quality, without neglecting its economic and promotional functions. As one might expect in the context of corporate history, the question of authenticity from the perspective of the Company was of great concern. Interestingly enough, the HBC assigned its own historian, Douglas MacKay, to the script, the author of (among other publications) one of the first complete histories of the HBC, *The Honourable Company* (1936).[17]

But what were the motivations of the HBC headquarters in jumping on the "Hollywood does Hudson's Bay" bandwagon of the entertainment business? The HBC was eager to become known outside Canada and expand its commercial activities throughout North America, and it saw in the glamour of Hollywood a way to reestablish its rather shaky and controversial image as a colonialist corporation. In the ensuing beaver craze that hit Hollywood, the race for the Hudson's Bay Company tale was quite fierce. According to HBC correspondence, two different projects solicited the approval and collaboration of the company: one led by Paramount Pictures with Cecil B. DeMille as director, and the other by 20th Century Fox. Following a bloody battle between Paramount and 20th Century Fox, a cat fight was reported in the papers as comparable to the two-year epic battle that pitted the same two leading studios over the southern colonial sagas, *Jezebel* and *Gone with the Wind*.[18] The abrupt withdrawal of the star director DeMille from the *Hudson's Bay* project[19] forced

Paramount to cancel the production, and Fox quickly stepped in. Meanwhile, DeMille and Paramount were busy producing the feature film that would end up scooping Hudson's Bay on its own territory: *North West Mounted Police*, starring Gary Cooper and Paulette Goddard, which premiered in Canada three months before *Hudson's Bay*.[20]

Beyond the territorial studio fights, the political and cultural context prevailing at the time was extremely favorable for the production of a film naturalizing the commercial and cultural ties between Great Britain and Canada. Given that *Hudson's Bay* was released at a moment when participation in the war effort was dividing the country, the advertising displayed by both 20th Century Fox and the HBC itself each in their respective chains across Canada betrayed a common national effort to stimulate patriotic, colonial feelings. As much as *Nanook* was all about the exotic Other, *Hudson's Bay* was about the contrasting points of the internal other: the French and the British becoming one unified couple, fighting for progress, and the preservation and triumph of the British/colonial presence in the "peace" of the new country. Billed as a film about reconciliation between men of all nations, 20th Century Fox received incredible support from the HBC officers. The Company also managed to involve various federal officials and agencies in documenting and advertising *Hudson's Bay* as *the* film about Canada. As I will show in the following pages, the close collaboration offered by the HBC and its employees in the production of the film raised important issues about the intermingling of corporate national history with that of sexualized embodiment of the nation. Moreover, the very specific homosocial representation of the birth of the Canadian nation under the sponsorship of the HBC unavoidably led to the gendering and sexualizing of Canada the nation as a fur babe. If men were always at the forefront of the Hudson's Bay tale, women were closely involved in the materialization of the national history as a fur romance. Fascinating documents relate to the complex elaboration of a faithful and sympathetic corporate narrative, along with the urgency of addressing ethnic and sexual issues – what came to be known as the all-important "woman's angle" in the initial Paramount storyline.

This matter of the "woman's angle" had less to do with a historical concern for representativeness of the invisible skin of the fur lady, than with the marketing and distribution strategies of the film. While the HBC people were more concerned with addressing women as consumers and shoppers in their retail stores and promoting households goods and fur for a female market, the Hollywood producers were clearly obsessed with the marketability and seductiveness to a female audience, first-class consumers of costume dramas and melodramas, of a film about a bunch of boys in the woods with their raccoon hats.

This gender interplay between the company and the Hollywood studio demonstrates the extent to which the film, in spite of its fur environment, was mostly a male action movie. As a way to displace the fact that they were overshadowed in the film, women were strongly involved in the making of the film. From the outset and in a clear gesture to bring a woman's touch to this buddy-buddy tale, women were invited to bring their labor in the shaping of the story, both as storytellers and guardians of the spirit of the nation and the colonial adventure. Miss Grace Nute, a historian from the United States, was involved from a very early stage of the project, and despite the battles between the two Hollywood rival studios over ownership of the story, managed to stay on as a consultant – on the initiative of the HBC – through to the end of the production.[21] And before Fox jumped in to produce the actual film, Jeanie MacPherson, researcher and scriptwriter for Cecil B. DeMille, gathered an impressive amount of information for the project, soliciting the participation of the HBC personnel for the script on a regular basis. Notably, MacPherson played a crucial role in collecting documentation about the Canadian North, initiating and maintaining a close contact with MacKay, literally fleshing out the anecdotal and fictitious tones of an authentic fur story, and translating the exoticness of the foreign north country into a suitable Hollywood project. Ironically, while fulfilling her role as empathic Canadian fan, McPherson would be instrumental in the drastic withdrawal of Paramount from the HBC project.[22]

At the Canadian end of the story, women were also key agents in making the HBC story into a national comedy. Most of the office employees of the HBC in Winnipeg were men, of course, but one woman took over the public relation function with the Hollywood studios: Alice MacKay. The first contact with HBC seems to have involved Douglas MacKay, her husband, author of the bible used by the Hollywood producers to sketch a first draft of the screenplay. After the sudden death of Douglas MacKay in a plane crash in 1939, Alice succeeded her husband as the HBC public relations representative – interestingly, there is no official trace of this passage of power, but the correspondence continues with Alice MacKay acting ex officio. Following Paramount's decision to abandon the *Hudson's Bay* movie, in a clear PR strategy, Alice formally became the Company lady assigned to the Hollywood producers.[23]

In order to avoid a second aborted project, many initiatives poured from both sides with the clear intention of easing tensions between Hollywood's vision of the birth of the Canadian fur nation, starring French buddy adventurers, and the company's own agenda of highlighting the British and romantic investment in the building of colonial Canada. Following one of her Penelope's odysseys, Alice MacKay traveled to Hollywood to visit the production set in November 1938, practically holding "salon" with the producers of the film. Her diplomatic mission was to maintain friendly relations with the producers, to marvel before the magic of Hollywood, and eventually smooth things over during the bumpy period that would follow the involvement of Clifford Wilson in 1939. Wilson, editor of the trade magazine *The Beaver* – an unofficial HBC promotional vehicle – was assigned as special historical advisor for the production of the film, and his contact with Hollywood, though friendly at the beginning, turned out to be quite frustrating.[24]

Unlike Wilson, who was bitter about his Hollywood experience, ceaselessly complaining about the lack of historical authenticity in the entire enterprise, and Hollywood's "dilettantism" vis-à-vis Canadian specificity, MacKay was seduced by her movieland experience. The abundant and ladylike correspondence between Alice MacKay and executive producer Kenneth MacGowan showed Alice's strong commitment to honor her husband's desire for the production of the film at any cost and by any means necessary, as well her genuine gift for exploiting her diplomatic charms. Her letters to MacGowan intermingle business talk and fan confessions, framing her Alice in Hollywood adventures as that of a pure fairy tale.[25] In between marveling at the ingenuous Hollywood sets, swooning before star studios, or shopping frantically for Shirley Temple collectable items for her daughter, Mackay was also busy establishing alliances with the producers on behalf of HBC. In this context, MacKay's trustful role went beyond that of diplomatic wife and the glittering surface of the transnational hostess, and to a certain extent was more instrumental than Clifford's. Her unique and paradoxical sense of allegiance to both the crown of England and English-Canadian nationalism was straightforward and passionate, and informed by a desire to add her two cents (or should I say five cents) to the screenplay.[26]

For example, she persistently encouraged a narrative angle that would privilege the most prominent Western seigneur of the HBC, Sir George Simpson, whom MacKay hailed as "a complete success story", over 20th Century Fox's choice of the elusive rascal Radisson.[27] Whether furnishing details of the HBC's mode of paying respect to the King of England or highlighting other jewels of the HBC's colonial legacy, MacKay was clearly invested in making the film into a celebration of the British colonial enterprise and Canadian Anglophone culture. Her role as Britannia's daughter reached its wildest expression in 1939 during the royal tour of the King George VI and Queen Elizabeth to Canada and Winnipeg, when she bombarded the Hollywood producers with details of the beaver ceremony (also known as the rent ceremony) and its ritual and historic importance in the culture of the Company. To the dismay of the producers and for her pure pleasure, she describes the rent ceremony in the following terms:

> Big things are happening in Canada this year, as the King and Queen are paying us a visit in May and June. One phase of this may interest you. For the first time in our long history (?) we are to carry out one of the terms of our Charter by "yielding and paying two Elks and two black Beavers" to the King when he enters our territory. Fortunately, he has graciously signified that he will accept a couple of elk heads and two black beaver skins instead of the traditional rent, though it might have been more dramatic to present him with live animals.[28]

As much as this nationalist taxidermist exhibitionism may appear to be limited to the expression of one royal family fan, MacKay's patriotic "drives" were in fact shared by most of the governors of the Company, and her emphatic understanding of what should constitute a success story was truly informed by corporate colonial romanticism. Ironically, the combo of English-Canadian nationalism and loyalty to the crown would have been widespread at the time (and is so even now). In this sense, MacKay's attitude towards Hollywood's imprint of HBC history was a mixture of ambivalence and fascination moving between colonial reminiscence and nationalist fever for the beaver land. Her voiced fear that the film would be more American than British, and that the Britishness of the Company of Adventurers would be overlooked by the irreverent attitude of that reckless and wicked French "rascal" Radisson (her own words). Alice's profound skepticism about tying the birth of her beloved company to that of a couple of French renegades – which was attractive for Hollywood – reveals the extent to which the HBC was playing gatekeeper of the corporate national story informed by British colonialist influence.

A squaw for rent

The ethnic elitism expressed by the HBC about the British vis-à-vis American narrative did not translate in the same way with respect to the gendering of the narrative. As conceived and represented by the officers of the HBC, the gender edge was unquestionably framed within a white context and the woman's angle was unsurprisingly framed in terms of ladies. Despite memoirs and travelogues written by governors, adventurers, or company's employees (Factors) discussing at length the politics of native skin in the customs of the company, the Hollywood fur lady could not by any means be a native woman, no matter what history, so to speak, had to say about this. Unlike the North West Company which made the country marriages an intrinsic part of a fair deal for the fur trade, HBC had always maintained an official position against inter-racial marriages and mixed "bonds of love." Henceforth, traces of native women in the culture of the company have always been perceived as tainted scratches on the English stock of the HBC, or with mixed feelings in the best of all cases.

This official position would find a new challenge when Miss Islay Ramona Sinclair, a Cree-blooded woman living in Winnipeg, wrote to MacPherson on 4 August 1937.[29] In blunt terms, Sinclair offered her services for a possible role in the forthcoming Paramount picture, then the primary producer on the project. Sinclair's request created excitement in Hollywood and commotion in Winnipeg as it raised a series of issues around sex/uality, race and trading customs.[30] Not only had the sensitive, quasi-silenced issue of the country wives as an intrinsic part of the history of the fur trade reemerged in contemporary dress, but so had the positioning and agency willingly embraced by the native woman in relation to the trading market. Sinclair's bold and unusual request was all the more challenging to the racial and sexual economy of the company as she was offering to perform and to masquerade for the producers as an authentic and legitimized Indian figure, reappropriating and recirculating the market value of her skin within the economy of Hollywood.

Sinclair's legitimate claim to embody the native side of the story relied on two elements: genetic legacy that made her a natural heir, and representational physical qualities that increased her marketable value for Hollywood. In a fairly detailed letter, Sinclair introduces herself as a daughter of the country whose family have been connected to the history of the HBC for nearly two hundred years. Having spent her childhood in the "historic Fort Norway House" (an important fur post in the north of Manitoba, home province of the company headquarters), Sinclair's legacy began with her great-great-grandfather who, as Chief Factor at York Factory, had married a Cree girl named Nahoway. Her father kept the HBC trail alive and in the family, working for the company for thirty-five years. Having disclosed her credentials as an HBC child, Sinclair went on to discuss in the most dazzling and detailed way the market value of her interracial genealogy from the standpoint of the sexual economy. She proudly advertised her "type" (emphasis by Sinclair herself) as a fulfillment of the "Indian" or the "Oriental" other for a Hollywood production, displaying at once a "bodily trademark" (Coombe 1996) and the performative quality of her true "origins." As an additional treat, Sinclair portrays her stage experience, insisting on the assets that her Indian performativity might contribute to a range of Asian cast characters. Sinclair depicts her racial traits and economic value in the following eloquent terms:

> Do you think this set up would be of any use to you in your forthcoming picture? It seems to me it might have some advertising value. If you are at all interested I should be glad to send photographs, press clippings and so on. I am five feet in height and weigh one hundred pounds. Dark skin and hair – features sufficiently of a "type" to lend themselves well to Indian or Oriental make-up. My speaking voice is low-pitched, though I sing soprano, and my diction is supposed to be very good.[31]

Beyond the businesslike casting-agent tone of her letter, what constitutes a total surprise and a wonderful piece of racial performance is the way in which Sinclair frames her value on market for the Indian performance just as any white Hollywood agent would. Sinclair's letter is not only a striking piece of salesmanship of racial features for advertising purposes and self-promotional valorization, but it also unfolds the complex and contradictory position of the subaltern body in the context of skin exchange. On one hand, Sinclair's letter to MacPherson and the Paramount studios betrays an uncanny sense of self-awareness about the physical value of the Indian body in the trading and promotion of the forthcoming film, bringing as she states in her own terms "some advertising value" to the white beaver narrative. On the other hand, Sinclair's racialized self-representation exposes the paradoxes of the mixed body on the trading market: in order words, the market value of the Indian woman lies in the commodity potential of "passing" as native for Hollywood, no matter how much "Indianness" was embodied in Sinclair's "type." Sinclair's skin value for a film about the fur land was due as much to a mixture of authentic genealogy as to the possibilities of fitting into the cultural and economic re-appropriation of the Indian woman's dark skin and hair, to conform to a perfect pristine stereotype of the Indian woman. If, as Stuart Hall (1997) rightly points out, stereotypes are the quickest way to access the Other,[32] the access to Otherness in the Sinclair story involved the masquerade of authenticity and the trans-formative display of authentic biological features as excessive and spectacular, i.e. perfect in the tradition of Hollywood "racial politics."

In vivid terms, Sinclair's letter raises crucial issues concerning both the visibility of the country marriages and the mixed body for a story of the origins of the company, as well as the sexual economy of the female body in relation to a corporate market. While Sinclair's letter enticed the Hollywood producers' taste for exotic tales, the HBC seemed more inclined to leave to Hollywood the decision on whether to crossover history, fiction and experience. As MacPherson confessed to Doug MacKay in the correspondence between Paramount and the HBC over Sinclair's tale, the value of the interracial snow romance was attractive to the Hollywood producers, and it promised an original (read "authentic") way to insert the famous "woman's angle" into this boys-club story. As MacPherson phrases it:

> What is your reaction to this lady? If Mr. DeMille should decide to use her in the picture, would she be of any help to me on the WOMAN'S angle of our subject? It is possible she might have some personal incident at York Factory that would be colorful. I notice that she seems to be part Indian and this might indicate some early romance between an Indian lady and a Factor. (Along the lines you and I once talked.).[33]

In the end, Sinclair was not cast in *Hudson's Bay*, in other words, the native body was excluded from Hollywood's final story as imagined by the 20th Century Fox people. Instead, Lamar Trotti, the studio's screenwriter, and the Winnipeg HBC office concluded a gentlemen's agreement that secured a British romance through the "addition" of the fictitious Lady Barbara. HBC and Hollywood traded Lady Sinclair's skin for Lady Barbara's seventeen minutes of screen fame, bringing an ironic spin on the fur trade company motto: a skin for a skin's worth. The gendering of the story served to mask the racial edges of the history of the fur trade, particularly a classic fur country tradition: the country wives, i.e., the native wives that fur trappers "collected" from one trip to another. Even the free promotional kits for window displays provided by the HBC on the occasion of the release of the film silenced the racial/native issue, as one local manager's remark states: "no 'Indian' or 'Esquimo' materials for display were available, but old company calendars, copies of the *Beaver*, fur trade maps and company photographs."[34]

Lady Barbara's trail and Radisson's monumental body[35]

Despite the presence of Clifford P. Wilson as a "special technical advisor" for the production of the film, *Hudson's Bay* never quite reached the level of historical accuracy that the trading company originally sought.[36] On the contrary, Hollywood did everything to assure that the film would cross the borders of local history to attain the "universal" stature of any other Hollywood story. As advertised in a fifteen-minute promotional segment for *Hudson's Bay* broadcast over the radio the night before the premiere at Winnipeg's Capitol cinema in January 1941: "Let it be said at the outset that the scriptwriter, Lamar Trotti, was not concerned with writing history. The picture is a tale of high adventure, with a warm, glowing love story running through it."[37]

In fact, Trotti managed to deal with love on many levels, playfully dislodging the sexual edges of bonds across gender within and beyond natural frontiers. If the requisite and predictable heterosexual love story figures in the romantic fling between Lord Crewe, special emissary of the court of England, and Lady Barbara, the film's biggest love affair is the most naturalized of all: the very special emotional and physical bond between Radisson and the dark treasures of the *real* Hudson's Bay. Throughout the film, Hudson's Bay the land and cradle of the richest beaver pelts of the colony, is serenaded with all the devotion usually dedicated to a lady/woman, powerfully echoing a colonial narrative tradition that shapes the ladyland as the Other: the land as an object of colonial lust becomes a mysterious "absent" female.[38] In conformity with the Hollywood lonesome hero, Radisson's carnal love translates through his special bond with nature: Hudson's Bay, a bound of love that is too intimately shared in the company of men, specially that of Lord Crewe.

The romantic ladyland prose is channeled through a homoerotic duet starring Radisson and Lord Edward Crewe (John Sutton). The scenes between Radisson and Lord Crewe are articulated in a double entendre that echoes the travel diaries and papers on the homosocial eroticism of fur country, as well as the ironic joke among voyageurs and explorers that HBC stood for the "Horny Boys Club."[39] That the male protagonists are all "others" from Hollywood's perspective, i.e., French, Native and British, only reinforces such an ironic double entendre. While heterosexualized on the surface, most of the scenes that intervene during the fur expeditions in the wilderness are shot like romantic homosocial interludes with a profusion of cross-gazing between the two heroes. Alone with Lord Crewe, Radisson praises his attraction for the wild lady, speaking of the blissful moments that the land has brought him countless times. Carried away by such passionate love poetry, Lord Crewe stands as a privileged confidante/lover. "This country is like a woman: waiting for a big man to take her," Radisson raves to an admirative and obedient Crewe. In another tête-à-tête, when Crewe inquires of Radisson why he would not marry, Radisson replies that Hudson's Bay is the only woman that he has ever loved. Crewe nods pensively, staring affectionately at Radisson. Ultimately, the ladyland metaphor of Hudson's Bay clearly articulates a link between the female body and its natural fur resources, at the same time that it sexualizes the relationships between men and the land. "Hudson's Bay, she is Canada," the butch macho Radisson adds with a sly smile to the dandy Crewe. As sexually challenging as Radisson's passionate panegyric for the beaver land sounds, this is not the marketable narrative that the promotional and advertising campaigns for the film pushed. *Hudson's Bay* was billed as an epic encounter between Muni (Radisson) and Tierney (Lady Barbara) from one hand, and Lady Barbara, and Lady Hudson's Bay – the metaphoric articulation between skin and fur in the construction of corporate national history. Ironically, the leading lady of the film is Lady Hudson's Bay, and Lady Barbara stands in a supporting role.

The contrast between the advertising campaigns featuring Tierney and her actual screen-time participation in this homoerotic, buddy-buddy narrative is amazingly stark, to say the least. Lady Barbara is to *Hudson's Bay* what the gown is to Greta Garbo in *Queen Christina* (R. Mamoulian, 1933): a drag. According to rumors, Hollywood sought out a "real" historical character to bring in the famous missing "woman's angle," and research was conducted to uncover some of the real ladies of Charles II's court that might fit the fur lady role. A certain Lady Mary Kirke seemed mysterious enough, until Nute looked closer. As Alice MacKay explained to MacGowan:

> [Miss Nute] also was vague about Mary Kirke, for the reason that she had found there was a notorious courtesan – presumably they are all notorious – named Mary Kirke of Charles's court. Either way it is a good story, and if you want to pursue Mary, write Miss Nute.[40]

Ultimately, the Hollywood producers would not settle for the good courtesan narrative so often exploited in Western film genres, and went instead with a more domesticated fur lady. Pure invention of the Hollywood producers, Lady Barbara was the necessary Venus in furs that any 1940s epic drama with a market edge for attracting a women's audience would demand. In a romantic farewell to her beau, Lord Crewe, Lady Barbara wanders with equal elegance from the king's court ball to the "no lady" land of the London docks. With a fur cape and a candelabra as her sole escort, Lady Barbara captures all the civilized world in one pose in one contrasting image to the wild and savage Hudson's Bay (Figure 2.3).

If the film gives spectators barely a glimpse of Lady Barbara, the publicity campaigns that accompanied the release of the film transformed and essentialized Tierney into one of the first fully-clothed Venuses in furs of all

Figure 2.3 She came from the snow: Lady Barbara (Gene Tierney) in furs, 1940.
Print courtesy of the Hudson's Bay Company archive.

American colonial creation. As wartime culture dominated the screen, Tierney faithfully posed as the fur pin-up of snow land. Whether featured on the cover of trade magazines such as *The Moccasin Telegraph*,[41] or in a full-colour amorous embrace with Lord Crewe on the cover of the *The Beaver* (Figure 2.4), Tierney genuinely played the lady that this love-in-a-fur-country called for. She proudly embodied the skin to be traded off for the sake of the new world and the future of a nation. With an anachronistic opening that blasted the Canadian national anthem (as the war effort obliged), *Hudson's Bay* built itself on the frank and patriotic camaraderie uniting manhood, a white manhood of course: British, French and French-Canadian. Alas, the film ends before we get to see Tierney play the diplomatic wife in the colony, suggesting that the men returned to their favorite country wife: lady Hudson's Bay.

Ultimately, this is what the movie is all about: intimacies between beaver men, and the male solidarity that reunites members of the beaver club. *Hudson's*

Figure 2.4 The perfect couple: Lady Barbara and Lord Crewe, *The Beaver* December 1940, cover photograph. Print courtesy of the Hudson's Bay Company Archive.

Bay stages an encounter between the wild world, embodied by a ruthless Radisson, and the sophisticated civilized world, portrayed here by a glittering Vincent Price as Charles II. The high profile of Charles II in the film is at odds with the historical founding of the Hudson's Bay Company. This raised questions about Hollywood's grafting of the character of Charles II onto Rupert's personality, slipping Price into Rupert's fur slippers. Given the fact that Price impersonated Charles II, this masquerade comes as a queer extra-textual crossing between Price and the actual Prince Rupert. As historical authenticity was far from the main motif of the Hollywood production, Prince Rupert, the brains behind the creation and drafting of the Company Charter in 1667, is confined in the film to the perfect subject of the king, an obedient civil servant of the British court. The film glorifies the fur saga as one involving two personas strongly attached to the beaver tale, and as the publicity and promotional campaigns led by the HBC headquarters show, there was no attempt to go against this traditional way of envisioning fur history. Paul Muni and Vincent Price became the odd couple of the fur trade, leaving Gene Tierney to personify the fur lady behind the furpost counter offscreen.

Clearly, the star status attained by Price and Muni at the time of the shooting was determinant in the marketing and promotional strategies deployed both by Hollywood and the HBC. The correspondence between the producers of the film and HBC headquarters in Winnipeg showed the extent to which the HBC was eager to endorse a fictionalized account of the adventurer's fur journey, providing Price's and Muni's participation was secured. In their questions about the script, HBC people showed a great deal of concern to clarify that Paul Muni/ Radisson had the insignia of the HBC – and NOT that of France – tattooed on his heart. This issue created a fair tension between Hollywood and Winnipeg, mainly due to the extreme control exercised by the studios over the commercial use of their star images at the time. On one hand, the HBC was still trying to digest the fact that Muni ended up as the logo of the company; and on the other hand, the Hollywood producers were determined to defend their vision of the fur trade as a one-man business, in the pure tradition of the Hollywood lonesome hero. This is why Muni/Radisson is presented as the good white father, a seventeenth century early version of the Lone Ranger/Davey Crockett of the Northwest, attentively listening to his fellow Indians, a necessarily benevolent figure for the survival of native culture and customs faced with the savage imperial manners of the British. In so many ways, Radisson stands as the transgendered "daughter of the country" – a role that should have been incumbent on Lady Barbara. With his fake French-from-France accent, Muni's Radisson embodies the exoticness and wild trait of the French *coureur des bois*, half-domesticated, witty, yet "roguish" nonetheless, the perfect beaver man.[42]

Muni, the stud voyageur, became the funny girl of the day, or should I say the beaver of the company, as seen in the glamorous posters featuring a larger than life Muni as half-Hercules, half-Daniel Boone, an iron-fisted adventurer. An ad for one of the Canadian opening venues features a quite sensationalist and ambiguous caption of Muni as the nation-man, which seems to address the homosocial texture of the film as well as its heroic colonial entreprise, all at once. "With the Drop of a Withered Twig, he . . . took a friend's life! Broke the heart of a woman in love [Lady Barbara] . . . saved a new world for the ruler who had ordered him hanged!"[43]

The national publicity campaign preceding and following the January 1941 trans-American release illustrates the extent to which the producers and the HBC sought to equate the creation of the HBC with the birth of the nation. The *Hudson's Bay* promotional campaign was not limited to the traditional advertising networks, window displays and radio shows, but also reached into the educational sphere through a national essay contest across Canadian elementary and secondary schools.[44] Interestingly enough, the film, promoted as a corporate fiction, came to be dressed up as the national Canadian window to the world, and talks were even initiated between the Canadian government, the HBC people and 20th Century Fox to acquire the film for the National Museum of Canada.[45] And as if the movie's message was not straightforward enough, in an ultimate concession to corporate nationalism and trans-American financial power, Fox even considered closing the film with a shot of the Company flag flying over the store, but withdrew the idea at the last minute.

Beyond its totally conventional epic dramatic format and insertion of a supposed heterosexual romance, *Hudson's Bay* constitutes a unique fabric to link the Canadian cultural industries, national corporatist discourse, and the display of testosterone. The actual release of the film culminated in a frantic campaign that hit the country coast to coast with wide window displays wherever the film was premiered.[46] The highlights of the Hudson's Bay publicity landscape and various trailers featured Muni's pecs and Price's gigantic wig, with Lady Barbara hugging and clinging to her furs in the backdrop.[47] The exposure of Muni and Price maintained the masculinization of the nation – as well as providing a transnational reference to the local story. Yet Gene Tierney's astonishing off-screen visibility is informed by the paradoxical attempt to address both contemporary predicaments regarding women and the fur market, along with the traditional desire to embed the *Hudson's Bay* story in a homosocial order. The fact that Tierney's character, Lady Barbara, is fictitious and fleshed/skinned out to give "the film some female allure" (Newman 1995: 193) does nothing to conceal the fact that the film was all about beaver men, leaving fur ladies and other girls on the side. This drag/masquerade did not fool anyone, from Clifford Wilson[48] to *New York Daily News* reviewer Kate Cameron, who wrote in one of the first film reviews of *Hudson's Bay*, that:

Pretty Gene Tierney has little to do in the story, although as Lord Crewe's fiancée she has the leading feminine role. This is a man's picture and all the ladies including Virginia Field as Nell Gwyn, are overshadowed by the male characters.

(Cameron 1941: 42)

Even Jerald (Morton Lowry), Lady Barbara's 'sissy' brother, usurped Tierney's position as wife of the country. Jerald, who volunteers to make the journey to masculinity and go to Canada to make a man of himself, masterfully plays the sissy boy of the Club. Cowardly Jerald, the only "femme" among this group of butch machos, does not fancy the cold nor the wilderness, longing instead for the glitter of the English court's sumptuous and sumptuary dress code. Jerald does not understand the real man's rule for a fair/square deal with the natives and prefers instead to trade pelts by cunning. His face and body are depicted as so tenderly precious that he becomes that favourite prey of the hunters: a beaver. In one of the best one-liners of the film, upon being bitten by a mad and prissy Jerald, Groseillers exclaims: "This fellow got some sharp teeth – like a beaver!"

With such homosocial texture, the presence of Lady Barbara in the promotional trailers constitutes an evanescent reminder for spectators, producers and sponsors that fur is better worn with a white lady's touch, and that the fur market is a woman's affair. To the bestiality of the *coureur des bois* and voyageurs, and their unfashionable raccoon hats, Lady Barbara's overshadowed sensuality, tamed eroticism and fancy furs adds class and feminine taste to the beaver mens' story. Gene Tierney is proudly portrayed as the fur lady *de service*, the fetishistic beaver displayed as a trading commodity travelling from magazine covers to billboards and marquees around the country. Framed as a fur (wartime) pin-up from head to toe, Tierney savoured this fur show, a compensation for the meagre screen time she was granted in the film itself. But Tierney had to share fame and glory with another skin: the point blanket.

The point blanket doll

In this section, I further consider how the production of the homosocial value of the *Hudson's Bay* story is premised on the condition that female skin be "treated" like any other fabric. In fact, Tierney became the corporate skin of the production through the HBC's most famous trademark: the point blanket. How did Lady Barbara's skin touch the trading fabric to transform herself into a domestic corporate good? The point blanket gained in surplus value in contact with Tierney's skin, and vice versa. While peripheral to the storyline of the film, Tierney's skin was central to its circulation, and to the representation of the *Hudson's Bay* as fur story.

The HBC blanket was introduced in the nineteenth century as a token value for trading goods with the trappers (native and white "engagés"). Still used at the time of the release of the film in most Canadian northern trade posts, the visibility of this colonial trading token had the enormous advantage of capturing the economic dimension of the fur history in one artifact. With their famous colourful stripes, the point blankets have over the centuries become the trademark, the emblem that would come to signify HBC's imperial control of the North. More so than beaver fur, the point blanket marked the domination, if not quasi-monopoly of the HBC over the competitive fur trade in Canada. While marginal competitors were "sharing" beaver skins as trading tokens, only one possessed the exclusive use of the point blanket: the HBC.

How did Tierney and the blanket come to be reunited in one corporate skin? *Hudson's Bay* was premiered in Canada in Winnipeg, home of HBC headquarters, on 16 January 1941.[49] On this memorable occasion, Paramount, Famous Players (the Canadian distributor) and HBC teamed up to organize a national release of the film and to launch an aggressive promotional campaign in the various retail stores of the company across Canada. While the film was not a box-office blast or a critical success across the US,[50] it was a goldmine for Bay store managers, local businessmen and movie theater managers in Canada. The word was out that *Hudson's Bay* was a film about Canada that featured fur and Frenchies like never before in Hollywood. Despite her marginal part, Tierney stood proudly on the marquee next to Muni and Price.

One of the strategies used by the marketing division to promote the association of blanket/flag/Canadian nation was to display Gene Tierney's body as the ultimate fur/blanket flag. Tierney was seen draped in the blanket as though it were a fur coat (Figure 2.5). On the set pictures immortalizing Gene Tierney and the blanket in one symbiotic embrace metamorphosed the eternal fur moment in the Hudson's Bay narrative: a fur lady for a blanket. As a result, the HBC publicity department and theater managers reoriented their promotional tactics around two of the most popular national stars: the beaver and the HBC point blanket.[51] Given that fur was after all the original skin that brought the British colonial presence into the north and western areas of Canada, it came as no surprise that it should be displayed like a star. As illustrated by the correspondence exchanged between the various divisions of the store, the officials placed a great deal of emphasis on achieving international recognition for the HBC point blanket as a central factor in the launching of a promotional campaign for the film. HBC franchise stores responded with wild yet disturbingly creative suggestions for promotional materials, urging the Winnipeg Publicity department to collaborate in the staging of original (sic!) trading show performances. One suggested "a miniature parade of young men dressed as Indians and portaging canoes of that nature," for which "it would be a good idea for the Hudson's Bay Company to make up some inexpensive costumes and furnish these to the dealers so they can put on a parade."[52]

Indeed, fur trade associations across the country and even in the US were approached to contribute to this skin show, mediating Canadian national resources, fur and beaver, in service of his majesty the beaver. Urban centers, along with the enthusiastic regional warehouses, were called to duty. In Montréal, for instance, the Fur Trade Office was asked to cooperate as closely as possible with local movie theaters. J. C. Atkins, Manager of the HBC Blanket Division, in a letter to Henry Morgan & Co. Limited in Montréal, mentions that arrangements have been made with the manager of Loew's (a famous

Figure 2.5 Tierney poses with a blanket, a gift from the Hudson's Bay Company, 1940.
Print courtesy of the Hudson's Bay Company Archive.

downtown movie palace) for the January 24 premiere of the film 'for tie-up displays, and also the suggestion as to bringing furs – skins and garments, into such displays.'[53] It is interesting to note that during the same period as the film's release, there was a significant increase in fur advertisement in selected city/local newspapers. Across impressive ads featuring Muni as the Daniel Boone/Davey Crockett of the North, appeared advertisements of ladies in furs for local retailers.[54] Because the film was scheduled to open in the New Year, advertising campaigns in the print media coincided with the holiday season shopping craze.

The film was then used by HBC to promote the ultimate corporate skin and pride of the company: the point blanket (Figure 2.5). In this sense, Hudson's Bay and her dark wilderness could not compete on the same terrain as Lady Barbara, queen of all for style. While fur was a luxurious fabric for the nation in war, the blanket suited perfectly the Company's wish to reach the international/ North American market through the most national of corporate skins. On screen beaver fur stood as the promotional and cultural marker of the Company of Adventurers; off screen it was the blanket and its strong colonial reminiscences that came to signify the historic link between the company and the Canadian nation. Hence the desire to expand the Company's visibility beyond the borders by using the blanket and Tierney's skin as a joint venture, if not a common thread. In a memo from Winnipeg to retailers, the blanket was presented as "la belle du jour" and tantalized as "the ideal Christmas gift," and Frank Ryan instructed HBC partners that "every bride covets a pair; for they represent the ultimate in blanket merchandise."[55]

But more than commercial circulation, the company hoped for a more intimate embodiment of its star fabric. With the presence of two company representatives on the set, the official ceremony that traded blankets for blanketed stars was initially designed and staged by HBC as a publicity stunt.[56] However, unable to tie up an agreement that would allow the company to obtain real/free publicity out of the stars' shots with the blankets, HBC went after the fabric of the colonial enterprise, using the original design sent to the stars as a fair substitute for the absent bodies, literally making the point blankets impersonate each star of the production. In an attempt to increase the international value of the Company skin – and as a poorly disguised bribe of the actors in exchange for public endorsement of the blanket – each actor received genuine HBC blankets, the same ones that had assured the company its colonial status of negotiation. Accompanied by the famous Company trademark slogan *With compliments of the Hudson's Bay Company*, point blankets were showered over the actors and executive producers of the studio in one of the most important (and costly) seduction campaigns coordinated by the Winnipeg office. The point blanket goes to Hollywood saga reached epic proportions. The Winnipeg Blanket divisions went through a tremendous frenzy in order to accommodate Price's taste for royal blue, Tierney's fondness for pink and yellow stripes, and Muni and Crewe's butchy taste for dark colors. While blankets were generously distributed to every single member of the cast, Gene Tierney and Vincent Price were the only actors to choir over their adoring fondness for the HBC blanket. The actress, in a handwritten letter to the HBC Department Publicity Head, F.W. Gasston, praised the blanket and confessed longing for the completion of reshooting, so that she might wrap herself in the corporate fabric.[57]

> I received my beautiful sets of blankets quite some time ago but I have been so busy with retakes on the picture that I haven't ever had time to write you off a thank you note. They are are too lovely and I can't tell you how glad I am to have them. They match my room at home in Connecticut perfectly, so I'm taking them with me on my vacation with the hope that I shall get back there pretty frequently and get lots of opportunity to use them.

Even if the fear of being sued by the Actor's Guild stopped the studios and HBC from using a series of publicity shots featuring the actors with the blankets, including Tierney's (Figure 2.5) other initiatives were encouraged, and suggestions were offered on how to give "shape" and bring life to stacks of blankets, and to arrange windows and interior displays of blankets in the most intimate, cosy and homey ways. While the quasi-anthropomorphic visuality of point blanket was a response to the studio system injunction that limited the free circulation of star images outside the economy of Hollywood, especially in a non-domestic space, there is something definitely sensual in this trading of skins, this almost organic troubling of fabrics. True, in the intense correspondence exchanged by HBC and 20th Century Fox on the matter, it was obvious that HBC was desperate to marry the Company's financial and human involvement in the production of the film to that of the blanket, the corporate skin. In this sense, the point blanket-Tierney coupling emerges as an effective and affective alternative to blur the boundaries between fabrics. The blanket and its doll Tierney secure against all odds the marketability of domestic and female skins as trading goods, each skin providing a feminine touch-ing to a men-in-furs story.

Beaver tales of the city: the Beaver Club fairy tale

As Peter C. Newman argues (1995), the commercial and trading success of the film was tied to the direct involvement and partnership of the HBC in promoting this perfectly ethnocentric history of the Company's debut in the fur trade. *Hudson's Bay*, unlike many other short films produced and funded by the company to promote their commercial activities in the development of the trade, playfully reappropriates the wilderness of Canada as a masculine homosocial nation, and a feminine fur gig. The film's grand finale culminates in the spectacular scene of the signing of the Charter of the Company of Adventurers, seceding a quasi-full control over the fur market in Canada to English interests. This blissful royal moment glitters with an imposing display of wigs, beaver boys and dandies in a touching family portrait that captures the spirit of the man-made fur country: that of the King surrounded by his entourages of Princes, the grand seigneurs and men of the fur trade (see Figure 3.1). And no lady blanket could get in the way.

If *Hudson's Bay* constitutes a fantastic expression of corporate national history in which the homosocialization of the fur trade played a central role, the prominence of beaver boy associations and fur trader clubs creates a new tangent to the perpetuation of the beaver economy as the dominant historical narrative of the man-made nation. In this final section, I discuss how the homosocial aspect of the trade has been immortalized through the gentlemen's club culture, and specially that of the Beaver Club.

While fur narratives maintain a nostalgic politics of location regarding the "wilderness," replete with romanticizations of the North and its Inuit and native communities as makers of fur products, the city appears remote from the beauty of the colonial enterprise and as a representational site of fur trade history. For example, in the course of touring a number of sites on the trail of various fur archives and museums for this research, I visited an exhibition at the Musée de la civilisation in Québec City with the theme of "Memories: Identity and Nation."[58] I was struck by the fact that, while fur was abundantly portrayed as the eminent original fabric of the nation, it has faded from contemporary discourses on the industrialization and "modernization" of Québec. Various economic and financial reasons might partially account for such an "erasure" of fur from the national contemporary landscape. However, I argue that this missing link coincides with important changes that occurred within the twentieth-century fur market: in particular, fur truly became the modern urban woman's second skin, as well as coming to signify European immigrant labor and capital in the activities of the fur trade in Canada. In other words, the disappearance of fur from narratives of the nation and economic success stories converges with the permutations and emergence of a "racialization" (i.e. non-Caucasian marking) and gendering of the fur industry, now defined as an urban space. This feminization and racialization of the fur economy directly impinges on the fashioning of a new geographic configuration of fur narratives outside the liminality of the traditional white masculine sexual economy deployed in scenarios of wilderness and purity.[59]

Paradoxically, in this gendered and racialized context of selective urban and national production, one group managed to assure the interconnections between nation, nature and urban development in the most efficient and successful way: the Beaver Club. The Beaver Club, founded in 1785, is to Canadian fur history what the French can-can is to Parisian nightlife: a zany institution that has less to do with a national romanticization than with the sexual economy and bodily trademarks of the nation. The Beaver Club's popular tales and the way it has come over the centuries to illustrate and embody male fur culture merits a mention in the fur lady family album in and of itself. A social and political institution vaguely acquainted with Masonic organizational culture, the Beaver Club is unparalleled in Canada as an exclusive male association. Founded by three hard-core North West Company (NWC) partners and comrades in arms

Thomas, Joseph and Benjamin Frobisher, along with their buddy James McGill, the Beaver Club has its roots in the specifics of the ethnic and class politics and geographies of the economic development of the fur trade.[60]

Unlike dozens of other social clubs shaped by a French-English ethnic separatism, the Beaver Club never claimed to technically be a Canadian-Anglophone only institution. It counted among its nineteen founders eight prominent Francophone fur traders, the others being Scotsmen (six), Englishmen (three) and even two Americans, including Jacob Astor, the American fur tycoon, as an honorary gentleman. This demographic distribution encompassed an accurate portrait of the fur economy at the time, as well as hinting at the already transnational nature of the fur trade and its important ramifications for the United States. Whereas the HBC perpetuated a pristine image of mother England and British Culture, the NWC stood as a more local and regional formation, serving a local and national elite inflamed by reveries of wilderness, rather than fancy glittering banquets. Their governors lived in-colony – not abroad – and the alliances between French, Scottish and sometimes American traders were considered a sign of autonomy for the colony/ies against the all-powerful London-based colonial power. While the HBC governors were known to be British dandies and not inclined to get their hands dirty on the fur trail – in other words preferring to wear fur rather than to hunt it – the Nor'westers relished exposing their colonial roots. Indeed, the NWC officers were praised and admired for being "real men." But not just any sort of real men: *dressy* real men. The officers were truly buff bear boys in tuxedos.

My interest in the venerable and centennial club draws from my larger questioning of the sexually discursive movements that have marked representations of fur as *the* Canadian landmark. It marks a troubling and comforting site in the context of my research of women in furs because of the ways in which the Club, as a gentlemen's affair and in a very ambiguous fashion, deploys a continual revival of the past and a totally schizophrenic experience of the grand adventurers' expeditions in the fur country. Historic staging and role-playing of the grand adventures was the ultimate experience for the Beaver Club members, exposing at once the homosocial boundaries of the sexual economy of the trade, and the performativity of its economic agency. The membership of the most select of Montréal's elite is tied to the masculinity of the industry in terms of national discourse: the nation as a fur business featuring tuxedo-wearing bear boys performing their ultimate roles as fur traders. Following the tales of the beaver trade, it seems appropriate to devote some attention to this famous men-only club in which rumours of gargantuan dinners, drinking extravaganzas, and performances of metaphoric bestiality, testified to a continued "taste" and "touch" for homosocial fur gatherings among beaver men.

The Beaver Club, heir to the Northwest ideology of building on a local bourgeoisie eager to contest the supremacy of London over the colony, encapsulates both the resistance of a national political elite and a powerful promotional vehicle for the development of a national fur economy and other commodity goods on the continent.[61] With its fancy-dress men performing a fantasized *coureur des bois* legacy, it constituted an unprecedented manifestation of the growing interest in marketing the colony as a more independent economic structure, hence its extreme popularity as a "national men's club." Contrary to British gentlemen's clubs who represented the epitome of civilization, the Beaver Club was all about nature and the reinforcement of "going back to the wilderness" as a sense of belonging.

Yet it is not so much the constitution of the Beaver Club that arouses my interest in this famous institution. As a genuine colony of male beavers, its excesses and its dedication to men in furs mark its originality. For instance, in looking at the eccentricities of the club and its ritualistic *mise en scène* of the grand voyage into fur land, one finds an incredible dramatization and romanticization of fur culture as a masculine space. The dinners and meetings organized by the club were staged as a perfect urban reenactment of life in the wilderness – the restaging of *le grand voyage*, to reappropriate Newman's expression (1995). Only princes who could prove that they had spent one winter in Indian Country were officially admitted and initiated to Beaver Club culture. The valued experience of wintering in fur country was the most valid way to judge if one had the right stuff (*l'étoffe du pays*) for Beaver Club members. For the rich and prominent businessmen living in Montréal, this treasuring of life in the wilds contributed to the production of an abundant folklore about white men in fur country . . . and the so-called knowledge acquired from trading with the natives. The club magnified fancy tastes for passing and dressing as proud fur hunters in order to elevate the social value of belonging to the bourgeoisie and commercial elite of Canada. This performance of furry drag masculinity culminated in a cathartic romantic journey to the North. The romance of passing as members of the same wedding (the fur trade) was the soul of this social and economic institution.

One newspaper columnist recalls that:

> Each meeting was opened by passing round the calumet, or Indian pipe of peace. When the members, [with their gold medals engraved with the club motto "Fortitude in Distress"] had filled the room with a genial smoke, an officer of the club would make a speech recalling his adventures of the North West.
>
> (Collard 1963: 16)

This ceremonial staging of the historic journey to fur country was the "centerpiece" of the club gatherings. Built as an homage to the athletic and homosocial bonds among hunters, and between men and beasts, the narrative reached its crescendo in the expression of longing for the life "out there." The ritual of *le grand voyage* performed by the members of the club at each of their meetings enhanced the magic and added an original dimension to the homosocial fur country. As Collard relates:

Later in the evening came the boisterous symbolism of the "Grand Voyage." It was a ceremony to recall the excitement of shooting the rapids in a birch-bark canoe . . . All the members would seize hold upon firetongs, pokers, or walking-sticks in place of paddles, and would seat themselves upon the floor. Then all would make a roaring pretence of sending a canoe through the most appalling spray and down the most treacherous passage, while the songs of the voyageur would make them swing in motion as the member at the end of the line would shout his commands.

(Collard 1963: 16)

Given that Club dinners were notorious as extraordinary drinking events, it is not difficult to imagine all those men sitting in rows, swinging and singing at the top of their lungs *À La Claire Fontaine* (probably in the most dubious French), a touching spectacle of colonial homosociality. Not only did these dinners mark the ritualistic and romantic scope of the historic origins of the white explorer/adventurer fur episodes, but they also provided a unique expression of male bonding. Interestingly enough in this all-male circle, the bachelors were the true ascendants, i.e., the masters of the ceremony. As part of the ceremonial code of the gathering for the top twenty-five Beavers of the city, married men were excused early and the other guests could then carry on with the festivities in peace until morning. This signified the exclusion of any trace of the social order liable to interfere with the masculine carnaval-esque, i.e., marriage and the presence of "the feminine." It was also an explicit expression of the constitution of fur as a manly local business. If chivalry was hailed, it was as a fair expression of male courtesy. As Clifford P. Wilson observes in an article for *The Beaver*:

Montréal in the hey-day of the Nor'westers was as gay and hospitable a place as one could wish for . . . while the lakes and rivers were frozen commerce was pretty well at a standstill, and it was then that the Montréalers setted down to the cheerful business of entertaining each other with card parties, teas, dances, concerts, assemblies, plays, sleigh drives, *visites de civilités*, and dinners.

(Wilson 1936: 19–20)

In this club for men only, the fur ladies, wives of the proud beaver boys, were naturally reduced to the size of the brooch they were asked to wear: a beaver token.

After interrupting its activities for more than a century (i.e. in 1824), the Beaver Club resumes its decadent gatherings in 1959, the year Queen Elizabeth II blesses Canada with a royal visit. For the occasion, the Club is relocalized in the Grand Salon of the Queen Elizabeth Hotel, a popular and chic venue that coincidentally happens to be a 1950s favorite hang out for 'bachelors' in the core of the gay village. As Sylvain Gingras, in his popular history of hunting and fishing in Québec, *A Century of Sport*, observes: "Old customs were restored: especially the five traditional toasts: to the Mother of all Saints, to the Queen, to the fur trade, to the wives and children of the voyageurs, and to absent members" (Gingras 1994: 14–15). Many decades later, the active and influential role of the Beaver Club in the economic and financial structures of urban life still have traces all over the city. Once a Masonic, "athletic tux club," and a fortress of manhood, the club now regularly welcomes ladies to its annual winter bacchanalian feast complete with live animals and stuffed taxidermy, extending symbolic and elite membership to both women and men.

In 1993, when the Club reunited to celebrate the thirty-fifth anniversary of its contemporary revival, tradition called for an impressive and lavish fancy dress dinner, with men in beaver hats and ladies in crinolines. At the centre of the official banquet was outgoing president Lise Watier, a cosmetics tycoon and former top model and first woman ever to be baptized "beaver man," surrounded by other prominent female agents of national economy, namely government ministers and artists.[62] Ladies were no longer displayed as brooches – a tradition with the wives of Beaver Club members. Instead, the fur ladies now performed the gendering of national entrepreneurship. Moreover, blessed by a renewed fur economy after fifteen years spent in the doghouse due to animal rights activism (see chapter 5), the banquet was celebrated with more than a hint of revenge. So long banished from the portrait of the fake fur lady, the beaver now came to the rescue of the Club and the Chamber of Commerce. The presence of Watier, founder and head of a prominent North American cosmetics company yet to ban the animal testing of its products, came as an ironic demonstration of fur immortality.[63]

The spectacle of the powerful association between beaver men and wilderness on one hand, and fur and skin on the other hand, both "extremes" being so central to the culture and economy of the Beaver Club, is captured incisively by French-Québec filmmaker Pierre Falardeau in *Le Temps des Bouffons*. Shot during a 1985 banquet of the Beaver Club, the film unravels like a hate poem to the impossible Other, here the Scottish and British ascendants of the financial nation. Falardeau's disdain for the Anglo-Scottish money lobby is palpable in his incisive portrait of the banquet as an example of colonial grotesque. A forceful document of colonial decadence, the film perpetuates the male agency of the economics of the nation, where white men – mostly Anglophones and Francophones – "passing" as Anglos perpetuates the ritual of the grand conquest. Narrated in voice-over by Falardeau himself, in a standard French-Québec nationalist rant against elite Anglophone control of the national economy, Falardeau attacks the colonial masquerade of a so-called modern institution. Citing Jean Rouch's landmark film on African colonial subalternity, *Les Maîtres fous* (the opening scene of *Le Temps des Bouffons* is an excerpt from the possession scene in Rouch's document), the film embraces a traditional ethnography of cinema (Shohat 1991) where the culture of the colonized is scrutinized, magnified, and deformed into an excess of masculinity, social intimacies, and bestiality all at once.

Falardeau centers his critique of the Beaver Club culture as being about ethnic economic separatism and enactment of hundreds years of linguistic servitude. Condemning how the French [white]-Canadian elite invited to the master's banquet are costumed as "bicultural nigger kings" (*les Canadiens français costumés en rois nègres biculturels*),[64] Falardeau denounces what he feels is the complicit participation of French magnates in colonialist English domination. Contained and constrained by its format and tone – a 14-minute radical charge against the English establishment gathering around the famous political table symbolized by the Beaver Club – the beauty of Falardeau's document is that it relies on the same gender-bent display as Pichel's *Hudson's Bay*. The same white male buffoons dominate the scene, only the language has changed. The native chiefs (including Max Gros-Louis, Grand Chief of the Huron-Wendat Nation)[65] and the women-brooches present at the banquet – the true freaks of this show – barely get a glimpse, the camera stubbornly, masochistically dragging on the wigs and drag of the Beaver Club's honorable company of men, in a sort of male homosocial compliance.

Interestingly, beyond the cultural, gendered and social changes in the club membership, the carnavalesque fancy dress culture of the galas has been maintained. Tales of the wealth of the nation are reinvented here in all their glory, and if the presence of a few female skins now informs the constituency of the chamber of commerce, the perpetual eighteenth-century dress and decor resurrects the glamour of the first "urban" male sporting club of the city. For all the lady Barbaras that the club now counts as members, only one can occupy the queen's seat: the lady beaver herself, figured here as a unified Canadian nation. Once deeply anti-British, the club is now just as strongly anti-independentist. Among its prestigious guests and members, one can barely find a single pro-independent Québec member. And the women invited to the Beaver Club's table are no exception. In this sense, Watier, a well known federalist, and her presence at the head of the historical club is a barely disguised call for the maintenance of the links between nation, women and prosperity. Watier appears as a late but true daughter of the club and the nation, curiously embodying the multiple functions of the traditional Canadian beaver: mother, guardian and money-maker.

Still a private club, the Beaver Club stages a curious live fur display, in which bears, Venuses and beasts all gather together in a sort of post-Victorian fancy dress ball. Despite contemporary female contamination, the fur trade's male legacy still impregnates Beaver Club culture and still contributes to its aura as a male gender-bent spectacle. In this sense, it is similar to the male athletic clubs of the same name that were created in the early twentieth century by the HBC stores to initiate HBC staff members "in bonds of good fellowship by means of social gatherings, games and athletic sports." (Farquharson 1934: 34). Beyond its staged marketing, the Beaver Club stands as a display of the economic power of testosterone in the regulation of the nation, and to me, perpetuates the beaver tales that such "rogues" as Hollywood's Radisson managed to create. What the Beaver Club economy speaks to is to a sexual economy within which is recapitulated the historical and economic bounds between fur and nation. What homosociality provides here, is a point of entry to the contrasting elements that compose the close encounter between nation and fur as a process of development of national embodiment.

Part II

BEAVERS

3

THE EYES OF JUNE SAUER

For a sexual economy of fur fashion photography

She met Georgine Skeene there who was cultivating her voice which some thought was quite a pleasant one. Helen Furr and Georgine Skeene lived together then. Georgine Skeene liked travelling. Helen Furr did not care about travelling, she liked to stay in one place and be gay there. They were together then and travelled to another place and stayed there and were gay there.

Stein (1923)[1]

January 2000. I am sitting in the National Archives of Canada, all eyes and fingers as I thumb through hundreds of fur fashion photographs by June Sauer. One photo in particular leaves me breathless. A black and white three-photo strip documenting a studio photo shoot (Figure 3.1). A story vividly unfolds before my eyes, a fur tale . . . The top photo shows the model and an assistant struggling to find the perfect look for the camera, striking an extravagant pose. Something is not quite right, does not catch the eye. Then another woman enters the frame. June (on the right, middle photo). The assistant adjusts the model's posture; the photographer steps in to establish a perfect and seamless contact between the model's skin and the fur coat. Suddenly, a transformation occurs: the model is no longer just a model, the fur coat no longer just a fur coat. Everything becomes skin and touch, the model transfigured by the expert hands that guide the skin through fur. Seeking out the perfect touch, the perfect gaze. . . .

June's photographs bear this enchanting tactile quality of revelation beneath the glossy traits of perfection. They open up a totally new set of representations of fur ladies, images that touch me, that draw infinite tangents of desireable encounters. All of a sudden, it strikes me that this little woman, with whom I have shared coffee, red wine, lunch and a few – very few – confidences over the past two years stands before my eyes as a totally new, uncanny persona. Beneath the prints, proofs and posters, June again and again reinvents the

Figure 3.1 Three women at work: the model, June Sauer and her assistant. Max and June Sauer, print courtesy of NAC PA 200982.

pleasure of looking at fur ladies, "just for me," I foolishly believe. Through the photographs, I fantasize about being one of June's girls. I am surprised by how easily I surrender myself to her fierce gaze, expert hand and lens, how I let her skilfully arrange my posture, a trustful accomplice in a synchronic abandonment. Waves of mixed feelings, of bemusement, desire and identification overcome me, as I let the distance between "history" and stories fill the entire room. This sensual interlude is subsumed by my awareness that such publicness is consumed by intimacy and desire, the latest being after all a "relational force among individuals" (Probyn 1996: 25), and that the individuals in question happen to be 2-D stunning and dashing ladies in furs.

I perform the complex gesture of unveiling and carefully manipulating each photograph with diligent, flirtatious fingers, butterflying through hundreds of proofs, avid to find the best angle, the sexiest gaze, the most sensual posture, holding my breath here, smiling there, barely able to reach for the pencil that allows me to document and mentally collect such treasures. June's models, Carmen, Olivia, Leslie, Jackie, Peggy, Carole, Phyllis, Pat, Renée, Sylvie, Nicole and Naomi dance before my eyes in a furred choreography. I suddenly become the gazer, the taker, the photographer. I long for the pleasure of pushing the button, fixing the camera, the light, I am obsessed with the camera obscura – or should I say camera *chiura*. I am driven by the simple thought of achieving the magical, the marvelous and the forbidden, in just the simple act of capturing the delicate papery texture of skin and the sensuality of the fur in the frame. In a moment of excessive delight and emotion, for the first time since I have started this research, I understand fully the web of mediations that converge to construct women in furs: the spectacular materiality and incandescent public and "private quality" of the fur ladies tease my brain and senses. Through the tiny and limited surface of my fingertips, through the protective white gloves, I caress the skin and fur all at once. Sitting silently, yet talking to myself so loudly that my whole body is aching, all my senses vividly bubbling *à fleur de peau*. I am riveted by this aberrant bliss of fur and skin. I mentally route each image in a process of composition, correcting a hand, a head, smiling at the perfection of the gesture, amorously contemplating the astonishing results of woman made fur. At this moment, I wish I was June, I want to become Lady June Sauer.

This chapter is about June Sauer and her eye(s) for fur ladies. It seeks to rethink expressions of desire in the figuration of the nation as a tactile quality.[2] The very gesture of touching, being touched by the fabrics – skin and fur – as desirable surfaces and interfaces, transports the flatness of fur and fur ladies into a physical and mobile embodiment. From the touches between the texture of fashion photography and that of sensuality, it is not only the obviously erotic visuality associated with fur, but also its materiality, its texture, its "presence." I had to wait to meet June Sauer, to flesh out the fur ladies and understand how they have impinged on the exquisite complexity of the sexual economy of fur. The eyes of June Sauer capture a series of enchanted encounters and odd couplings, which is what the infinite points of contrast and contact between skin and fur are all about. Sauer's photos are tactile tales, touch-ing tales: since I can only touch through her eyes, I have to rely on sight and imagination to reach for the complexities and paradoxes of the intimate touch between skin and skins. The tactility of fur revealed through the eyes of June Sauer acts as a fabric of representation, drawing and redrawing the gestures and acts of women in the fur trade.

This chapter unfolds through various gestures of touch and touch-ing. The tactile dimensions extend through my encounter with the real photographer. In this context, tactility also describes a series of encounters – real and imagined – with the first woman photographer to run a commercial studio in Canada and to specialize in fur photography: June Sauer. As Jane Mulvagh recalls in her "unauthorized" biography of British fashion outlaw Vivienne Westwood,[3] nothing prepared me for my encounter with June Sauer. Meeting June opened a dream life for me: the fur ladies that had thus far been limited to a two-dimensional iconographic flatness, suddenly became three-dimensional. The vivid aroma of women in furs gained a peculiar materiality in the "live" presence of Sauer herself, reinjecting texture to the series of commercial fur portraits. June Sauer's urban fur post came late in my research on women in furs, yet in so many ways it is the closest to home and to my heart. My perpetually renewed encounters with June recirculate and transgress narratives on the business of fur and skin: of fashion photography as a business, a business where money and success are a matter of looking right. More importantly, it is a business where the intimacies between female bodies and fur pelts makes the trade look right. As part of the economy of female subjectivity, Sauer's thousands of photo documents of women in furs are priceless, particularly for a critical questioning of the modern nation and the agency of the woman entrepreneur in the post-World War II era.

Sauer's economic and domestic strategies also fit into the crucial women's role as "mediator in the fur-trading process" (Menzies 1990). By framing women such as Sauer as both mediators and cultural producers of the fur economy, I question and pinpoint some of the key elements that inform the articulation between fur, nation and the professionalization of women's labor in the circula-tion of the bonds between women and fur in the national economy. While it is true that the commercial relations of a significant contingent of women to the trade was once informed by forced encounters (see *Les Filles du roy* and the country wives), many others came to fur commerce on their own terms. This was the case for fur trader Madeleine de Roy de Bon d'Allonne, fur retailers Claire Labelle and Jeanne Sirbain, passing female-to-male trapper Isabel Gunn, immigrant Canadian-Lebanese fur trader Annie Midlige, and indeed commercial photographer June Sauer.[4]

I wish I could write a bio epic about June's famous eyes, but Sauer, like her British alter mater Westwood, the other *enfant terrible*, is an elusive one. As much as Westwood instigates and relishes public outbursts as intrinsically linked to her rebellious look, June Sauer fancies elegance, class and privacy as her professional and personal trademark signature. Behind the combative businesswoman wearing vintage Chanel and selling classy images and snapshots of ladies stands a very private individual, fiercely opposed to any intrusion. Sauer, a prominent and popular eye on the Montréal and North American fashion scene in the 1950s through the 1970s has managed to keep her influence and privacy one of the best secrets of the industry, constantly tricking dates, moments and spaces in order to make any straightforward narrative about her a riddle. In the rare interviews she gives to the media, Sauer has mastered the art of elusiveness, making good use of de Certeau's *"la perruque,"* i.e., this *art de faire* of telling stories that incessantly dislodge, displace and de-center her subject position so as to stress the contours of her re-production (de Certeau 1990: 45–8).

The only patches of subjectivity that June Sauer overtly confides are her darting blue eyes: for me, they became my central point of entry to her, hence my fascination for the eyes of June Sauer. Sauer's blue eyes have, in the most powerful way, captured the sexual economy that reunites pelts and skin, maneuvering back from skin to pelts with the same sharpness and irony. Her intuition and career decision to shoot ladies in fur have made her among the most important commercial fur photographers of the postwar period in North America. If "fashion is not art, it is a trade" (Mulvagh 1998: 6), then fashion photography is also about trade: the fur and skin trade. June Sauer made fashion photography all about the sensuality and eroticism of capturing skin and fur at once. The fact that Sauer's photographs function as both art and trade broaches the need to think them through the sexual value of fur as skin for a national economy. My investigative journey into June Sauer's phenomenal production coincides with a critical desire to understand the dynamics of female com-plicities in the shaping and circulation of national bliss. By framing June and her photographs in a complex web of proximities and intimacies we not only the question productiveness of fur and ladies, but also the modalities of recording and thinking scratches as traces.

June Sauer's career spans a thirty-year period (1954–87), and her work can be counted among the most important in twentieth century Canadian com-mercial photography production. Sauer's career and life, as for so many other business fur ladies, blossomed within a female homosocial space: few men were around her, and her practice, though marginalized and marked by gender and sexual stigma, nevertheless participated in the development of a regional and national sexual economy of fur. In this sense, this chapter constitutes an attempt to think through the urbanization of the trade from the other side of the looking glass, a looking glass traditionally saturated by princes, merchants, adventurers and Beaver Club boys. Against the homosociality of the bear boys who embodied the official history of the trade, the homosociality of the fur ladies as imagined and represented by June Sauer suggests a quite different set of representations of women in furs. As the first commercial photographer to

71

own a professional studio in Canada, Sauer represents an original furlady in this regard, being at once a privileged eyewitness and fur lady maker. Moreover, Sauer's case is one of the few that offers a way to disrupt the romanticized links between fur and nature/wilderness (HBC), or fur and social status (Notman), suggesting on the contrary that fur was a commodity.

In this sense, the only way to approach the mystery of June Sauer has been to "trade" some sense of realist authenticity or investigative biography for tales, piecing together the various portraits that punctuate her career and the various stories that popularly circulate, with the secret wish that these portraits give texture and materiality to the lady. In so doing, my tactile detours take me through a series of portraits of fictional odd couples (Stein, Verne) along with the bear boy of Canadian photography, William Notman. I use these portraits, or should I say "portraits of marriages," to reappropriate the popular narrative of the tumultuous relations between Vita Sackville-West and Violet Trefusis, as a strategy to dislocate and relocate the economic and sexual ties that necessarily shape private and professional ties. For instance, Gertrude Stein's depiction of the portrait of marriage in "Miss Skeene and Miss Furr" transposes my own intellectual and personal fascination and relation with June Sauer both as a person and a subject of investigation. Stein's wicked title for this short story of female intimacies is too perfect: the words skin and fur playfully trouble the encounter between the two odd women. Miss Skeene's and Miss Furr's peculiar ways of being "gay together" and apart, yet still part of normative "good" society, speaks to the specific conditions of my production of an affective investment towards a genealogy of women in furs. Additionally, Jules Verne's odd portrait of Miss Madge and Paulina's adventurous taste for the North also captures a certain mode of being and feeling – intimate, yet distant – that best reveals June's adventurous edge in the fur business.

I propose to revisit my encounters with June through a dilettante and interior conversation with three remarkable projects: Mulvagh's biography of Westwood, McRobbie's vivid analysis of the British fashion business, and Mavor's own encounter with Clementina Hawarden. While very different in their scope, the three projects all carry an acute sensibility regarding the mechanisms at work in the encounter between object and subject, and a fierce desire to go beyond representation as a matter of visibility. Although my references to these texts are not explicit, they are formative to my way of reaching for June Sauer's body of works. From Mulvagh, I borrow a self-conscious sense of fairy tale; from McRobbie, an urgency to frame a national business in relation to women's signature in the textile trade (fur is now marketed as a textile and taught as such in fashion colleges); and from Mavor, a driving (homo)eroticism and a fascination for the object and subject of my research. As Mavor eloquently suggests when describing her feeling for a certain nineteenth-century amateur photographer, "Clementina Hawarden's photographs have always been erotic to me: they make finger-words write desire" (Mavor 1999: xxv). The desire to write of Sauer's production is highly affective and feeds by a longing to revisit an environment so unfamiliar, yet so close: Montréal's fur district activities as captured and revitalized through June Sauer's production. The physical proximity of June, yet her palpable distance, makes this chapter at once a sensuous quest and a reflection on the role that women, particularly white female entrepreneurs, have strategically occupied in the dissemination of nationalist iconography.

In other words, in a paradoxical and sometimes irreconcilable fashion, through June's eyes emerges the opportunity to glimpse the sensuality of fur, and to confront the fur ladies in their most transparent commodified apparel. Sauer's stunning collection echoes how sensual and sexual representation constitutes a perverse way of thinking through the investment of women's work in the promotion of national resources. Sauer's work is compelling because it challenges the relation between value and commodity through a double expression of labor: commercial and artistic. The fact that Sauer was the first woman in Canada to own her own professional studio raises important questions with respect to the construction of a professional market of fur ladies. While commercial photography as a culture of production is about "the visual economy of feminine display" (Solomon-Godeau 1996), we need to recognize its value in producing desirable proximities within sexualized national identities. This latter point is all the more true given that the circulation, marketing and exchange value of the commercial fur photographs are part of an international and standardized market dominated in the 1960s by a strong social and sexual stigmatization.

As part of the framing of an analysis of the modern fur trade, along with the gender and sexual slippages and racial shifts that mark its new face, I wish to offer a reflection on the conditions and strategies of female professionals as part of the visual and sexual economy of fur display. Retracing the seams of the fur country left by such women as June Sauer, is tightly shaped by the representational strategies that document the nation as a simultaneously popular and commercial practice, as a qualitative relation to the publicness of fur ladies. How do professional and commercial practices participate in women's cultural production of national imagery? The professionalization of the domesticated female body is a key factor in the authority and double representation of fur ladies as economic agents of the trade. In this context of commodification and control, women's relation to capital is primarily informed by the fetishization of both their bodies/skin, and their practice/labor. Commercial practices of documentation by women of women (especially in commercial photography) exploit these contradictions in unique ways.

Among the mountains of archives that I consulted for this research, very few documents speak to the obvious modulations in value and quality that were undermined in the popularization of the twentieth century trade, and what those modulations generated in the commercialization of the links between women, fur and nation in urban industrial space. This sort of half-silence is all the more ironic given that the popularity of fur in the twentieth century is intrinsically linked to the growing presence of women in the work force, and the wide implementation of credit for working class consumers. Moreover, as a double irony, it is in the most widely circulated site for the cultural association between fur and ladies, i.e. fashion, that this most visible and abundant documentation was also the most deceptive and the most challenging to make sense of. In this sense, Sauer's use and practice of fur photography constitutes not only an eccentric example of woman-made fur, but also a rare contemporary example of disenfranchisement from an essentialist iconography of woman-fur-landscapes. Sauer's collection proposes on the contrary a transnational vision of women in furs – the urban space being by definition a space where identities collide, even in their absence of crossings.

Sauer's production coincides also with the postwar inter and intranational renaissance of capital, and this fact enacts the celebration of the so-called modern nation (i.e., urban and industrial) and the revitalization of a colonial industry (fur). Sauer's outstanding and prolific production coupled sensuality and commodity inside and outside the commercial trade culture of the 1950s, 1960s and 1970s, and this Canadian flavor was best captured through women in furs. This coupling of sensuality and commodity was not estranged from a set of social and sexual relations specific to the market of fur consumers, urban fur subjects, nor the envisioning of the Canadian nation in the 1960s. Sauer's fierce eyes beg the following questions: what kinds of representation of the fur lady economy does Sauer's commercial photographic practice capture and reveal? What kinds of mediated representations of the nation do Sauer's collection and practice deploy in the market of skin commodities?

Portraits of a marriage take one:
June and Max

Helen Furr had quite a pleasant home. Mrs. Furr was quite a pleasant woman. Mr. Furr was quite a pleasant man. Helen Furr had quite a pleasant voice a voice quite worth cultivating. She did not mind working. She worked to cultivate her voice. She did not find it gay living in the same place where she had always been living. She went to a place where some were cultivating something, voices and other things needing cultivating.

(Stein 1923: 563)

The 1950s. In those days, June Sauer was unable to cultivate her photographic eye. She did not mind working. Max did. She did not find it possible to cultivate before tragic circumstances triggered her career. The sudden death in 1954 of Max, her husband of five years, created the place and the space in which to cultivate her eye. Inexperienced, young (between twenty-four and twenty-seven), she decided to train and cultivate her eye.

Max Sauer (1912–54) was already an established commercial photographer with a certain stature before he married June in 1949. Born in Niagara Falls, Ontario, talented and described by *Mademoiselle* magazine as a Gregory Peck look-alike,[5] Sauer was first destined for a career in engineering, before the poor economic conditions of the 1930s and his growing interest for photography triggered a change in career plan. Sauer sold his first pictures in 1931 as a free-lance free spirit, but opened a commercial studio in Montréal in 1942. His dramatic style led to commissions by many commercial and governmental agencies to immortalize the modernization of the country, as well as the culture and goods produced by the nation.

Over his career Max built a genuine archive and his work, an eclectic collection of prints and nitrates, related mostly to Canadian industry and commerce. Since 1989, 69,000 photographs have been catalogued at the National Archives of Canada as part of the Max and June Sauer Studio Collection.[6] Sauer, despite a strictly trade profile, had a pretty camera and for that he could be considered in the company of great men. Companies liked his photographs, and Max was keen to include more companies in his portfolio: Bell Telephone, Hudson's Bay Company, Aluminum Company of Canada, Molson, Dupont and CIL were all members of the wedding of the great nation. Like William Notman and Robert Flaherty, Sauer could also be regarded as a legitimate witness for the nation. The comparison of the three men offers some brotherly parallels. For instance, a decade after Flaherty went North, commissioned by Révillon Fourrures to realize his one-time landmark *Nanook of the North*, Sauer also journeyed North, this time with the blessing and support of the grand rival of the French furriers, the Hudson's Bay Company.

In the company of sailors and men aboard the *Nascopi*, a company ship, Max took documentary photographs during a trip along the coast of Labrador that lasted for almost two years. The result was two photo-reports of Max Sauer's trip to Churchill Falls published in the company trade journal, *The Beaver*, in 1933 and 1934.[7] Something of a Canadian novella, the photo-report offers an original twist on the documentation of the nation as a corporate image. This time around, Nanook is relegated to the backdrop. The romanticization of the North transpires in the deeds of the company and ship workers wearing furs. In the pure spirit and aesthetics of corporate ethnography, the pictures include government officials, icebergs, Inuit communities, HBC outposts, Révillon Frères trading posts,[8] cargo posts and Royal Canadian Military Police (RCMP) stations.

The *Nascopi* photo-report by Max speaks to a practice that favors the scenic views and spectacular settings of corporate history, recouping the tradition of a masculinized national photography, where male bodies seem always at work, in motion. His studio work reproduced the landscape of corporate culture in miniature. Most of the photographs available at the National Archives of Canada demonstrate his taste for the gigantic, the industrious and the spectacular, i.e., the marketable. The fact that Sauer built his business on advertising and publicity for Canadian industry and commerce only further perpetuated the popularization and spectacularization of the genius of industry and male labor as the official document of the nation. When confined to the scale of studio work, his photographs nevertheless maintained their edge for the gigantic. Despite important contracts with such prominent names in the fur fashion industry as Grosvernors and Alexanders in the late 1940s and early 1950s, Max was not very interested in fur fashion scenery, and the fur trade photographs represented only an infinitesimal part of the studio contracts. Women and furs were accessories for the Max Sauer Studio.

Then, in 1954, June entered. And the studio went through drastic changes in style and management. The gigantic and sensational industrial portraits became less and less prominent. June favored intimacy, fantasy and champagne tastes. Somewhere along this transformative trajectory, a touch of fur was added to studio production. June very quickly became a leader in commercial fur photography: The Fur Trade Association, Grosvenor Fur, Irene Hats, Simpson's, Natural Furs and Leclair Furs became regulars of the Max and June Sauer Studios, as June imposed herself as *the* signature of the studio. Yet as a member of the national family album, Sauer privileges a much more intimate and subtle mode of documenting the nation: contractual intimacies between bodies and pelts became the new landscapes featured at the Max and June Sauer Studios. Lakes, mountains, boats, exotic communities and sceneries were replaced by women in furs, a luxury tapestry of skin and furs. *Domestic chic* would be one way to describe the strategic new trends adopted in the make-over of the studio.

One of the most significant changes that took place with June's takeover of the direction of Max Sauer Studios was a distinctive division of work and contracts along gender lines. While contracts with traditional industrial patrons such as Bell were vital to the survival of the studio and were mostly executed by employees, June came more and more to monopolize the fashion/ladylike aspect of the business. Sauer also decided that she would be the girl behind the camera. In a very short period of time, Sauer was able to gather significant contracts from the trade sector as well as from the cultural industries, heightening the studio's reputation nationally and internationally.

Of those early years, there is little documentation. The period seemed to be one of mourning and grieving the sudden death of Max, as well as keeping the "family business" afloat. Surrounded by faithful assistants, June actually increased and diversified the activities of the studio. Around the mid 1960s, June decided to move the Sherbrooke Street studio to the business district, to the art deco-styled Power Corporation building, headquarters of one of the most important companies in Canada: the Desmarais' Power Corporation. Such changes in the location and the setting of the studio clearly responded to the imperative of increasing the visibility of the studio and establishing possible alliances with both the fashion district and the wider business world, conveniently located next door. Sauer was poised to enter the most prolific years of her career.

Portrait of a marriage take two: June as June

Helen Furr was not needing using her voice to be a gay one. She was gay then and sometimes she used her voice and she was not using it very often. It was quite completely enough cultivated and it was quite completely a pleasant one and she did not use it very often. She was then, she was quite exactly as gay as she had been, she was gay a little longer in the day than she had been.

(Stein 1923: 567)

My encounter with June Sauer was quite unexpected, and belongs to the domain of the fantastic. It was first during a research trip to the National Archives in Ottawa in November 1997 that her name first surfaced in my research. Consulting the visual archives for twentieth-century fur illustration, June Sauer's name quickly caught my attention. Interested in popular representations of fur ladies more than in artistic works, I could not believe that a woman's name could actually be associated with the commercial photography business in the 1950s and 1960s. Records of commercial shootings for important Montréal fur retailers were carefully preserved. But the fund was a new acquisition, and due to reorganization and relocation of the collections at the Archives, most of the documents were difficult to access. I decided at that point to keep an eye out for Sauer's production and privileged associations with fur. Further investigation confirmed my intuition: no entry in any biographical dictionary of Canadiana, nothing about Sauer in the different databases, other than the new fund at the National Archives. I decided to wait.

Sauer's name came up a second time in researching the McGill archives for *My Fur Lady* in January 1998 (see chapter 4). A significant number of the publicity shots of the actors and producers designated for promotional material featured the imprint of Max and June Sauer Studios. Thrilled by the coincidence, yet without any additional information about June Sauer, I experienced this June moment as a personal reward, a glimpse at another unknown fur lady: another beaver tale/trail leading to a dead end. However, later that spring, during a visit to the McCord Museum, Jackie Ross, archivist in the Archival and Documentation Center, suggested to my research assistant Tamara that we should talk to June Sauer about fur. This came as a shock. Sauer was not only alive, she was living here in Montréal, literally next door, on the very bourgeois rue de la Montagne in the downtown core, right next to the fur district, as she had for most of her life, in what she calls "her favourite city in the world." Her name was listed in the phone book (as Mrs. Max Sauer). Sauer was real, Sauer was right next door, and I would soon meet her.

The woman I met that sunny hot day in July 1998 – so much sun for fur – surpassed my expectations: tiny with huge blue eyes, very elegant in her vintage designer ensemble (Chanel?), Sauer waited for us in the lobby of the McGill faculty club, the rendezvous point. However, through a wicked irony, we were soon disinvited from the venerable club: a film shoot of Jules Verne's adventures in Canada was in progress, and the foyer of the institution was restricted to men at work. I was bemused. Another queer encounter.

Verne's novel, *Le pays des fourrures* (1985 [1869]), a landmark nineteenth-century colonial novel and second in his Canada triptych, had not only been one of the first fantastic fur tales of the country that I have read, but was also memorable for me for its powerful queer subtext.[9] Introducing Canada as the Hudson's Bay country, Verne's account of a fictional expedition led by the HBC army is festive in its longing for homosexual intimacies.[10] In this nineteenth-century science fiction narrative of fur discovery, Mrs. Paulina Barrett and her faithful "companion" (*dame de compagnie*) Madge fight the dreadful and pitiless winter like men in order to participate in the grand adventure of the Hudson's Bay Company in the North.[11] Solo women abroad, they quickly become true fur ladies of the company, adventuring in the numerous dangers of the Canadian wilderness, inventing exquisite and hearty "Canadian" cuisine dishes from scratch for their companions. More than the others, Mrs. Paulina, who in Verne's words "ain't quite a lady" arouses admiration and curiosity among the men of the company and the aboriginal guides recruited for the northern expeditions. In this all-male environment, the presence of the two ladies seems gay and queer all at once: othered, yet accepted as reluctant members of the Beaver Mens' club:

> How could a woman dare to venture forth where so many explorers before her perished? But the stranger, stationed at fort Reliance for the time being, was not a woman: it was Paulina Barrett, laureate of the Royal Society. One might add that the famous traveller kept company with Madge, a maid, better than a maid, an intrepid and devoted friend, who lived only for Paulina, a Scott from olden times. A Caleb could have married her in good standing. Madge was a bit older than her mistress – about five years. She was tall and well-built. Madge addressed Paulina as "*tu*," and Paulina addressed Madge as "*tu*." Paulina looked up to Madge like an older sister; and Madge treated Paulina like a daughter. In sum, these two souls were one.
>
> (Verne 1985 [1869]:16)[12]

Just as Groseillers and Radisson were the couple of adventurers portrayed in *Hudson's Bay* (see chapter 2), Paulina and Madge formed the fur lady couple of the trade. Verne's fascination for Hudson's Bay Fur Country is tailored mainly by predictably exotic visions of the fur business and its gendered and racialized configurations and figures: beavers, polar bears and all kinds of beasts share the spotlight with the good colonizers. Unlike his contemporary British alter ego, Sir Richard Burton, for whom the exotic country was always an opportunity to intermingle scientific discovery and sexual experience (and vice versa), Verne had a relatively sanitized approach to the North and the exoticness of a country.

Verne's naive glimpse of the North in many ways coincides with Flaherty's fascination for the Nanook lifestyle: both "explorers" depict the North as a fashionable space for "feeling cold" and fur as the ultimate Canadian experience. While in Flaherty's *Nanook*, masculinity embodies the authentic fur moment, for Verne the fur moment is troubled by the powerful – and sexual – presence of the white European woman, Paulina, acting as the emissary of European Enlightenment. In this colonial man's world driven by money, Madge and Pauline incarnate "scientific sex," or sexualized scientific bodies. Their imperial knowledge and savoir-faire for the survival of the HBC expedition as daughters of the empire is disseminated through a uniquely female homosocial bonding.

The story of Madge and Paulina – who are both so deeply gay – is not only fantastic, it is a queer portrait of a marriage. Given the systematic erasure of women from the written history of the company, Verne's sensibility in his depiction of Madge and Paulina's *amitiés particulières*, devoted as it was to Madge's scientific project, offers a keen portrait of the ways that gender, sexuality and bodies conflate in the sort of homoerotic geography (and cartography) of the fur country – this time with a female touch. Mrs. Paulina loves science and nature, is critical of the fur fashion craze that seems to possess Europe – and more specifically her dearest Britannia – and does not hesitate to see her intervention in the North as one of preservation, i.e., the promotion of the British 'discovery' moment through the expansion of HBC fur trail and other economic imperial missions.

Verne's account of the ladies in fur country was clearly inspired by the social transformations accompanying the expansion of the colonial fur routes in Canada, and in the envisioning of the economic enterprise as a merging between tourist science and the colonial imperatives of trade. The fantastic journey of Paulina and Madge situates the commercial and corporate ties between bodies and skins in which women acted as prominent figures and agents. The fact that Paulina is portrayed as a scientist, a *"femme savante"* attests to the growing influence of women in public affairs (*"la chose publique"*) in the British colony. At the same time, the depiction of the lonely explorer gal is one of a woman with her own agenda: an expert, yet a marginalized one. Science becomes an interesting substitute for economic agency at the same time that science impinges on a new dimension of women's subjectivity. However, Paulina's heroism in the North is already contained in relation to her womanly skills that embrace domestic bliss: cooking, cleaning and sewing. Paulina, while a true partner in the colonial enterprise, also stands as a fierce manager of an extended domestic space. Paulina, with her romantic environmental sensibility – including a sympathy for the "indigenous" – ain't a traditional business woman, which is best for the sake of the company and the fur country. The romantic scope of Verne's rendition of the HBC's pioneering mission in America is paradoxically enflamed by the presence of the supposedly "asexual" Paulina Barrett.

Back to McGill. Fade from Verne's snow land. I dream June is Paulina, I am Madge. I follow her around the fur district, smiling, my heart pounding, imagining that I am on some sort of wild domestic beaver trail. In the heat of the day, Lady June finally settles for the lobby of the Ritz Carlton: after all, fur is a classy and downtown business. To add to the seduction, Sauer has brought with her some samples of her work, along with a powerful and charming determination to keep details about her personal life secret. After a random one hour discussion, followed by girl talk over coffee, we depart. I am hooked, yet frustrated and confused.

There are few facts about June Sauer, and a lot of tales. June was born in Thunder Bay in Northern Ontario in either 1927 or 1924, depending on the source and Lady June's desire to keep a sense of mystery about her. Lady June's youth may have been gay, perhaps not. June apparently moved to Montréal at the end of the 1940s, prior to her marriage in 1949 to Max Sauer native of Thunder Bay, longtime resident of Montréal. A straight route. She keeps family life secret, she does not discuss her childhood, her teens. In the National Archives I found a family portrait. Is it June's? Max's? There is a blond little girl frowning at the camera. Is it you, June? Don't ask, don't tell. I suspect that she likes me to think that she was actually born in 1954 at the age of 24. Or is it 27? Her birth was a process of learning and training in photography techniques, "discovering" a fierce eye for fur and fashion. Entrepreneurship went along with the apprenticeship, and Sauer took public relations courses at McGill University and in Toronto to keep the business close to home. Even her career is a tale. A fur tale. A national fur tale. An international fur tale. June's eyes took her around the world in eighty days, to work for Valentino and Chanel, and gained her awards from numerous associations, including a prestigious Merit Award from the Professional Photographers of America and the National Society of Art Directors. June was the first woman to receive such praises. June was the first to have a commercial studio. June was the first in her field. A fur hero.

Throughout her career, Sauer furiously documented ladies in furs. Like Paulina, June sought and cultivated the science of black and white photography. Her fur photo collection is by far one of the most important in North America, and it offers a unique and original showcase of thirty years of fur fashion in Montréal and Canada, documenting the most popular and most opulent period of postwar fur retail. Queen of fur photography, renowned for a fierce eye and incomparable touch for furs and ladies, Sauer was the obligatory stop for whoever wanted to enhance the commercial value of their fur garments. Pro-fur June? June smiles. June does not like barebacked models, does not care so much for the fur. June likes the fur ladies, the models, and the models in fur like her. Sauer's contribution to the promotion of fur only reinforces what I have argued in previous chapters: that without the contribution of women to the colonial enterprise and national formation, fur would never have survived and remained today one of the highlights of international design, with the billions of dollars that the fur businesses – pro and anti – generate. Sauer's marketable fur expertise, as well as her proximities with the raw materials – skin and fur – brings a complexity to the exposure of women within and beyond the production of colonial/national imagery. June's eyes unveil the sensual property of the national fabric; and her photographs enable a sensuality that is not fact, but possibility and promise.

Sauer's use of the camera entices sensual proximities between fur and model, between the fur ladies and the woman behind the camera. This softness textures her signature. If some photographs reproduce stereotypical fur shots, others stand as thoroughly original takes on the encounter between fur and female skin. For instance, this two-shot series of Pat McKillop posing as a reincarnation of Botticelli's Venus not only demonstrates a sense of pure fantasy and irony, but also renders the sensuality and playfulness of the naked body rubbing against the most precious animal skin. In the two shots (Figures 3.2 and 3.3) McKillop defies the camera, surrounded by sable and mink, springing from a sea of pelts. The image is stunning and telling: the quintessential fur lady rising from the animal skins. The encounter is magic and the performance sexualized. The touches between the model and the pelts create another fabric, yet recognizable: the fur lady par excellence.

When asked about her interest for fur and ladies, Sauer talks of her approach as *mise en scène* of fur and modeling in a totally different manner than male photographers. Her greatest concern is to transmit the exquisite bond between women and fur, a bond defined first by the metaphoric quality of fur. The erotic aspect of fur is not her motif – that would be left to the boys as she has said – what fascinates her is the capacity of fur to make women look different, look distant yet intimate with the pelts. For Sauer, the mobility within and between the skins is a crucial motif: women's skin espousing the caprice and imperfection of the pelts; fur revealing what is beneath the skins. Whether on location or in studio, her aesthetic configuration is truly defined by bringing life to the dead.

Many of her pictures play on this tension between the inert and the mobile. In particular, Sauer's publicity shots transmit this constant movement between the recognizable public images of women and fur as circulated in popular media and fashion magazines, including the glamorous dimension of star images, and the necessarily elitist, classy approach to fur so associated with fur fashion. But this exclusive treatment of women in furs seems less informed by her elitist vision of who should wear fur – in the traditional pro-fur way, she claims that "the mink doesn't mind who is wearing it" – than by her desire to capture the symbiosis between the goods and the subject, making then into a perfect marketable representation of women and fur. Sauer's eyes for women in furs brings a true element to the sexual economy of the nation: for her, both skin and skins compose the representation of Canadian fur, and fur only exists within the boundaries of skin touch. This proximity brings a fantastically touch-ing quality to her work, a tactile quality that resides in this papery frontier linking

Figure 3.2 Pat McKillop as a reincarnation of Botticelli's Venus. June Sauer, print courtesy of NAC/J.

the two fabrics, the two textures. Against the raw, if not primitive association traditionally enhanced by commercial pornographic representations of the beaver, Sauer's skinning, exposition of the beaver fur marks the richness of the white female body at the same time that it troubles the value of skin. This necessarily calls for a critique of class and race; in other words, of the corporeality and incorporation of the sexual economy of fur in a homogeneous whiteness. Sauer occupies a privileged position in the diffusion of whiteness and fur as

Figure 3.3 Pat McKillop. June Sauer, print courtesy of NAC/J.

the most popularized and nationalized expression of the fur nation and the stature of the trade from the late 1950s to the 1970s.

Sauer's prolific and long-term association with the fur fashion trade is distinguished by the numerous contracts she held for dozens of important furriers across Canada, including the powerful Fur Traders Association. Twice, in 1958 and 1964, Sauer did all the furs in the city for one of the most important economic fur trading forums in the world, organizing dozens of photo sessions, mechanically reproducing thousands of prints and proofs of ladies in furs for nineteen different furriers. Although vaguely tainted by the artificial aesthetics of corporate trade that makes a model look like any dummy mannequin in flesh – a good example being the fiftieth anniversary issue of the *Canadian Fur Review*[13] – Sauer's photographs radiate a sense of ambiguity that disrupts the stereotypical iconography of the model as coat rack for fur. For instance, while some of her models did share the high-market slim-blonde features à la Lisa Fonssagrives, the model du jour back then (I am thinking here of Phyllis Clapperton as she appears in Figure 3.6), most of the girls were selected for their strong divergence from the usual fifties and sixties pin-up stereotype, sporting dark hair, stylish cuts, strong features and original make-up. Two of Sauer's favourite models from the period, Carmen Lister (Figures 3.4 and 3.5)

Figure 3.4 Carmen Lister in a seal and beaver coat with a cigarette holder, late 1950s. June Sauer, print courtesy of NAC/J.

Figure 3.5 Carmen Lister in a touch of mink for Holt and Renfrew, 1950s. June Sauer, print courtesy of NAC/J.

Figure 3.6 Phyllis Clapperton for Hollinger Furs. June Sauer, print courtesy of NAC/J.

and Pat McKillop (Figures 3.2 and 3.3 and book cover), best embodied the Sauer style. Caught, even trapped, in furs from head to toe, the whiteness of the skin shines and contrasts with the dark fabric. Three decades of models paraded before her eyes in mink, seal and beaver (a favorite) and were immortalized on four-by-five, five-by-seven, and eight-by-ten black and white images, Sauer's preference over color photography.

The photo shoots appear to have been conducted like experimental living displays, with a new spin on the old boy fur tales. The portraits that emerge are disruptive yet recognizable: they trouble the borders between modernity and wilderness, the stiffness of the traditional model and the women in movement, in brief they secure and spoil the natural link between fur ladies and landscape. Whether tantalized by the playful lady on the verge of departing at the gate (Figure 3.7), or the performing fur queen conquering the Île Sainte-Hélène (Figure 3.8), each tableau comes to disrupt a taxidermic national image of the fur fashion trade where the dead beast and the busy land collide to constitute the two faces of the nation (and of Venus). Herein lies a definite paradox in Sauer's style and production: it speaks both to the international/transnational trade and local cultural markers. The photos clearly belong to the tradition of transversal commercial fashion photography, yet some local reappropriations are clearly at work. Several of June's girls adopted Lisa Fonssagrives' recognizable touch and some of the photo compositions clearly belong to the tradition of major international fashion trade magazines such as *Vogue* (see Phyllis Clapperton,). The fact that Sauer herself was commissioned by international traders and magazines and went frequently on assignments around Europe (Zurich, Milan, Paris and London) and North America have contributed to this sense of everywhere-ness, yet the photographs betray local and national flavors. The mapping of the city is contingent on a negotiated transnationality with regard to specific Montréal sceneries recognizable from both within and without: the fur ladies travel and route the city, conferring a sense of both reverie and abrasive commerciality in their ladies' footprints.

The crossovers between the local and the national, and the national and the transnational, are wonderfully captured in hundreds of vignettes of the "modern" lady in the city. In fact, the collection radiates a contemporary look at the so-called modern Québec women. The women in furs immortalized by Sauer reveal the ways that female skin has been the main economic vector for local retailers. This was necessarily anchored in a construction of women moving into the modern corporate/business world, a world where mobility was a key element. Either as travel (airport), education (McGill) or pier (Île Sainte-Hélène), sites of mobility were covered with models in fur. Fur is no longer a symbol of masculine wilderness: fur is now an urban thread. Sauer's photographic compositions reveal something about the Québec of the 1950s, 1960s and early 1970s that goes against a traditionalist representation of women in the domestic space, tied to the family environment. June's girls were

Figure 3.7 Fur lady in downtown Montréal in a seal Alaska coat. June Sauer, 1950s, print courtesy of NAC.

bachelors, playful, involved in homosocial complicities. They show a large degree of sensuality that was quite bold for the time, expressing a singular view of women in the Québec postwar period. Among this accumulation of fur and skin, Sauer's world emerges as a powerfully homosocial and homoerotic space channeled through a small group of mostly female accomplices and collaborators. The sense of humor, and self-derision in the posture of the "Beauties

Figure 3.8 Conquering fur lady in a rabbit purse, hat and coat ensemble at Île Ste Hélène. June Sauer 1958, print courtesy of NAC.

of Montréal" – the actual title for a fur fashion and tourist report for *Montréal* magazine in 1965[14] – defines Sauer's photographic contribution to this sense of exclusivity and confined homosociality in which the photographer herself, her crew and models worked. Ironically, the value of fur for the industry is tied to this incessant flirt with the tacky, yet sophisticated, texture of women and furs.

The interplay between the intimacy of the fabrics and the publicness of models in fur participates in Sauer's *art de faire* and her contractual proximities with the models. Her practice has been shaped by a complex network of alliances, complicities and sensualities between the models, the photographer and the customers. This created exchange of ideas about fur and nation responds to and is nourished by both the imperatives of the "real industry" and the creation of the sublime. Her closeness to the models was well-known, and is still considered her trademark. Models from New York's Ford Agency were regulars at her studio, but Sauer had her own family of fur ladies in Montréal. She worked with a limited team of models, recreating a homosocial working space that transpires throughout her entire collection. As Sauer confesses, "The girls worked well with me . . . We had close relationships. They trusted me. They knew I wouldn't take bad pictures of them. I always tried to put them in the best light" (Monahan 1996: B6). To not take bad pictures in Sauer's language meant to resist a sexy iconography à la Hollywood, and to develop a new and different look, a gay look filled with allusive seduction and sophistication . . . "I would say that my models radiated something different with me . . . I was also a woman. The models did not feel the need to seduce and to be sexy at all costs. They were beautiful and elegant, that's all" (Roy 1996: C6). Beautiful and elegant they all were – most of all Carmen Lister, her professional muse and most intimate model who was more gay than any of the others.

Lister was a hybrid recreation of the Venus in Furs and Venus de Milo. A dark brunette, she starred in countless photo shots, delicately crossing the boundaries between human and animal skins, embodying the proximities and intimacies between skins like no one else. According to Sauer, Lister had the best acting abilities, and her extreme ease of movement between the skins, beneath the skin made her the natural star of Sauer. Unlike McKillop who was first a Grosvernor's lady, Lister, despite some "special" commissions for Holt and Renfrew, was one of a kind, freelancing for the most important Sauer clients. Whether modeling for luxurious lingerie in a sensual abandonment (for the Toronto-based fancy shop Nylon Lingerie); or wearing a touch of beaver with "panache" and a butchy edge for the most important and powerful fur retailer (Figures 3.4 and 3.5 in a beaver coat for Holt and Renfrew), Lister *was* the lady-made-fur, the fur lady par excellence in June's eyes. Sauer's longtime companionship association with Lister (already under contract with Max) is revealing of June's style: a hint of mockery, and a wicked sense of performance that only Pat McKillop (Figures 3.2 and 3.3 and book cover) could also capture. But there is something else with Carmen: an unparalleled sensuality. The Nylon Lingerie advertisement for which Lister modeled made me gasp, and the series that also features other models (including Clapperton and McKillop) appears almost as an aberrant moment. Furless, the skin triumphs, rendering even more sumptuous and desireable the absent skins. I had to verify the copyright date to realize that in fact June was the photographer, not Max. Here Carmen is engulfed in a panorama of gazes and screens, sensually half-naked, smiling cockily at the camera; there, Carmen is beheaded in a stereotypical close-up pose, offering her body to the lens in a troubling abandonment. The skin has the strangeness of invisible fur, as June's eyes reach beneath the skin.

Through Sauer's eyes I see a profound sense of commodified femininity encased in a set of trading gestures peculiar to the encounter between image and self-image. In particular, I envision a troubling moment that exposes the business of fur and skin as one of desirability, one that fleshes out the intimacies of the sexual economy of fur. The value of Sauer's work for a sexual economy of fur resides in this fragile ambivalence: on the one hand, Sauer's commodities and commercial production are bound to the gendered commercialization of the nation through fashion and other cultural events.[15] On the other hand, Sauer's photographs are embedded in the homoeroticism of the popular history of fur, a popular history always reminiscent of the British legacy. It was not by chance that Sauer was commissioned in 1959 and 1967 to immortalize a centennial tradition of Canada, the beaver ceremony, a fur trade ritual that commemorates each visit of a British royal family member by a governmental gift of a beaver coat, in this last case Queen Elizabeth II.

Sauer maneuvered inside and outside the trade: from within, her photographs enticed the fur ladies as bodily trademarks; outside, she invented an image of Venuses walking on the wild side of the domestication of beasts and belles. Sauer's photographs simultaneously materialize female bodies, industrial and cultural/political values. Her style obeyed a range of cultural contrasts. Her practice succeeded in sexualizing one of the most conservative and traditionalist, even essentialist, features of the nation: the fur lady. I imagine that Sauer was not interested in the invisible, and was rather constrained by the contours of the visible. Her strong ability to conflate skin and fur as part of the same texture in order to define the sexualized publicness of the trade confesses an exquisite sensuality towards women, but betrays all the same that without skin there is no fur. Sauer's graceful way of framing her models, partially skinned or lightly wrapped in lingerie or furs, allowed her to stretch the value of women in furs beyond the materiality of the fabric. In a rather exciting way, whether as lingerie master or fur hunter, Sauer defines a singular Canadian panorama. In so many ways, Sauer reinvents skin and fur, yet she also dislodges the conventions attached to the representativeness of women in furs in the national panorama, exhibiting the double movement between skin and national geographics within the context of the industry and the trade. Because it celebrates the intimacies between fur and skin, Sauer's work reinscribes the double articulation between dead flesh and live flesh as an intrinsic component of the national sexual economy. The merging between skins and the locations produces cultural and economic vignettes that enhance the intimate belonging to a local geography, while instilling a desire to situate national landmarks within a transnational movement.

Less sanitized than the quintessential *Vogue* girls à la Lisa Fonssagrives, June's girls had a presence that was enticed by both the homoerotic composition of the camera and their heteronormative exchange value on the market of commercial fashion photography. They were defined through the movement of local trade traveling on the transnational stock exchange. Acting as "trade" icons, tourist hostesses and mediators of the intimacies between/beneath the skins all at the same time, June's fur ladies possessed exhilarating and dangerous capacities to make the pictures hide as much as they reveal. This constant in-betweeness emerges from a linked set of representational moments to constitute a unique vignette in the family album of the fur ladies. June to me is a member of the wedding, of the homosocial marriages that troubled official accounts of the fur trade. If Sauer was a business libertine, she is nevertheless an eager member of the Canadian federalist/nationalist family. Most of her productions and geographies are encompassed by a shared commitment to English Canadian culture and a strong federalist nation. A self-declared pro-fur lady, Sauer was also a Trudeau Girl, like millions of other Canadians, her Dominion building studio guarded by a gigantic framed portrait of the pin-up prime minister of Canada.[16] As though June thought that the only Prince that could be invited to the photo shoot was the modern reincarnation of Prince Rupert.

Portrait of a marriage take three: June and Notman

> There were some dark and heavy men there then. There were some who were not so heavy and some who were not so dark. Helen Furr and Georgine Skeene sat regularly with them.
>
> (Stein 1923: 565)

My strategy of analyzing the works of June Sauer through William Notman's (1826–1891) legacy participates in this conflation of the commercial and the historical that asserts the naturalized value of fur in the artifice of the national.[17] Notman's fur portraits produced a unique cultural value in the process of historicizing and immortalizing the nation in the nineteenth century. Among the substantial tableaux of wilderness and other composites destined to capture the narrative of white colonial power and national wealth in a glimpse, including fantasia scenes such as an amazing in-studio reconstitution of a seal hunt,[18] Notman's portraits offer a unique point of entry to domestic spaces as mediated through commercial aesthetics. Here fur is introduced simultaneously as a matter of private property and public belonging. Yet today, Notman is largely remembered as a commercial preservationist of bear boys and fur ladies.

Unlike William Notman, photographer to the queen and father of Canadian commercial artistic photography whose photographic activities were primarily commissioned by different societies, individuals and even institutions, Sauer has never had her work exhibited in a major museum. Her dazzling photographs appeared mostly in the popular press, international trade magazines, or were highlights in major retail store catalogues and publicity pamphlets (among them, Holt Renfrew, Simpson's, Ogilvy, The Bay). While Sauer was prolific, her work was considered to be commercial and trade material, and she was never invited to become a member of the exclusive and select club of documentary guardians of Canadiana. Max had, of course; so had Notman. As a commercial production, Sauer's work raises questions about the conditions of circulation and validation of selective images in the commodification of the nation. Both inside and outside the conventions of the trade, Sauer's photographs need to be situated at the threshold of the borders of the sexual and the national. As raw commercial material, June's photographs call for analysis of particular regimes of circulation that operate in the market of skin and fur: "[those] conjunctural linkages of discourses and institutions which allow the regulation of what and who circulates, how, where, and when" (Grenier and Guilbault 1997: 214). Interestingly enough, while Notman's collection is valued today for its ethnographic contribution, Sauer's work, as a product of professionalization, troubles the fine line between authenticity and fictionalization.

Prior to my encounter with June, I was convinced that the iconography of the fur nation was man-made. Notman's amazing collection of socialites in furs made him the fur man of Canadian photographic history. His fur collection confers the value of legitimacy to fashion and the fur garments, dresses and coats fancied during the Victorian and Edwardian eras. His collection is enshrined into a naturalization of the Canadian body as a fur body: the myth that every Canadian is born with a fur coat. Fur is everywhere and part of the everyday: children, men, married women, single women, debutantes and curling ladies all proudly display fur. For instance, with his gallery of "true" people, Notman's work authenticates the essence of fur. Every single domestic or social activity was wrapped in fur, social bounds were fur bounds, and couples were sealed in furs (see Figures 2.1 and 3.9).

In contrast, Sauer made a gendered and sexual fantasy of fur, a uniquely raw sensuality/materiality that transpires from the seamless relation between female skin and fur. Her abundant documents of fur ladies from the end of the 1950s to the early 1980s sexualizes the proximities created between fur and female skin. In other words, Sauer and her passion for fur and skin speaks to what Notman's work cannot: that the regimes of circulation of skin and fur are intimately tied to the points of contact between fur and skin. What delimits Sauer's fur work is her repetitive yet unique way of documenting women in furs outside the folkloric moment of traditional sites of the fur trade, forging an association between fur and the nation as one of *modernity* and *urbanity* based on popular consumption. June's trade fantasies of excessive skin(s) unravels the idea of fur and female skin *as* nature. Gone are the landscapes, the forests and the wilderness: here the professionalization of the representativeness of fur ladies becomes a crucial aspect of urban culture and national trademarks. While the documentary aspect of Notman's work and production is constantly praised and legitimized as a unique contribution to the archive of the nation during the Victorian and Edwardian eras,[19] Sauer's linkage of fur, identity and geography exacerbates the "artifices" that intervene in the naturalization of the relation between fur and nation. The staging of professional models wearing fur in Sauer's photographs – in opposition to the officials, socialites and "real" people who compose Notman's impressive frescoes – is marginalized in the construction of a national identity, or the documentation of a national culture of fur. As Rosetta Brookes suggests:

> For historians and critics concerned with isolating "great" photo-graphic images and according them enduring significance, the commercial sphere of photography – the domain of the everyday image – represents the debasement of a conventional history of photography. Fashion advertising, in particular, is seen as negating the purity of the photographic image. We see the typical instead of the unique moment or event.
>
> (Brookes 1993: 17)

The encounter between Notman and Sauer reveals a great deal about the modalities of production of the national archive and the recording and preservation of popular history. Asked why she did not send her rich collection to the McCord (which would have been a logical choice, given that McCord is the most important repository of costume and dress archives in Canada), Sauer confides some hesitations about the facilities offered by the McCord Archives and Documentation Centre. As McCord already possesses the Notman fund, the decision to donate the Sauer funds to National Archives of Canada in Ottawa is all the more surprising. Or perhaps not. The Max and June Sauer Studio did not have the historical stature of the Notman Studios, and Sauer's commercial status overrides any artistic, archival one. Sauer is as much a socialite as an artist, and her insistence on situating her work at the crossroads of trade and art challenges the classificatory regimes that intervene in the industry of remembrance on many levels. In other words, the coupling of commercial value and fur ladies stands as a paradoxical instance of Sauer's participation in the documentation of the nation, one that, I argue, is based on the performative quality of the narrative that Sauer's fur stagings suggest. Yet June Sauer's work, because it is about the media, the popular, the trade, the commercial, and because it is about a woman seeing the nation through fur ladies, provokes important questions concerning the articulations between representational strategies of sexual economies and the circulation and dissemination of imagery that act as markers of the national. The sensational texture of national identity is captured in its excessive qualities through the commercial value and circulation offered by Sauer's fur ladies. The tensions between Sauer and Notman do not only emerge from differences in fur gazing; they also lie in the marketability and the knowledge of their work in the circulation of a national tale, particularly with respect to the representational value of Canadian identity (and Canadian beaver) for American and European markets. What distinguishes Sauer from Notman is the possibility of de-fetishization of fur as fur, fur is nothing per se, fur ladies are a more valuable fabric.

Although Notman actively sought out the globalization of his activities – his assistants toured Canada and the United States, opened studios according to need and demand, taking thousands of portraits for the posterity of American institutional gems such as Harvard, Vassar, Bryn Mawr – he was nevertheless truly the eye of the nation. Notman's impressive collection and production of commercial and tourist material reveals the ubiquity of the marketing of the nation through events of national interest. For instance, his composites – those incredible fantasmagoric frescoes chronicling balls, celebrations, and outdoor events – offer a fantastic journey into the retelling of the origins of the nation. What made Notman famous and what elevated the Notman style to the level of national history is also at work in the mythic national fur tale: a sanitized vision of the nation enticed by homogeneous imagery. His portraits of Canadian winter scenery, whether fancy dress balls, sporting events or family gatherings had the quaint quality of tourist postcards, yet the tenderness of a family album. Notman's signature on the nation sells both commercially and historically because it captures an unproblematic representation of Canada as a white snow country: a kaleidoscope of creative imageries of fur, snow and ice, ideally portrayed together in ways that transform and reinvent a fantastical narrative of the everyday. Despite his spectacular expressions of odd occasions and gatherings, he offers a secure representation of the fur nation: the nation according to Notman is a family portrait; while for Sauer it is a queer coupling both within and beyond the frame.

Notman captured people as events, and this is certainly one of the reasons that he managed to gain such popularity. His portraits constituted a way of simultaneously retelling social and economic progress, elite prowess and other aspects of social life. Notman was part of the Scottish elite of the city, the same class that had seen the birth of the North West Company and McGill University, the same elite that threw annual charity balls at the Windsor Hotel, participating in the governor's fancy dress balls, reconstructing Montréal as a continental Britannia. Notman's acquaintance with the Scottish bourgeoisie clearly reproduced the class and ethnic divisions that separated the French and English speaking communities of Montréal. Most of his portraits featured members of prominent Anglophone families, revealing the domination of British capital over finances. In this context, his production offers an interesting way to look at the paradoxical ties that sometimes link nationalism and colonialism. In fact, Notman's work cannot be dissociated from a form of mercantilist Scottish nationalism that was so much part of Northwestern culture. Unsurprisingly, Notman's photographs were the evidence of the success encountered by a certain Scottish elite in Canada. Most of his scenery cards/and landscapes were sent back home, as proof of the shining and the dynamism of

Scottish culture "overseas." "Colonized" in their own country, the Scots who came to Montréal occupied a double position in relation to colonization: colonized at home, they were paradoxically accomplices with a form of British imperialism (even colonialism) in the context of Montréal.

In the spirit of pure Victorian Britannia, domestic space intertwines with public knowledge, in a mode that is both commercial and asexual: the photographs reveal nothing but distance and a lack of skin, buried under fur and fabric. Intimacies are fittingly contained yet accessible, a matter of abundant display and exhibition of the fabric of the nation. In most of the portraits of ladies in fur, women do not touch fur, do not perform the women-made-fur moment: no sensuality towards furry materiality is made visible. Fur is clearly established as a layer, an excess, and not as a (second) skin. Among the photographs catalogued at the McCord Museum, only a few offer a disruptive approach to the rigidity of the pelts over fur. Among these, two portraits caught my eye: Miss M. Burley and "friend" (1881), and Miss Legge (1876) (Figure 3.9 and Figure 3.10). The queerness of both photographs attract me: Miss M. Burley and her "friend" (the caption reads as such) look like "sisters," an odd couple immortalized in a fur moment. The absence of a name for the friend echoing in a devilish way Verne's depiction of Paulina and Madge as faithful "companions." Meanwhile, Miss Legge stands proud: in the most sensual way, the photograph renders the texture of fur. If Miss Legge's portraiture barely suggests the brief encounter between her skin and the wild pelts, the eye caresses the richness of the dark fox. Yet something is not quite there: the encounter between fur and skin is not materialized. Miss Legge, Miss M. Burley and her friend wear fur, they do not touch it. These are photographs of mummified women in furs, actualizing the gap between fur and skin.

In the same spirit, Sauer's commercial fur photographs reveal as much about the circulation of goods and commodities over the span of three decades as about the materiality of women wearing and performing ladies in furs. Although seduced by Sauer's singularity, I cannot resist dislodging and relodging her incandescent style here and there with that of the Notman studio, especially the 1920s "high fashion" line of production. What is fascinating in the realm of liminalities and the containment of sexual economy is how the corporate work of Sauer fulfilled a similar purpose to that of Notman's so-called commissioned works. For Sauer, the vocation of the studio called for contracts with prominent national (and international) corporations featuring professional, i.e., fictionalized fur ladies. With the Notman studio, bourgeois families, social clubs and associations, as well as national/natural tourist attractions, offered their faces to his family fur portrait, bringing a sense of authenticity to his documents. Sauer is remembered as an agent of the fashion fur industry, as numerous contracts with the Fur Trade Association testify, while Notman appears as the artist, a taxidermist managing to capture splendid vignettes depicting national and local scenery, in which fur acts as the quaint landmark of Canadian winters. Sauer as the private figure, Notman as the public one.

Figure 3.9 Miss Burley and "friend", Montreal 1881. Print courtesy of NPA/MMCH.

Figure 3.10 Miss Legge, Montréal 1876. Print courtesy of NPA/MMCH.

Sauer's studio was an essential stop for fur retailers; Notman's, a space to perform mundane activities, including posing in furs. For Sauer, fur was a necessity of business; for Notman's, fur was the final touch on a parade of famous local and national personalities having their faces immortalized for prosperity. As Bara explains, "A visit to the Notman studio in Montréal was almost obligatory for the many visitors from Britain, and the studio record-books are filled with portraits of almost all the well-known personages of the era who came to Montréal" (Bara 1991: 187).

Ironically, Sauer also had an eye for royalty and other colonial remains, and her work occasionally flirted with the economy of souvenir and commemoration. Sauer's work was often used by different governmental agencies in the production of tourist, commercial and national materials, also becoming photographer of the royal family. Like William Notman, "photographer to the queen," Sauer also documented a very important moment in the development of the fur trade in Canada, and even America: photographing the queen's second skin. It happened during the preparations surrounding the visit of Queen Elizabeth II to Canada in 1959. Sauer received the commission by the Canadian government to take the official photograph of the royal gift – the traditional fur coat – presented to Queen Elizabeth as part of the "rent ceremony" (see chapter 2). However, as the fur was about to be offered to royal blood, and as sumptuary law of diplomatic British protocol prohibits touching the Queen ("to touch royal skin") no one could wear the fur in advance, even for fashion modeling purposes. Accustomed to working with models, Sauer was constrained by sumptuary rules to shoot the mink fur coat without the lady, substituting a chair in the hall of the Fine Arts Museum for the Queen. This episode contrasts with Sauer's technique and touch of/for fur: the objectification of the royal subject by a chair disturbed Sauer's use of touch-ing for erasing the boundaries between skin and pelt, but making skin and pelt one. In the absence of body, royal or not, to give life to the pelts, the mink coat stood as a textureless, valueless fabric. In other words, the mink coat had no value per se without the skin (here the blue skin): i.e., no cultural value, no value as national staple. Deprived of the sexual quality of the trading skin, the mink becomes a banal and static object of contemplation instead of being a powerful mediation of the transnational economy.[20]

All things considered, Sauer was a leader in fashion photography, one of a kind, artistically gifted, but marketed as "commercial" nevertheless. The first woman in Canada to receive a degree from the Professional Photographers of Canada Inc., Sauer has always walked the fine line between commercial work and artistic approach. Even if some of her works have been touring commercial venues, and many of her prize-winning photographs are in permanent loan collections throughout North America (notably at the Carnergie Institute in New York), Sauer's work has never crossed the threshold of a museum institution. No catalogues, no institutional retrospectives exist to record her production; no entries in any journal or photography magazines. Only the exhibition awards, prizes and trophies gathered from different professional competitions, such as the Professional Photographers of America and the National Society of Art Directors bear some traces of her work. When the upscale department store Ogilvy's celebrated its 130th anniversary in 1996 by sponsoring the first retrospective of 150 of Sauer's best fashion works commissioned by the famous retail store and important fur depository, it was the first exhibition of its kind in the career of the photographer.

In this context, her participation in the fur national economy and representation of the nation operates on a different and estranged scale from the work produced by Notman's national, cultural enterprise. Notman photographed the elite in fur, Sauer photographed professional women (models) in fur. Both series of photographs were staged: one for family posterity, social recognition and the historical glamour of the city and the nation, the other for the splendor of consumers, for the sake of the business, and the triumph of fur ladies. Notman has become the mandatory reference for anyone interested in the history of costume and Canadiana; Sauer an unspeakable detour for anyone titillated by the crossover between the private and the public, skin and fur. Notman's fantastic collection is featured at the McCord Museum, Sauer's work of fashion extravaganza at Ogilvy's, a department store. No wonder they never crossed paths.

Epilogue: The Queen and I

June 2000. Like Gertrude Stein's Miss Furr and Miss Skeene, I dreamt that June and I were an odd couple who had found each other. As for Helen Furr and Georgine Skeene, whose togetherness came through being gay and gayer every day, each encounter with June – whether in flesh and bone, or more often through the tremendous volume of photographs she produced – was exactly like theirs, while not quite like it: a gay moment filled by gay thoughts, gay memories, gay fantasies. In our whimsy (how queer! little Alice in Wonderland would say) – either in politics or sexuality – I imagine our skins as part of the same fabric. And because she was gay enough, I could not help but always be gay in the same way. Because June/Helen Furr:

> [. . .] was gay enough, she was gay exactly the same way, she was always learning little things to use in being gay, she was telling about using other ways in being gay, she was telling about learning other ways in being gay, she was learning other ways in being gay, she would be using other ways in being gay, she would always be gay in the same way, when Georgine Skeene was there not so long each day and when Georgine Skeene was away.

(Stein 1923: 567)

My reconstitution of Sauer's career and contribution to the sexual economy of the nation transpires through a strategy of encounters, as a means to produce both an affective and effective portrait of an inscrutable yet "real" subject – Sauer "happened" and "happens still" (Morris 1984: 46). Because there is no historical documentation that offers traces of Sauer, there is no "official" catalogued archive of Sauer as a historical figure, she remains a "missing link" from the very record of Canadiana primarily occupied by such photographic figures as William Notman. Instead, traces of Sauer are routed into the thousands of photographs she donated to the Archives, and to the other thousands that she jealously keeps at home and in a secret repository. Sauer's (national) identity defies historical reconstitution: it is on the contrary by juxtaposing stories and tales of other "unfit" and outcast ladies that she gains representativeness.

Paradoxically, Sauer's elusiveness in official Canadiana stands in stark contrast to her omnipresence and extreme renown in various informal circles of the Montréal fashion scene. There, Sauer is a sort of legend, a lady of tall tales. Any woman who has been involved in one way or another with Montréal fur culture knows of June Sauer, from costume historians to journalists, to fashion scholars, to fur businesswomen. In other words, Sauer is known as a popular figure rather than a historical name. Until very recently, professional fashion design schools would invite her to give seminars, even after her retirement, and she was for a very long time a regular of various professional associations, among which are found the prestigious New York-based Fashion Group International (Montréal branch), and the National Society of Art Directors. It is due to her very status as a popular and commercial figure that I am compelled to weave her story through encounters, by stealing other people's fictional and real life accounts to make them an intrinsic part of June's fantastic elusiveness as a pioneer of commercial fur photography.

Sauer's non-traditional way of displaying and "looking" through the skin of both models and fur patches challenges strategies of production in ways that trouble long-standing debates about tradition versus modernity, as well as artistic practices versus commercial ones. In contrast to official canons of historical and cultural documentation from which the fur ladies' productive labor remains absent, Sauer's authorial, popular and subjective approach reverberates in a cultural moment that unveils the gendered structure of the business. This becomes all the more acute when we contrast Sauer's eyes as a concrete site of documenting the nation to William Notman's industry of national commemoration and celebration, as encapsulated in his famous composites.[21] Sauer's popular representation of the nation in the context of the commercialization of documentation shines because of her own unique way to reach the skin beneath the fur.

In Sauer's work, what I see is the skin through the fur . . . the moment of juncture of a conceptualization of fur as skin. Sauer's interpretation of the uniqueness of beaver in marking the value of the female body in the national economy reasserts the sexual and paradoxcial value of white skin within the commercial fur trade. This is why I choose in the following pages to analyze

Sauer's work and practices transversally as part of both the homoerotic and heterosexual commodification of the nation. By arguing that Sauer's work calls for a homoerotic and heterosexual transversality, I suggest that her national imagery is at once informed by normative contingencies – the trade – while it also opens a space that can be consumed and looked at queerly. June Sauer's photographs are triumphantly inside out: inside the heterosexual economy of the trade – the fashion posture and staging – and yet outside of it, homosocially composed and queer looking. A strange sense of in-betweeness, of impenitent crossovers between the commercial and high fashion scenes are harbored in her work, dominating its construction/production and the way we are able to reach for it. As Mavor puts it in relation to Clementina's photographs: "Hawarden's photographs, like all photographs of family members, live in a magical intermediary area of transitional space: they are 'me' and 'not-me' objects par excellence" (Mavor 1999: 77). June's photographs not only capture the many ways that fur touches skin. They also unveil how ladies and fur touch each other to reveal a tissue of proximities that reinvents our ways of seeing women in the nation.

4

MY FUR LADY, OR CANADA'S LIBERTY

Into a new world,
My hopes so foolishly high,
I fly,
Into a new world.
Into the blue
Where a new heaven must lie.

Into a new world,
Where nights of loneliness
Are quite unknown,
Into a light blue world,
Sunny and bright new world,
Into the arms of a love of my own.
(*My Fur Lady*, Act I, Scene 2)

Snow pies and pretty beavers

Feminists such as Ware (1992), Stoler (1997), McClintock (1995), Lewis (1996), Shohat (1992), and Brody (1998) have recently analyzed representations of white femininity as a means to address conflicts between colonial transnational movements and domestic space, stressing in particular the importance of the association between home and the nation for the preservation of the imperial order and economy. Either through such social means as educational programs and missionary work, or through glittering cultural events – such as fancy dress balls, humane societies, and social purity organizations – white women were key actors in the development of a complex and dense network in which ties to the empire were channeled into a strong national colonial system of governance.

Victorian imperialism is often cited as one of the most spectacular and excessive performances of gendered and racialized colonialism, dominated by the obsession for ethnic purity, reproduction and women's contribution to the circulation of natural resources. On the other hand, as a way to counterbalance the skin hunt, one might argue that the Victorian period (1837–1901) was marked, among other things, by an extraordinary refusal of skin – but certainly not of fur. According to Ewing (1981) and Toussaint-Samat (1990), the late nineteenth century was fur fashion bliss. Canada as a white settler country[1] was knitted together by cultural and social regimes of governance over sexuality, race and the family – and this state of affairs was not estranged from the dominant role assumed by the Roman Catholic Church in the European origins of the nation. The ultimate goal of the religious orders and communities of nuns who held an important share of fur capital (through landed property) was the transformation of the wilderness into white European civilization and the domestication and moral education of the beasts.

The remainders of this colonial sexual economy persisted in the development of the nation-state at the turn of the twentieth century, while a burgeoning economy of social morality, sexual education and state provisions on sexuality proliferated. Native communities across the Americas were confined to "civil-izing," in other words, assimilationist programs. Meanwhile, in Canada, the growing nationalization of private issues, from family rule to unruly beavers – notably through laws framing female sexuality as an ethnic and moral impurity[2] – became a national sport and was practised indifferently by the government, Christian religious orders and impressive numbers of women associations, constituted by bourgeois and middle-class women. As I demon-strate in my analysis of the anti-fur movement (see chapter 5), this culture of cleansing, apparently peripheral to the fur economy, was *a contrario* a key factor in the contemporary deployment of the sexual economy of the nation, via its clear commitment to reproduction and racial containment. In chapter 1, I discussed the degree to which the colonial network unfolded as a complex mixture of official and unofficial rules, a textural "ensemble" of material and symbolic references through which the scope of imperial discourse was con-stantly reinserted, adapted and modified to suit the new contingencies of the development and "progress" of the future anterior colony. Interestingly enough, it was very often through official functions and status that "Canadian" women were given opportunities to perform for the project of colonialization through nationalist representations. For instance, Canadian associations such as The Imperial Order of the Daughters of the Empire (IODE), or animal welfare/benevolent colonial societies, such as the Society for the Prevention of Cruelty to Animals (founded in 1869), offered a great deal of exposure and agency for middle-class and bourgeois women at the same time that they were securing the economy of invisible fur.

The case of the IODE is worth a pause here, meriting a star in the fur lady album. Under the national motto, "One Flag, One Throne, One Empire," the IODE's mandate was:

> To promote in the Motherland and in the Colonies the study of the history of the Empire, and of current Imperial questions . . . to promote

unity between the Motherland, the sister colonies, and themselves, to promote loyalty to King and Country; to forward every good work for the betterment of their country and people; to assist in the progress of art and literature; to draw women's influence to the bettering of all things connected with our great Empire and to instill into the youth of their country patriotism in its fullest sense.

Aims and Objects of Order nos. 4 and 6
(The Imperial Order of Daughters of the Empire 1900–50: 9–10)

The IODE is the logical continuum of the Victorian female economy. As Pickles argues, throughout the twentieth century, the "IODE has represented Canadian colonial history," and the various patriotic, caring and educational tasks fulfilled by the members went beyond benevolent initiatives. Positioning themselves above other women's charity organizations and women's auxiliaries, the members of the still-existing Order were actively involved in fundraising to finance their activities as well as organizing social and entertainment events to inspire patriotic fervor and support naval and military efforts. Marketing strategies were mostly focussed on preserving the British Empire at any cost, even if that meant marginalizing so-called domestic/national issues (Pickles 1996: 233). The Order, on a smaller scale, was simply following the grand cultural and social mobilization that the Governor-General's ladies had long decreed for the daughters of the country. Pageants, plays, musicals and popular variety performances were staged from coast to coast, praising Anglo-Celtic culture as informed by colonial history in the preservation of the Dominion of Canada. Following in the path of the colonizers, the Order became the best ambassador to America that the Queen of England could have dreamt of. Rather than simply mobilizing people around colonial pride, the daughters disseminated the Empire throughout the country. Their so-called social and cultural role was actually supported by an important financial infrastructure that would allow the Order to play an important role in such transnational events as war, education, and Imperial interests in Canada.[3]

To further pursue the skin-trading of patriotism, both common-law marriages bound by royal order (i.e., *Les Filles du roy*) and corporate gentlemen's agreements blessed by the fur trade companies (the HBC and North West Company) were also sites of important commerce and paradoxical agency for women, white and native: the legal trading of skin for skin. As Irigaray observes, "A commodity – a woman – is divided into two irreconcilable bodies: her 'natural' body and her socially valued, exchangeable body, which is a particularly mimetic expression of masculine values" (Irigaray 1985: 180). Finally, the economy of diplomatic wives contributed to a rampant but necessary fair deal for the fur business. It extended from Beaver Club Grand Seigneur's wives who fancied the beaver brooch as a sign of social standing (as discussed in chapter 2), to the aboriginal country wives, to the Lady Excellencies – the official name given the wives of the Governor Generals of Canada who functioned as supreme representatives of the Queen in the dominion countries. The colonial apparatus was extremely diversified and creative in renewing its territorial and colonial resources in the establishment of a communications network based around a strong sexual economy, in which women were both commodities and agents of an important sector of the politics and economics of the nation.

In this sense, the Victorian period had a strong influence on the ways that women – mostly white and European – have been asked to contribute to the colonial effort. If, on the one hand, the official activities of the daughters of the empire have received a fair amount of attention from feminist postcolonial work (see for instance Lewis [1996], Ware [1992], Shohat [1992], McClintock [1995] and Stoler [1997]), little concern has been addressed, on the other hand, to the way that the nationalization of colonial culture has mediated a racialized sexual economy under the "fetishization" of native bodies to the colonial project. In other words, the sexual economy of the nation is always understood as racially exclusive. For instance, while the country wives are seen as natural components of the colonial economic landscape – that naturalness being indeed monitored through invisibility, or wilderness – the diplomatic wives and governmental ladies are praised for maintaining a level of cultural and social visibility appealing to the grandeur of the country. In this chapter, I propose to question how white female agency is achieved through a strong mixture of racial performance and sexual nationalization, commanding the sexualization of the white body in order to mask the native one.[4] In this sense, the 1958 Canadian musical *My Fur Lady* will be analyzed as a historical and cultural expression of the marriage between fur and skin, race and sexuality, in the fabrication of the nation. Rooted in the Victorian tradition of "screening" mixed blood as politically unfit, the play celebrates the triumph of one nation under one flag: the Eskimo/snow lady. Moreover, in the most vivid way, the discourse in and around *My Fur Lady* confused the boundaries between the trading modalities of fur as skin, and skin as meat/beast.

However, before I analyze in *My Fur Lady*'s interracial musical, we need to consider the fancy dress ball culture and economy that prevailed in the late nineteenth century in Canada, as it contextualizes the extent of the display and mannerisms of racial and sexual passing as a fundamental strategy of nation-building within colonial allegiance.

Fancy dress ball culture, or women made nature

In the postcolony, the very display of grandeur and prestige always entails an aspect of vulgarity and the baroque that the official order tries hard to hide, but which ordinary people bring to its attention – sometimes intentionally, often unwittingly.

(Mbembe 1992: 12)[5]

Long before the balls entertained by governors general, the traces of colonialism were often channeled into Empire entertainment, and frequently commodified through the touring of the "other," an other brought home and exhibited on the domestic market. The balls themselves raised important issues regarding, on the one hand, the local commodification of the colonial market and, on the other hand, the creation of a national event through a practice of imperial transvestitism. In the Canadian Victorian economy, the wife of the Governor General, the First Lady, occupied a key role in the performance of national duty. Local queen, she was the darling of the social columnists and the *maître d'oeuvre* of the society world necessary to the stability of the political establishment. At once queen and "*soubrette*," the Governor General's wife represented the contradictory nature of the colony: a satellite, yet an autonomous structure.

One of the most dashing figures of the late 1800s was Lady Aberdeen, who managed to take over Parliament Hill with her talent for *frou-frou* and a fierce eye for national performativity (Figure 4.1). Lady Aberdeen's longing for fancy dress balls that went beyond their aesthetic attractions could be seen as a powerful forum for colonial materiality, a commemorative experience comparable in so many ways to the celebration of nation/colony that was driving various World Fairs and Museum Exhibitions. Shamelessly inspired by Queen Victoria's dress balls, the colonial fancy dress balls were an exquisite and ambitious opportunity for the vice-regents to recreate the glamour of the British nobility within the colony, while knitting from a strong sense of identity for the colonial nation. Beyond the mere display of the "treasures" of colonial enterprise, the fancy dress balls were a unique occasion for the ladies to bridge the economy of the nation to the racial, sexual and class markers encompassing the new "nation." On the one hand, the fancy dress balls allowed a celebration of the creativity of the wives of the new country and their commitment to the success and longevity of British culture within the new and still quaintly acculturating country. On the other hand the balls, as imagined and designed by this army of ladies, made the encounter with the Other into pure spectacle, a masquerade, a performance tantalizing the sexual and racial edges of the other.

However, beyond dilettante entertainment and the *frou-frou* (rustling; frill) of "passing" extravaganzas, the fancy dress balls were a complex texture of material patriotic excess and representational otherness, where the bounds between skin, costume and the land were at the core of the success and the economy of these balls. The two most popular figures of fancy dress ball culture during the Victorian period, Lady Aberdeen and her predecessor Lady Dufferin, were not only vivid examples of the means undertaken by country ladies to fulfill their colonial duty as wives of the country – they were also successful in inscribing the value of skin in the organization of political society. In the traditional model of pure society ladies, Lady Aberdeen left traces of her patriotic devotion and communal sensitivity to both the fit and the unfit, as her numerous initiatives to create ladies' foundations and associations showed. Unlike Lady Dufferin, Lady Aberdeen relished her primary role as a true fur

Figure 4.1 Lady Aberdeen costumed for the Chateau de Ramezay Ball, Montréal 1898.
Courtesy of NPA/MMCH.

country lady. In order to extend my analysis of the economy of the 1950s *My Fur Lady* moment beyond the context of the postwar period, I want to frame the fancy dress balls within the commercial and trading market of the theatrical, the "spectacularization" of the Other, and the domestication of national belonging. The balls, although "memorable" were also scenes of the everyday.[6] Although exceptional and staged, the balls were "banalized" as popular events, events to which "the people" were invited (under conditions of restricted entry, of course) to mix and rub elbows with the local, and sometimes national, elite. In other words, the balls were well-orchestrated regimes of containment of excesses of sexuality and race under the tight supervision of the official fur lady, in this case, Lady Aberdeen.

As Cynthia Cooper observes in *Magnificent Entertainments: Fancy Dress Balls of Canada's Governors General* (1997), the first study of the fancy dress ball tradition and culture in dominion Canada:

> While Lady Aberdeen extended her influence to politics and other matters more than any other Governor General's wife, she knew how to make her role in the feminine sphere serve the same ends. She had a sophisticated understanding of the meaning of dress and of how her own clothing could inspire patriotic feeling in others.
>
> (Cooper 1997: 68)

What Cooper, as a costume historian, overlooks is how this *chiffon patriotism* was channeled through the closeness of skin, fur and subjects attending the balls. Her illustrated study shows numerous costumes by the daughters of the Empire that discursively and politically replicate and marshall the intimate association between the female body and the potential richness of the land, including valued contrasts between the skin colours. Mummified, almost taxidermic in their texture, these costumes did not have any materiality, did not have any trading value per se on their own. Not, that is, until Lady Aberdeen, in two "dominion" chiffon extravaganzas that she staged for the Governor General, captured the spirit of Ottawa-the-docile-dominion-child in scenes of colonial bliss.

For the final ball entertained by the Aberdeens in 1897 in Toronto, under the operatic theme "One Queen, One Empire," Lady Aberdeen came up with the wildest sexualized representations of the nation that such an event could muster, asking women to literally embody the natural resources of each specific dominion, while men would proudly act as their discoverers and exploiters. "Women personified natural resources such as mines, forests, fishing, and fur – all creatively rendered as emblematic costumes. Their partners dressed as controllers and exploiters of these resources: miners, lumbermen, fishermen, and fur traders" (Cooper 1997: 101). Through female skin, male penetration and denaturalizing conquest, Lady Aberdeen captured the perfect expression of one country's richness, and the backbone of economic exchanges between Britain and its seven dominions, Canada included. While one might argue that the threads between skin, ethnicity and the nationalistic economy of the body could only be anachronistically read in retrospect, journalists assigned to cover the uncovered noted the fabulous connections. For instance one observer commented on the gendered aesthetics of the ensemble of tableaux: "The abstract, as usual, is feminine and the concrete, masculine" (Cooper 1997: 101). Meanwhile another newspaper described the racial passing of two performing Indians in these terms: "one looking exactly like a native and the other looking exactly like a white man dressed up as an Indian" (150). These performances of the essential origins of the nation were replete with racial and gendered constructions, and clearly the sexualized encryption of the mise en scène did not escape the observers attending the balls. The ball sought to offer a panorama of all colonies, and a description of the Canadian fantasia is worth some pause here.

Glorying among the North America tableau, Canada was featured as a flesh, fur, skin and fabric composition of seven resources, each "natural resource" diligently escorted by the men who brought them on the domestic and transnational markets. In a sort of live panorama of Canada, the parade introduced the natural resource ladies. At the centre, the Aberdeen's seventeen-year-old daughter came as the Forests of Canada, with her escort "A Lumberman" (David Erskine). They were followed by Miss Augusta Beverley Robinson in her salmon-can label dress who came as "Fishing," with her partner, "A Lower Canadian Fisherman." Edith Mowat came as "Our Lady of the Snows," "the title of a controversial Kipling poem written earlier in 1897 celebrating the preferential tariffs Canada had accorded to Great Britain" (Cooper 1997: 104–5). Finally, Miss Etta Macpherson splendidly embodied "Fur," partnered by "A Half-breed Fur Trader," "wearing a buckskin suit and moccasins and draped in furs" (Cooper 1997: 104). These national vignettes in their magnificent redundancy and glittering excess unveiled the extent to which the sexual economy of the nation was enacted in the relation between women, nation, politics and economy. Moreover, because the production of the balls made visible the strange marriage between female labor (the balls often took months to organize), white homosociality (the white female socialites) and the panoramic/tourist nation (performing the "other" skin), it is not hard to see in this wild operation of commodity fetishism a strong manifestation of nationalist homogenization and colonialist allegiance. In this sense, while performed regional references offered their predictable share of trappers, aboriginal pastiche and so on, *la coterie* was ultimately devoted to performing the Imperial Subject, and the celebration of the grandeur of Britannia for women and different women's societies that were spreading in the dominion. For instance, in Lady Aberdeen's farewell ball, Mrs. Edith Nordheimer, who would soon become the first president of the Imperial Order of Daughters of the Empire, showed up as "England, Queen of the Seas" (Cooper 1997: 106).

With her final fancy dress, Lady Aberdeen made transparent like never before the carnal lust behind the reenactment of the heritage and legacy of colonial grandeur through skin exhibitionism. In a mixture of museum-brought-home, popular display and carnavalesque celebration, topped up with plenty of skin and fur, she went a step further than her predecessors in fusing together entertainment, political and historical content. Her dilettante appearance as first lady of the King led to a missionary vision of her role as leader and curator of the British Commonwealth. The balls that she fancied were highly political, as were the happy bunnies who participated and contributed to the success of her dressed-up moments. Whiteness was indeed the dominant theme, and the historical tableaux created to depict and celebrate the (trans)national British colonial project was clearly inspired by the spirit of existing popular entertainments such as World Fairs and their freakeries, the touring of "natives" as Jewels in the Crowns of the Courts of England or France, or even public medical conferences about the anatomy of queer bodies (Kapsalis 1997).

The fancy dress balls allowed at least two complementary representations of women to be placed on display, one from within and one from without: as natural sexual resources of the colony, and as the colonial triumph of lady's club in the dissemination of the imperial order. The first one secured the link between female body and colonial land, the latter maintained the hierarchy between Mother-land and the daughters of the country. Lady Aberdeen's strongly colonial conception of women as "natural resources" and men as "exploiters" of these resources in her swan song in 1897 betrayed a powerful vision of the gendered and cultural resonances of the colonial legacy for the new nation. In many ways, the fancy dress balls captured the mediated aspect of female sexuality for women, revealing the excessive capital of the undressed nation.

In addition to the sexualization of imperial display, the balls offered a unique way to mediate race and ethnicity, making the other into the ultimate expression of political encounter and colonial masquerade. In line with historical and cultural reenactments spreading throughout America and Europe, where "repeated ruptures in the narration of the nation are smoothed by sanitized, sanctified versions of history" (Brody 1998: 6), the balls also acted as a performing post for Whites to embody the other. Not only were personas masqueraded, but entire scenes and tableaux were mounted depicting the most glorious moments of colonial/Victorian regency. For example, when Lady Aberdeen called her first ball in 1896 "Canadian History, from the Vikings to the Loyalists," she made no secret that the entire enterprise had a necessarily "educational value" over the simple entertainment flavor that characterized the Dufferin regency. Lady Aberdeen embodied the triumph of the European white women in the colony, fancying herself as a missionary, educator and proud apostle of the Queen, as wife and mother of the colonizing project. Aberdeen's elitist vision of her mandate as first lady of the Queen in Canada was not far from the salvation enterprises undertaken by various societies of Daughters of the Empire, who expended energy and time across the dominions and colonies of the empire in the spirit of "fertilizing" British values, as well as to foreground the reproductive reverberations of white women in the economy of domesticated land (Whitlock 1995).[7]

In this context, the balls were not only a matter of socialization or display of colonial culture, but also an amazing scene that intertwined economy, politics and sexualization in the domesticating of the new nation. The repetition of colonial vignettes like the one described above at each Governor General's ball perpetuated the national beaver tales that propogated a gendered discourse of the origins of national history. The fact that most of the costumes fancied at the balls were romanticized versions of history added to the fairy/beaver tale aspect of the *frou-frou* enterprise. When an item collected or acquired during a colonial assignation or travel was sometimes displayed by the ballgoers, the entire attire made even more explicit the crucial mediating role played by women in the transnational movement of colonialism. Not strictly mundane events, the balls generated an economy of national and imperial commemoration through *frou-frou* culture. The balls were actually a "domesticated," i.e., "feminized" version of a more official and legitimated display of colonial enterprise that one can find in the archives of the Smithsonian Institute, or the Paris World Fair. Elitist yet popular, resistant to commercialism, the balls called for a female entrepreneurship explicitly expressed in the production and the making of historical and commemorative artifacts, ranging from costumes, to food, to publicity and social promotion of the soiree. Ironically, the relative "playfulness" of these colonial ceremonials was only made possible through a set of strictly hierarchic social relations and political allegiances, in which class, race and sexual markers were emphasized. Moreover, the obvious sexual division of labor upon which the success of the soiree was based only made the sexualized production of national tales that was at the basis of colonial glory more explicit. In this sense, the photographic documentation of the balls – including the William Notman Studios in Montréal (see chapter 4) – made visible the contribution of bourgeois white women and women's societies to the circuit of the balls, relegating native women to a role of performed other.

Over half a century, *My Fur Lady* espouses exactly the same contours of this paradoxical, yet complementary mode of sexualizing and racializing national representation: *My Fur Lady*'s popular appeal and political and economic success lay in its capacity to at once address the reverie (marriage) and the banal (national politics) of the country. In addition, because it also echoed the gendered and sexualized configuration of modern trading, the musical charted the sexuality of history in a most traditional and predictable way. The fact that the fancy balls were primarily popular with the white Anglophone political and social elite is certainly not estranged from the fact that – almost sixty years after the great Montréal Historical Fancy Dress ball held in 1898 – the McGill Red and White Revue featured the theatrical revue *My Fur Lady* for its final year show. Still considered today as one of the most popular theatrical revues ever produced in Canada,[8] *My Fur Lady* offers a rich "moment" in which to consider how national subjectivities are channeled through the sexual dynamics of imperialist and colonialist culture, as well as practices of substituting skin for fur. A medley of political revue, fancy dress ball, postwar Nanook of the North and commodification of colonial history, the beaver politics of *My Fur Lady* are clearly forged into master narratives of sexuality and nation. Looking back on both the original event, as well as its twenty-fifth anniversary commemorative reunion in 1982, I want to dance with the princes and ladies that made *My Fur Lady* the perfect fairy/furry tale for trading identities in a colonialist historical and political context. I propose to approach *My Fur Lady* as a contemporary expression of the national performance of miscegenation, a musical can-can that offers peculiar expressions of the relations between race and sex, human and animal. If Canada was really made of beaver, of white beavers and snow pies, *My Fur Lady* would be the queen of them all, the double embodiment of the empress fully-clothed, and fully-skinned. She could dance all night and never again be afraid of being outed as Other.

My Fur Lady: an "Eskimo" tale

Teach me how to think Canadian
How to greet and eat and drink Canadian
Be and ski and skate Canadian
Teach me how to mate Canadian.
        Princess and Rex, Scene 3, Act I[9]

Even in my wildest dreams of discovering a virgin female terrain in my *flâneur* reverie of the beaver trail, I could not imagine a more extravagant fur post to explore than *My Fur Lady*. When I first expressed my excitement about McGill's 1957 theater revue (see Figure 4.2), most of my friends and colleagues would hear that I was interested in *My Fair Lady*, which they thought was a peculiar way to hail the "*{savoir} faire*" of the fur ladies. The initial confusion became an inspiring pun for "fair fur" as well as a subjective tactic to move between the different layers of skin narratives. Most of us are familiar with George Cukor's 1964 Hollywood screen adaptation of the Broadway show, starring a dashing Audrey Hepburn in a gigantic hat, speaking and spouting perfect English for the sake of British culture. The ultimate embodiment of Victorian fair culture, Hepburn also stands as the quintessential image of the colonized female body. Like the land, a rude, rough, wild Hepburn undergoes the different phases of progress and development: she is tamed, groomed, scrubbed, revamped, domesticated, ready to be displayed to the British elite society, half-debutante, half-species exhibited before the eyes of the British court. Not only does a furless Hepburn get her language right, she also gets her skin clean and silky, honoring the deeds of "square deal" between trading parties. Her body and tongue are exchanged for a pristinely clean dress, under which the

After 10 sold out weeks in Montreal

Opens July 22nd
for two weeks
at the Avon Theatre
Stratford, Ont.

Matines 3:00 p.m.
Evenings 8:30 p.m.
Prices $3.00 - $2.50 - $1.75

Presented by
The Graduates' Society
of
McGill University

A Canadian Musical Satire
Directed by
BRIAN & OLIVIA MACDONALD

Figure 4.2 Poster for *My Fur Lady*, Stratford 1957. Print courtesy of MUA.

whiteness of the skin radiates. The grand finale of the film celebrates the new Fair Lady as the greatest achievement and discovery of civilized taste: the stunning trophy of the Great British Explorer (Rex Harrison). Completely revamped under the expertise of the Great Explorer, the Fair Lady trades her still virgin body for the respectability of marriage.

The Hollywood adaptation of *Pygmalion* obviously was not available to the five creators of *My Fur Lady*, the Quince Brothers (or Princes) when they wrote this amateur-turned-professional revue.[10] But the Broadway adaptation, the tale of a groomed beaver who learns to speak "proper English" was definitely the talk of the town, inspiring the all-male Anglophone writing team of McGill's Red and White Annual Revue. As one of the creators confesses, "[The] cheeky gesture . . . [of] . . . misappropriat[ing] . . . the name of Broadway's reigning hit"[11] contributed to the national popularity of *My Fur Lady*, fur being the most Canadian way of all to address an interracial, intranational satire on "domestic" politics and national affairs.

The musical which began its professional career on 23 May 1957 was originally conceived as a college production to be produced by and for students of McGill University in Montréal. Featuring non-professional actors, the play enjoyed all-star wannabe professional artistic direction, lead by composers James B. Domville and Galt MacDermott and directed, staged and choreographed by Brian and Olivia MacDonald.[12] In other words, the play, featuring ladies in pelts (more so than in furs) and bear boys, was a fur-man made initiative. Interestingly enough, Olivia McDonald's participation in *My Fur Lady*, while it got full credits in the playbill, was always overshadowed by her husband's profile as producer and star-director of the play, maintaining a strong gendered division between performance (by the ladies of the play) and creation/production (by the boys). The double directorship of the McDonalds constitutes a micro expression of the institutional cleavage between the production of display/ performance on one end, and the production of national expression along the lines of gendered agency on the other end. In other words, what *My Fur Lady* made visible was the masculine creativity of the play; yet what was economically successful was the female sexual commodity of the fur ladies beyond the play. This is why, from the very beginning of the project, and as I shall develop in this chapter, the sexual economy of the play was as much informed by the text itself as by its conditions of circulation and consumption: i.e., by the availability of Olivia and other female cast members to perform as fur ladies outside the realm of the stage.

My Fur Lady premiered on 7 February 1957. Intended as a Canadian version of the Grace Kelly–Prince Rainier romance that saved Monaco from absorption into France, the storyline revolves around an *immigrant* (sic!) Inuit Princess, Aurora, performed by a Snow White amateur actress (Ann Golden) masquerading as a fancy Eskimo Pie – ironically a popular delight in the fifties made of vanilla ice cream coated with milk chocolate. Aurora goes south to find a young white Canadian to marry in order to save her people, the community of Mukluko which, in the event of dynastic failure, reverts to Canada. "Two acts, twelve scenes, fifteen songs and a thousand rewrites later," (McDonald *et al*. 1975: 124) Aurora finally weds the representative of the Queen in Dominion Canada, the Governor General, and, as a nuptial gift, cedes to Canada both her body and her land. In this sheared beaver and tabloid twist on the famous Broadway musical, the Quince Brothers manage in less than three hours to tour more than three hundred years of colonial legacy, producing representations of national identity conveniently cleansed of any trace of native female subjectivities. In order to proclaim a homogeneous national space, the review advocates for a commodification of the other – the Eskimo female – as essential to preserving and expanding Canadian unity. Through the furry Aurora tale in the south, the play recasts a nostalgic narrativization of the country wife economy so prominent and essential in the early centuries of the fur trade (Van Kirk 1980).

Ironically, neither the media (which covered the show extensively) nor the creators revealed how this discourse about domestic politics and national affairs became a postwar revival of beaver trade culture, in which the survival of an Eskimo community depended upon the trading value of the jewel of that community: Princess Aurora. The cultural and political references that informed the *My Fur Lady* project/product reveal the transnational and postcolonial nature of the play. Sharing a degree of complicity with a Victorian English theater tradition that celebrated and sanitized the mixed body, here the "metis,"[13] *My Fur Lady* represents/casts Princess Aurora as the Inuit maiden – the virtuous, ignorant princess – whose private body parts become public and federal property. My mode of analysis moves within and outside the conditions of production and circulation of the play so as to frame it in the following way: as a fancy dress ball perniciously embedded in the politics of the federation, in which the exposure and the education of the assimilated othered body becomes a truly cathartic moment for the stability of the white Anglophone nation. The play in this sense offers fantastic signs of ethnic, racial and sexual control, Aurora becoming the repository of the experimental postcolony.

In this sense, *My Fur Lady* belongs entirely to the corporate and incorporated culture of national identity defined within the realm of the fur trade. Like Nanook, Aurora is a fabrication of national corporatism. Like *Nanook*, *My Fur Lady* was a vehicle for the fur trade. The musical was a mediation of corporate nationalism, in which fur industrialists and governmental agencies used the skin of the fur ladies to promote and commercialize a strong vision of the Canadian nation, a vision that was totally inspired by the tradition of the corporate fur enterprise. Thirty years after Robert J. Flaherty, sponsored by Révillon Frères, went north to create *Nanook*, it was Aurora's turn to come south in order to be discovered by the genius of the white college man.

Interestingly enough, *My Fur Lady* relies on an excess of race and femininity which is channeled through raw skin and staged furs. The economy of fur in the play was provided less by the fur on display – there were few furs on-stage, but an avalanche off-stage – than by Aurora's skills at "passing" as a white fur lady. The transformative quality of *My Fur Lady* relies on the following: coming from fur land, from Nanook country, Aurora was nevertheless naked, and had no value on the market as a fur lady before she came south. Aurora eagerly plunges into the residues of British colonial culture, such as the debutante ball, where she is properly introduced to the governmental elite, instantly learning to perform the role of the perfect diplomatic wife. To become, in other words, Lady Aberdeen's nemesis. In *My Fur Lady*, the myth of the good savage is mediated through that of colonial femininity. Aurora embodies the multiple images of white women's femininity defined by Vron Ware, as simultaneously a responsible mother, missionary, pioneer and companion, but also "a defenceless piece of property" (Ware 1992: 120). In other words, Aurora is the rearticulation – through the passing Eskimo woman's body – of the white European woman traveler in the colony, conjuring endless references to historical representations of women and the nation. Like *Les Filles du roy*, Aurora leaves Mukluko to become a Fille (Daughter) of the Queen, in order to preserve the survival of her own Inuit colony. Aurora's journey to the south finds its essence in the marriage to the ultimate colonial authority: "GG," the Governor General.

The traveling Nordic Princess revisits the beaver trail, only this time north-south, bearing to the white community the value of her skin. As Caren Kaplan argues:

> When the freedom to travel is held to be a sign of liberation for European-American women, it is inevitable that the terms and histories of modes of transportation, the production of "difference" for tourist consumption, and the social construction of class, race, and nation become mystified.
>
> (Kaplan 1995: 47)

Reversing the traditional narrative of the fur adventurers and voyageurs leaving the civilized world to venture in the wilderness, it is the fur lady who this time departs from her remote/outskirt world to marvel before the bliss of the civilized world, a word full of domesticity that actually reveals her true worth. Both merchandise and subject of her deal, Aurora carries with her the conditions of a "square deal" with the dominant country: a skin (hers) for a skin's worth (the independence of her northern community).[14] Moreover, as a performed and masqueraded Inuit princess, Aurora is like a ranched mink: a pristine, perfect, virginal representation of northern female exposure. The value of her Eskimo skin on the national unity stock exchange is priceless, hence the yearning to have the Princess embrace the benefits of (con)federation. While Hepburn's ladylikeness was based upon her ability to "pass" as a bourgeoise, Aurora's ladylikeness was a matter of passing as a white who is passing as an Eskimo who is now passing as white. The skin that Aurora willingly trades is actually a perfect locus for transracial sexuality: the big white bear has eaten the little beaver. Transformed into the emblem of unity, little Beaver Aurora can proudly sing of her abandonment into the new world and the federal regime in "I'm For Love" and "I'm into a New World," two of the musical number's titles.[15]

Offering a powerful and symbiotic illustration of skin-trading for national survival, the musical asserts both the triumph of colonial enterprise and the commercialism of identity as part of the national project. This element is even more salient given that the play was written and produced as a response to the national debate surrounding the Massey Commission, or to use the *My Fur Lady* creators' words, as "a satirical comment of the post-Massey era of the 1950s" and "a search for our cultural identity" (McDonald *et al.* 1975: 123). Briefly, the Massey Commission (1949–51), spearheaded by the future Governor General Vincent Massey (in office at the time of the play), addressed the perceived necessity of establishing a better understanding of the two settler communities in Canada, i.e., the Anglophones and the Francophones. Among the brainwave of recommendations drafted by the Commission were the urge to adopt a national flag and the creation of major cultural agencies to give Canadians the means to proudly show to the world their unique identity.[16]

More than a fun fur trailer show in this context, the production, circulation and marketing of *My Fur Lady* was designed to redeploy the Massey Commission discourse on Canadian nationalism in the 1950s, in which "culture" meant unity and fidelity to the Queen of England and the triumph of the British legacy in the definition of the new dominion. The conditions of production and strategies of diffusion of *My Fur Lady* culture were informed by this colonialist representation of the natural links between women and beaver as a bodily trademark for the postcolonial space. At the juncture of the trading of skin and land for the sake of the federation lies the masquerade and the performativity of the Eskimo girl, replicated through the play in the recurrent image of "the igloo girl" and that of the multiplicity of the trading girls (see Figure 4.3). Hence, the following clear message to native peoples: tradition (the survival of an "Eskimo" community) and progress (the unity of the nation) are necessarily tied to the preservation of colonial institutions and the creation of white national agencies.

My Flag Lady

The pleasure of learning is attached to the song of a monarch or a flag.

(Williams 1983: 182)

My Fur Lady took on an incredible variety of issues related to the colonial legacy of fur in the construction of a narrative that took as its point of departure the corporate nature of the nation and its identity formation. At the centre of a federalist notion of the nation was a fetishistic obsession for the yet-to-be-created-flag (the Canadian Maple Leaf flag was only created in 1965). And in this tall flag tale, Aurora acted as the national flag, her skin stretched out from coast to coast and stirred through a patriotic song. Causing a commotion over the intimate association between the materiality of the desirable yet absent national flag and that of the fur lady's skin, the *My Fur Lady* flag tale added another layer of value to Aurora's skin for nationalist discourse. Aurora's skin was the fabric of the nation: her racial and sexual performance of identities allowing her to stretch out and trade her skin in order to recover all cultural difference and symbolize the one federation/one nation credo. In this sense, the flag becomes Aurora's second skin and stands as a bodily trademark – in much the same way that the Hudson's Bay Company blanket represented for so many years the commercial trade for the flesh and skin of the nation (see chapter 2). The flag became the most recognizable national trademark of *My Fur Lady*, mediating the lines between sexuality and nation, transforming the texture of the fur lady. Both fabric-ated, Aurora and the flag embodied at the same time the most effective dimensions of the commodity nation.

118

Figure 4.3 "Igloo Girls," residents of Mukluko (the cast of 1957). From head to toe: Elizabeth Heseltine, Josephine Stone, Liane Marshall, Judy Tarlo and Zena Shane.

In fact, the creators of the musical went so far as to ask an architect, McGill professor Gordon Webber, to design a flag for the play, "a New Canadian Flag" that would ultimately be used as the backdrop for the minimalist set design. With its naive, yet so "Canadian" wilderness iconography of polar bear, fish, boats, goose and indeed the little beaver, the two-coloured flag espoused the McGill Red and White Revue's colored emblem, red and white, soon to become the colours of the Canadian flag in 1965 (see Figure 4.4). It drew significant attention in the media, creating a true nationalist frenzy over the appropriateness, and even dramatic urgency of making Canada one nation under one flag. With a sense of national self-indulgence, the flag became the talk of the day, the rising star of an English-federal nationalism. Critics and journalists commented on how the new flag would make a decent alternative to the red ensign, then the ex-officio Canadian flag,[17] promoters for county fairs wanted the flag on display, and fans wrote to the production inquiring about getting a flag sample, often long after the musical had closed.[18]

Following the life of the musical, the pattern of the *My Fur Lady* flag completely integrated the market of national artifacts, reproduced on placemats, postcards and other play memorabilia. In this sense, this flag tale strongly informed the marketing of the play and its crew as agents of the new, "revitalized," postcolonial economy and culture. Intermingling local, national and international popular cultural references in a satirical musical, *My Fur Lady* was nevertheless reappropriated and legitimated as a pure "Canadian" discourse about the beauty of federalism and multiculturalism for the beaver country.

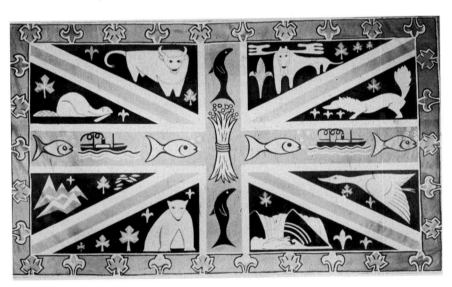

Figure 4.4 Looking for a new Canadian flag? Gordon Webber's design. Max Sauer Studio, photo by June Sauer, 1957.

The musical owed its success to the skills of the producers in selling the story as one of national interest in a time where national cultural identity was apparently insecure or non-existent. In the context created by the endless aftershocks of the Massey Commission, and the most recent visit of the Queen in 1957, the play not only offered a Mondo Canuck version of current affairs, but quickly became a site of intermingling between the different political and diplomatic issues at stake in the three-way marriage between English-Canada, French-Québec and of course, Britannia.

In light of the centennial fight about what constituted Canadian identity and the Canadian nation, the Princes of Quince Productions developed a story-line that chronicled in various tableaux the "immigrant" Eskimo Princess's discovery of the national identity crisis that afflicts maple leaf country, and more specifically the national capital. In line with this "creative effort" to reclaim the Canadian flavor and spirit of the fur trade ancestors that dominated McGill culture, the class issue so prominent in the Fair Lady transmogrifies into a racial and ethnic issue in the Fur Lady. However, the flavor of ethnicity and raciality was also punctually transposed in the play through the issue of language. The Canadian nationalist angle structured traditionally around questions of the "identity struggle" and sovereignty between French and English, is then rearticulated through Aurora as a metaphor of the French minority. In several moments in the play, Aurora's words are those of the necessary assimilation for both the survival and the unity of the nation. Plus, the French language is very often portrayed as the exotic and cute flavor on the fringe of the country, but never seen as a national. The fact that Aurora becomes "assimilated" in the end speaks with little subtilty to the political situation of Québec in relation to the rest of Canada, and does so through a dismissal of the native and Inuit communities' specific racial and ethnic politics.

Constructed as an "inside story" with a series of intrigues unfolded before the eyes of the naive "other," *My Fur Lady* manages to mock the paradoxes of the linguistic and constitutional political situation while implicitly praising the strong royalist tradition of one nation under one flag. The national identity that is praised throughout favors whiteness as the color of the federation, English as the way to speak the so-called new nation, and attachment to the mother country (i.e., Britain) as a sign of cultural and political maturity. By teaching Aurora about the peculiarly Canadian way to be Canadian, i.e., to give up any desire for independence, the Governor General and his followers convince themselves of the beauty of being Canadian, for the thus far independent community of Mukluko.

The connections to the fur business and national history of the McGill production brought necessary legitimacy and popularity to the play, explaining the "national" coverage that the production enjoyed, as well as its status as a cultural industry. The play opens with a historical allegory that heavily draws upon the development of the fur trade and the central role played by James

McGill in the shining of the business and the city.[19] In many ways, *My Fur Lady* could only be conceived in a context defined by McGill's cultural and economic heritage as the symbol of fur power in Montréal. Such legitimacy has its foundations in the history of McGill University itself: the first Anglo university in all of North America, McGill was founded in 1821 through fur trade money. The founding donor of McGill University, James McGill, was one of the most powerful and wealthy fur traders and merchants of the North West Company, the most serious competitor to the HBC in the eighteenth century. Not only a symbol of Canadian nationalism with a twitch of colonial nostalgia, in its most glorious days the North West Company gathered the elite of Anglophone culture in Montréal and Canada. These furry tracks, mummified from the colonial era, remain very much part of the elite social/ite status and economic power McGill still enjoys today. Visitors lucky enough to wander the central campus may pass by McGill's grave at the top of the grand entrance before entering the McLennan-Redpath Library and glimpse a tapestry chronicling the glory of the fur trader and his formidable contribution to the prestige of the city.

In this sense, *My Fur Lady* stood as a cultural industry both for the nation and the corporate public foundation: McGill University. The level of governmental representation attached to the play and its crew could only have been brought by the corporate culture and economy that informed the *My Fur Lady* economy. As revealed in the impressive amount of correspondence between the Quince boys, McGill officials and various institutional bodies, *My Fur Lady* was granted support from various governmental federal agencies and local socialites who gladly enhanced the ambassador role assumed by the crew in the name of the federation. Moreover, it became the diplomatic wife of the country through the prominent political figures of the local and the national scene as well as British ambassadors, Russian and American officials who attended the endless "premieres" of the play to experience real "live" Canadiana, including Governor General Vincent Massey.[20]

McGill authorities themselves capitalized on this prodigious, naughty yet dignified child of the cultural and economic legacy of the fur fathers, granting special leaves to some of its personnel and students attached to the production. While the five all-star male producers were "enthroned" in the Beaver Club tradition, the prominent *My Fur Lady* McGill women's circle also had its moment of fame, and enthusiastically supported a national initiative that pursued women's essential role as national caretakers and symbols of unity. Granted "unlimited leave," the girls of the show were freed to experience and perform the nation as part of their duty, to expand off-stage the symbolism of Aurora, princess of the nation. Such new spins on the diplomatic wife received tremendous support. As the Quince Production Princes reported in a special collective reminiscence of the *My Fur Lady* years, following the triumph of the opening night on 7 February 1957:

The most welcome and unexpected tribute of the evening came from the Dean of Women, Dr. Muriel Roscoe, who at the close of the show granted unlimited leave to all the RVC [Royal Victoria College women's residence] girls in the company.

(Macdonald *et al*. 1975: 123)

Roscoe's response is worth situating both within the overall institutional reaction to the show, and in relation to female engagement with the "trunk/truck showing" of the ladies across Canada. A key promotional and marketing dimension of the show was assured by women. For instance, professional modeling for important furriers sponsoring the musical was assured for Olivia McDonald and Ann Golden. In addition, a newcomer to the business of fashion photography was there to capture the fur moment: June Sauer. Sauer's collaboration with the *My Fur Lady* production went beyond the studio photographs of the cast members and the official photo-postcard of the flag. As documented in the Max and June Sauer collection at the National Archives of Canada (see chapter 3), Sauer signed Olivia MacDonald for a series of photo shoots for local fur retailers. The encounter between Sauer, the fur photographer, and MacDonald, the fur lady, though ephemeral, created exemplary conditions to intersect the commercial value and the "cultural quality" of women in furs on and off stage.

In addition to the production and commodity business, the publicity around the musical was clearly designed to attract a female audience. The media coverage of the play systematically reported on the loving relationship between *My Fur Lady* and its female public. The fetishistic aspects of the show were nourished by the female labor involved in the actual production and promotion of the show, along with the tremendous, almost ubiquitous quality of the fur ladies expanding their fur lady role off stage. They became an enterprise of their own as they made regular appearances at various social events, featured in the print media across the nation as a group of caring "fair ladies," touring charities and children's hospitals, entertaining the navy or the army as part of their professional duties.[21] This contribution to the national effort fit nicely with the spirit of the women's associations and clubs born during the Victorian period, whose faith it was to bring that touch of mink, i.e., the "female touch", to national affairs.[22]

Interestingly, such displays of feminine nationalism are religiously documented in the binders of the *My Fur Lady* collection, revealing the clear interest that the off-stage representation of the female cast signified for women's associations and socialites. Photos of the fur ladies (both the McGill cast and the professional one) "posing" next to local socialites in a cascade of fur, pearls and perms are abundant and carefully documented. They capture such officials as Secretary of State, the Honorable Ellen Fairclough rubbing elbows with the ladies of the Windsor Local Council of Women, all waiting to attend the local premiere of the musical in the southernmost city of Ontario, along with many anonymous yet respectable local fur ladies. Most of the visual documentation – some of it strategically "placed" in the Women's sections of local and national newspapers, as well as in the newspaper's weekly magazines[23] – constructs a female narrative/event around the play, conferring a distinctly feminine quality and taste to the enterprise, and to "those ladies [who] kept pouring in."[24]

Moreover, the endless puns in press headlines and captions reinforced how the intertwining of gender, class, sex and nation not only acted as a remedy to political boredom ("Lady Proves Canadiana is fun," "Don't Be Highbrow"),[25] but also as a means to elicit the sensuality of the nation through the consumption of the fur ladies. Sexy titles such as "My Fur Lady Delights Capacity Audience," "Audiences Love to Peer into My Fur Lady's Mirror," "Fur Lady Finds Furs Hot Here," along with the vague bestial kinky references "Mukluko Lassies," and "Furred Females," appeared next to pin-upish pictures of the fair fur ladies, licking ice cream, wagging their coats (fur or fake) like a piece of *lingerie fine*, or flashing their bare legs beneath parkas trimmed with fur (we are in the 1950s after all).[26] Echoing the popular and traditional analogy between female sex and food as the ultimate erotic yet domestic bliss, fur and ladies merge here to constitute the delight of new Canadiana: my-fur lady.[27] The "Eskimo pie" (vs. the beaver tail)[28] became officially channeled as the white pie, perpetuating the osmosis between the nation as sexual construction and the female body as a mediated terrain to explore its racialized circulation.

Clearly *My Fur Lady* is the darling child of a debutante/fancy ball culture that skins the girl in order to capture the lady. As a sort of reenactment of the tableaux vivants of elitist Victorian fancy dress balls, *My Fur Lady*'s racial and sexual visual trunk-show (a form of fashion traveling show) illustrates in a very distinctive way how the market of the nation was channeled through a living display featuring fur and skin as commercial and national goods. Significantly, this civilian national-guard role performed by the fair/fur ladies became all the more important after the play went "professional" and the McGill students (except Ann Golden) were replaced by professional actors and dancers. In other words, the corporatization of the *My Fur Lady* women's agency was only possible in the context of the commercialization and the professionalization of the play as an exemplary Canadian cultural industry.

For instance, it is no coincidence that this transformation of the local story into a national tourist fair furry tale happened after *My Fur Lady* was invited to participate in the Fringe Program of the international Shakespeare Festival in Stratford, Ontario during the summer of 1957.[29] The founding of the Stratford Festival in 1953 was celebrated as the most exciting moment of Canadian cultural life and was considered "to be a national coming of age" for Canadian national theater. But as Knowles ironically and paradoxically observes, Stratford and "its Shakespeare" responded perfectly to a contested version of Canadian nationalism, a version intermingling fidelity to the Queen and Mother country, and a desire to develop a truly national theatre economy

(Knowles 1995). As Knowles defends, from its very beginning in 1953 the Festival represented, "the solidification of a delayed colonial celebration of the nineteenth-century brand of Canadian nationalism configured on an imperialist British model (one that allows Canada's national theatre to be dedicated to the plays of the canonical British writer)" (Knowles 1995: 20).

Though performed in the Fringe programme, the producers of *My Fur Lady* made sure that the play would enjoy the treatment of a truly national performance. For this, they convinced Gratien Gélinas, the most famous French-Canadian playwright of his time (and indeed, a true federalist), to be the patron of the Stratford performance, assuring at once the legitimacy of their presence at Stratford for the theater milieu, and the visibility that Gélinas, a popular and populist figure of the cultural scene, would bring to the event.[30] Stratford, already a national venue with a nationalist tourist twist, was then a natural habitat for the play and for the stars and producers of the gig. After Stratford, the play became a traveling national exhibition of corporate tourism, with the fur ladies and the bear boys as main agents of the nation, even performing once at the Francophone Québec City mecca, the Palais Montcalm – under the benevolent eye of patron saint Gélinas.

Canada Co./Quince's tale and the fur business

The conjunctural richness of *My Fur Lady* in relation to the blooming of the fur industry in Canada in the 1950s certainly enhanced the visibility of the revue. In the 1950s, the fur industry in Canada and around the world was literally exploding – led by fashion designer kings like Christian Dior. The fur district in Montréal was at the core of the North American fur business, and the HBC fur houses welcomed the most important fur auctions in the world, second only to London. The cultural and political references that informed the *My Fur Lady* project/product reveal the transnational and postcolonial nature of the play. If the local references first appealed to its domestic/national popularity, what was actually praised was the incredible strength of a pro-colonial/dominion discourse in the representation of the nation and its different "constituencies."

Henceforth, the play succeeded in interweaving and troubling the specific localities between politics and fur business, creating for the latter a promotional window for local and national fur retailers who proudly advertised their participation in an all-Canadian beaver story – including the Hudson's Bay Company. My favorite advertisement by the HBC, which appeared in numerous programs, featured a model wrapped in a mink cape, with the following caption (for women only): "You'll be a 'Fur Lady' on your own merits and steal the show in stunning mink!" (Figure 4.5) Because the producers printed a new program for each new venue, local retailers were able to have their name tied to the musical in an early version of fur product placement. Montréal-based, the production nevertheless played the regional/local card extremely well,

Figure 4.5 A Hudson's Bay Company advertisement. Print courtesy of MUA.

emphasizing all the more the national, unitary aspect of the storyline, and fur as national fabric for cultural identity.

The interlinked political, economic and sexual values of *My Fur Lady* in relation to postwar domestic consumerism and transnational export were even more central to the ways that the fur ladies were asked to mediate the necessary exchange between nation and fur as national spectacle. Oddly recalling Buffalo Bill and his Wild West Show featuring "Indians" playing "Indians," the five male creators of the show toured the ladies and the Inuit Princess from coast to coast. Clearly embracing the postcolonial subalternity of native Women and the agency of white Women in the sexual system of exchange in the development of the fur trade, *My Fur Lady* hinges the issue of the commercialism of fur and skin on the promotion of a national discourse inspired by colonial nostalgia. *My Fur Lady*, and its unique way of framing the success of national business in terms of a marriage between the "Immigrant" and the Colonizer, ironically constituted a clear reference to the legitimized interracial pillow talk that dominated the first centuries of the trade, in which the intimate bonds between white trappers and native women were seen as a vital element for the economic prosperity of the fur business. As Heather Menzies argues, "without that legitimized interracial pillow talk, the transnational fur exchange that led to the development of an industrialized Canadian nation wouldn't have happened in quite the same way."[31] *My Fur Lady* is not only about the many tender ties between an Inuit woman and a white man, to echo Sylvia Van Kirk's ironic yet vivid description of "country marriages" during the golden years of the fur trade,[32] or about the whitening of the Inuit people, it is also about the exchange value of female skin in the context of a male nation-state in search of its true identity.

My Fur Lady illustrates the importance of the continual and repeated reenactment – despite racial, sexual and linguistic differences – of the integrationist model of imperial order. The fact that the revue was in English and primarily embracing British and colonial references made explicitly clear the imperial perspective that maintains that the cultural identity crisis could be solved not through recognition of cultural differences, but through the recognition of the British legacy for the future of the nation-state.[33] Mukluko is annexed to Canada ("qui prend mari prend pays"), as Aurora the Eskimo "immigrant" princess sings at the top of her lungs: "Teach Me How to Think Canadian."[34]

In this context however, we are very far from the country wives: Aurora belongs to royalty, and that is enough to solve the class distinction. No matter that Aurora is an Eskimo maiden, she is a true princess after all, just enough to allow the resurgence of royalist/national sentiment. In light of such ethnocentrism and racism, the nation cannot be threatened and is in fact secured by an immigrant Eskimo princess in search of a white husband to save her little remote northern community. In other words, there is no Eskimo in the Eskimo girl; what is subversively tamed though is the fact that Aurora's body is written on the representational edges of a racialized and sexualized wannabe nation.

The fabric of a nation

FUR goodness sake[35]
It's Live! It's Wonderful! It's Canadian! *My Fur Lady*![36]

An in-depth search through the McGill University archives reveals that behind the spooky national farce, *My Fur Lady* was actually an extremely well-structured cultural industry backed by different governmental and private interests.[37] As participants and agents for the national unity and identity business, the actresses attached to the show were ceaselessly invited to perform as the fur pin-ups of the nation and the fur industry. While the Princes of the production performed as the producers and creators of national narratives, the ladies were the stars, the fans, and the "official" archivists and guardians of the play. This sexualizing of *My Fur Lady* as beaver tale was palpable through the collusion between the different levels of government (national, regional and local) and cultural agencies to make *My Fur Lady* an all-Canadian national promotional vehicle, clearly built on the model of Hollywood stars praising the war effort. As a significant volume of visual and print documents testify, the fur quintuplets campaigned for a Canadian identity strongly tied and defined through the display of fur. Interestingly enough, the female cast became the centre of a multitude of commercial and official promotional campaigns, starring as the Canadian fur ladies/beavers of a national traveling heritage show. In the tradition of the Eaton's traveling fur shows that toured Canada with four hundred models for four hundred coats to celebrate the vitality of the fur industry in the 1940s,[39] *My Fur Lady*, with its fur babes and bear boys, managed through its 402 shows to stage and reenact the crucial relations between sexuality, nation and gender in the corporate economy. Authentic cultural industry, *My Fur Lady* also managed to play the political line all around, as the men of the production became the official spokespersons of Canadian unity, while the fur ladies adopted the dislocated posture of the diplomatic wives touring the nation, the naval ships, the city halls and prime minister's offices to promote the glamour of ladies in furs for the national industry.

The media representations of the fur ladies – from mothers of the land, caring ladies for sick children and charities, to industrial and national pin-ups for the National Defense Department, to hot fashion beauties at the beach, as epitomized by this amazing photograph of four fur ladies in bathing suits and fur coats à la Jayne Mansfield, in Vancouver during a heat wave in July 1958 (Figure 4.6),[39] show the extent to which fur was valued through the display of skin. If fur stars on stage, skin triumphs offstage to ensure that the fur ladies were Canada's best commercial goods, the most performative trans/national geographies, and the most spectacular tourist "features" of the nation. In other words, the ladies of the show became the center of commercial and official promotional campaigns, in which the Canadian fur lady, replacing the beaver as the national emblem, became the new queen of a civil army.

If the show was clearly promoting a federalist position in which Canadian identity was advocated as a unique identity formation, the positioning of the Eskimo female skin as a trading token for unity clearly echoed the colonial rules of the fur trade economy around the value of the beaver. Aurora trades both her skin – her people – and her fur (sexual and nuptial) in the preservation of the nation. Not only does the furry tale rely upon the specific conditions of the history of the trade, but it further asserts the centrality of sexuality in the

Figure 4.6 The *My Fur Lady* girls at the beach: Joan Stewart, Anne Collings, Carol Morley, Margaret Walter. Print courtesy of MUA.

processes of postcolonial enterprise and the survival of the nation-state (albeit a diminished one) in the commodification of exotic marginalities. What Aurora trades is the power to sell and represent her own identity as already constructed through the production of a corporate culture massively mapped out by the presence of the British colonizers through the Hudson's Bay Company. The practices of Inuit community governmentality and the allegory of independence were all subsumed to the one power/one institution culture of white federalism.

The conjunctural richness of *My Fur Lady* in relation to the postwar economy, domestic consumerism and transnational export appears even more central in the ways that the fur ladies were asked to literally mediate the necessary exchange between nation and fur as national spectacle. With just enough Eskimo fur references to garner fur retailer sponsorships for the four hundred shows of the play, *My Fur Lady* successfully reconciled the materiality, physicality and sexuality of fur ladies for the nation. Hailed as "Canada's Most Popular Gal,"[40] *My Fur Lady* represents a spectacular aspect of national sexual economy, where the true fetish-spectacle of the nation translates into the skinning of the Eskimo/exotic babe.

Epilogue: *My Fur Lady* revisited

For the twenty-fifth anniversary reunion of *My Fur Lady* in 1982, CBC, the national television network, produced a special called *My Fur Lady Revisited*. The documentary featured the two-day celebration commemorating the silver anniversary of one of the most famous of Canadian musicals, conferring the status of a truly national event. Beyond its nostalgic reminiscence, the twenty-fifth anniversary can also be interpreted as a representational strategy of the organizers and producers to highlight the role – both cultural and economic – that the play and the trademark of *My Fur Lady* had in national unity.

Two significant, irreconcilable moments for national politics occurred in 1982. It was the year that Canada officially became a sovereign country, freeing itself from British colonial control with the repatriation from London of the Canadian Constitution by Pierre Elliot Trudeau's federal Liberal government. At the same time in Québec, the 1981 reelection of the Parti Québécois for another four-year mandate kept the English establishment on their toes. The *My Fur Lady* gathering of federal agents and bodies at McGill was the perfect occasion to display federal unity over and above provincial separatism, the real threat to Canadian nationalism.

However, like the Beaver Club dinner, beyond its public face the reunion was a private McGill-only gathering. Even if some memorabilia was produced and re/produced (a second press of the original hi-fi record was put into circulation) to commemorate the event, and even if the press was invited to cover the comeback of *My Fur Lady*, the moment looked like any college reunion, with its share of memories, parties and the glittering exposure of political networks. And again this time, to no surprise, the ladies of the show were more than ever called on duty as a reincarnation of "Les belles du jour," while the beaver boys restaged the second life of the musical. In their reminiscence of the 1950s, the *MFL* Nostalgia Team, as they proclaimed themselves, made all the more obvious the double *raison d'être* of *My Fur Lady* as a cultural industry and nationalist vehicle. While the racialized and sexualized masquerade of 1957–8 skinned the girls to get the colony, the 1980s redeployment of Aurora as the white muse of the nation was a clear obliteration of the agency of the fur ladies of the play as part of the national enterprise.

Presented as "a child of her time" by the five male creators of the revue, *My Fur Lady* stands today as a fascinating and wild expression of national "taxidermy," taxidermy being after all about "seek[ing] to make that which is dead look as if it were still living" (Tobing Rony 1996: 101). In a paradoxical way, Aurora mediates and channels the excess of race and sexuality into the commercial value of the female skin as a beaver token. The beauty of *My Fur Lady* as both a patriotic vehicle and an intraracial narrative is its absorption of racial and sexual conflict into a postcolonial survival tale, in which the heroic agents are white Anglophones living in the house of the government. What still lives through the sexual economy of *My Fur Lady* is the manner in which beaver fur is entrenched in a double assumption of romantic popular national commodity and site of political reproduction. Far from being obsolete in the contemporary cultural moment, Aurora and the fur and skin tale can be said to be undergoing a new visibility, this time more than ever in the double mode of national vignette and producer of a culture of beaver fur. Sarah Mills's words give this redeployment of bodily trademarks in national unity an acute flavor:

> In many postcolonial contexts . . . discursive frameworks generated by colonialism are still in active circulation. This rather puzzling evidence of discursive remnants extending across historical locations and cultures leads me to conclude that discourses tend to lumber on through time, being activated in circumstances where their use is anachronistic.
>
> (Mills 1995: 73)

Aurora's interracial, intranational pillow talk in the Canadian wonderlands, although specific to the context of the 1950s, still translates today in the most unruly fashion. For instance, in witnessing the recent aggressive pro-fur campaigns led by the Fur Council of Canada featuring native and white women designers as the new spokespersons of the renaissance of the fabric of the nation (see chapter 6), it is hard to not think about Aurora and her masqueraded skin as national fabric, as national flag. At the same time that I resist any simple equivalence, I think of these two moments as part of the same thread: a thread that insistently ties up the female skin and the female body to the naturalization of the land. Just as Aurora's (and the other cast members') serenade tells us, "It's a great big wonderful [beaver] country!" a strange sense of familiarity, sensuality and warm domesticity colours the twenty-first century sexual economy of fur, in which a kaleidoscope of Auroras redeploy the natural links between skin and fur. As if Lady Aberdeen was once more designing one of her famous Canadian flesh and nature tableaux, one more time.

Part III

BARDOTS

5

BB AND HER BEASTS

Marguerite et Brigitte

On 24 February 1968, Marguerite Yourcenar, a long-time animal rights activist and now retired to Mount Desert Island, Maine, wrote to Brigitte Bardot to enlist her help and support in fighting against the baby seal hunt in Canada (Yourcenar 1995: 278–83). Bardot was at the zenith of her career, a Bardot whom Yourcenar clearly had yet to meet, a "friend" whose film career was likely as familiar to the future academician as the culture of the French can-can. One could not have dreamt of a better alliance in the history of animal rights. These two monuments of French culture could not have better represented the antipodes of what could be seen as the cultural capital of the French Republic. On one side, Yourcenar, serious, authoritarian, master of classic contemporary literature, lesbian; on the other side, Bardot, the sex kitten, tabloid queen, vibrant idol of a new generation, torrid sex symbol of the French cinema industry, and ambassadress of heterosexual culture. Strangely enough, in this letter released by the Yourcenar Fund at Harvard University, the two sacred monsters of French culture would seal their public image to embrace the same combat for animal rights.

While Bardot was still a fairly discreet and tourist activist,[1] Yourcenar was already notorious for her adherence to various animal rights activist groups. In this context, Yourcenar's letter to Bardot retains a special flavor. Yourcenar, in an elegant though formal and rigid tone, begs the star to use her magisterial public image to intervene in what she considers to be the most horrible massacre perpetuated by human kind against the dramatic innocent victims of a barbaric and futile practice: baby seal hunting. Yourcenar provides with vigor the graphic details of the hunting ritual that lead each spring to the killing of an estimated 50,000 baby seals, confessing to Bardot the sex kitten that such horrors are performed in the context of an international deal involving not only Canada, but also Finland and Norway. Yourcenar's carefully chosen words to describe the agony of the "*blanchots*" (the baby white seals) resonate with all the more intensity given that the same words would be reappropriated and recirculated by BB herself ten years later, when the star invaded the Canadian ice floes during what would become her most spectacular and effective anti-seal hunt crusade.

The existence of the letter and its nature is even more surprising as Yourcenar, who always styled herself as beyond the scope of the media circus surrounding the star business, clearly urges BB to use her media diva status to mobilize international opinion. Bardot's successful intervention in the media on behalf of slaughtered animals in France had already caught the attention of American animal rights activist groups, including a secluded Yourcenar. Yourcenar flatters Bardot's persuasive appeal to female fur consumers when she states: "I am convinced that you, more so than anyone else, can persuade women to stop buying fur garments and accessories obtained at the expense of the pain and agony of innocent animals." (Yourcenar 1995: 280)[2]

Yourcenar's carefully scripted plea attests to the resonance of the Vietnam war in the American media, particularly in the discovery of the immediacy of television as a tactic to confront the invisible. What was good for denouncing the atrocities of Vietnam – we are in 1968 – would be equally effective for the condemnation of savage Canadian disposal of baby seals. An inspired and persuasive Yourcenar writes:

> I dare ask you to intervene, even just to write yet another letter to the Canada Prime Minister [Pierre Elliot Trudeau, committed wearer of fur coats],[3] but primarily by making television appearances against the tragic use of seal pelts, such a useless practice. My call to you is quite timely as the hunt (which lasts three to four days, and spreads from the St-Laurent river to Labrador) opens this year on March 18.
>
> (Yourcenar 1995: 280–1)[4]

Yourcenar's words unfold, rich with statistics on the seal hunt and the status of international laws regarding the quota and trapping regulations. It is Yourcenar' eagerness to link the seal massacre to human catastrophies such as the Vietnam war (Yourcenar 1995: 279), to tie seal hunting practices to the dark ages of civilization, that shows the extent to which the rhetoric employed during the anti-fur campaigns was designed and tailored to articulate a discourse of survival (nature as nation) to that of women. A particularly vehement Yourcenar argues for maternal essentialism:

> As for me, I confess that this world in which we live, so atrocious on so many levels, seems all the more dreadful when I think that, at the very moment that I write this letter, more than fifty thousand babies scattered amongst the snow banks are condemned to become bloody carcasses by the end of the hunt . . . and that the mothers who feed these babies will strain to recognize their bloody bodies, their

cries filling the air following a fierce fight to protect them while still alive and bearing fur.

(Yourcenar 1995: 281–2)[5]

And Yourcenar, naive in the age of mechanical and mediated reproduction, refutes any accusation of overstated sensationalist sentimentalism. As she denounces it: "The interested parties have indeed mocked such sentimentalism, but the photographs speak volumes and the testimony is undeniable" (Yourcenar 1995: 282).[6] Yourcenar's personal papers do not reveal if Bardot answered personally,[7] though Bardot's memoirs hint at the fact that the odd couple had a fair amount of contact.[8] Nevertheless, ten years after this epistolary call, when the sex symbol, newly revamped as the animal fairy, would recycle the same rhetoric, pushing even further the social mission of women to preserve nature, Bardot fulfilled her role as the dream spokesperson imagined by Yourcenar. Bardot, prematurely retired and freshly self-appointed as the Marianne (the national French symbol) of animal rights, would propel herself into one of the earliest and most highly mediated animal rights crusades ever seen.

In addition to the media spectacle, Bardot, the so-called anti-paparazzi star, would use anything the media could offer to stage and publicize her campaign and her interventions, creating an economic structure for the entire anti-fur business. Auctions, television shows, photo-reports, videos, and most importantly her "special association" with *Paris-Match*, would all lead to the dissemination of thousands of images of the star hugging furry beasts. Bardot's Canadian seal crusades in 1977 and 1994, for instance, stand as a logical follow-up to a campaign launched in 1969 by the French weekly glossy to "save" the baby seal (Servat 1968). No wonder that *Paris-Match* and its fan tabloid format would for the following twenty years become the official voice of BB – The Garbo of Saint-Tropez, featured in worldwide commercialized animal embraces and hugs, would over the next two decades use the glossy pages of *Paris-Match* countless times to speak to the nation of France "on behalf of those who can't speak,"[9] embodying the contemporary version of Joan of Arc on the northern Canadian "ice floes." From sex symbol tabloid queen, Bardot would quickly remodel her image into the animal fairy tabloid diva, hunting down stars, fur coats, politicians and barbaric hunters with consuming and consumate sensationalism.

In this chapter, I propose to explore how anti-fur movements represent a sophisticated articulation of the existing relations between female skin, animal survival and the nation as the "natural" space to confront the essential role of women in the continuity and productivity of the nation as she-woman. To do so, I argue that two interesting and competing discourses occurring on the same terrain had a direct influence on the participation of women in the anti-fur agenda. First, the naturalization of the land became more than ever framed as a nationalist claim intended to revive women's interest in the national issue, urging them to preserve the roots/origins of the nation (recently expressed in Québec Premier Lucien Bouchard's call for French-Québec women to increase an alarmingly low birthrate during the 1995 provincial election campaign). Second, the technologization of the production and reproduction of new fabric and tissue (human and synthetic) has had a strong impact on the ways that discourses of preservation of the land and species inflected the anti and pro-fur advocate positionings.

In focussing on Bardot's campaigns, I want to demonstrate how the moral sexuality of the nation is redeemed through the sacrificial image of surrogate motherhood. The adoption of star tactics has become a traditional site in anti-fur campaigns, since the star economy is an important element of fundraising and public awareness. The fact that the anti-fur movements count on a majority of women as followers and supporters is not estranged from this mommy rhetoric, so prominent in many iconographic and discursive representations of anti-fur tactics.[10] The seal campaigns in Canada and Québec became a key site for the positioning of women in the perpetuation of the idea of the nation as a natural entity, if not a natural extension of the Mother-country – here France through Bardot. Moreover, the nation talked of here is one of unity, over-shadowing the ethnic and racial tensions that have historically mapped out the national economy, and the history and culture of the fur trade.

Through Bardot I am able to question how gender and sexuality have acted as *les deux mamelles* (literally, the two nipples) of national/ist discourse. Not only is Bardot's sexuality and body framed in terms of "liberation," but also in terms of "education" and "revelation." The liberatory dimension of Bardot's commit-ment to life and animals was part of a representational media strategy depicting the star as older, mature, less sex kitten and more *fée des animaux*, the godmother of the seal nation.[11] Bardot herself tirelessly depicted her commitment as the gesture of growing-up, of quasi rebirth. As part of the women's lib movement, Bardot would embody the necessary association between animals, babies and women.[12] Interestingly, Bardot's motherly image would constitute an asset in the production and circulation of a series of children's books (all published after the 1977 crusade) prefaced by the star herself. Featuring titles such as *L'agonie des bébés phoques*, *L'enfer des animaux*, and the titillating *Et Dieu créa les animaux*, this pro-animal literature consecrated BB as the children's godmother, the animal fairy, saviour of baby seals, a role that her Foundation and her allies relished. When Bardot finally authored her own children's seal tale – *Noonoah, le petit phoque blanc* – with the esteemed French publisher Grasset & Fasquelle, she definitively embraced this new asexual role of mother of the animal kingdom.[13] However, and as I will discuss later in this chapter, the fairy tale was also a cash cow for Greenpeace, then led by the animal rights guru, Franz Weber.

In this sense, Bardot's involvement in the seal crusade followed the usual animal welfare/rights tactics of using media, literature, films and direct-to-consumer venues to educate and gain the sympathy of the population, here mostly women and children. For a while Bardot even had her own pro-animal show airing weekly on French television: *S.O.S Animaux*.[14] Produced by her own foundation, the show was a mixture of pro-animal advocacy destined for adults, with an infantilizing twist targeting children. Bardot, who in real life was unable to gain any sympathy as a mother, aggressively played the sensitive caregiver on screen and in the media, close to both children and animals, from *Et Dieu créa la Femme* . . . (R. Vadim, 1956) to *Dear Brigitte* (H. Koster, 1965), where the star appeared as herself, kissing and hugging boys and puppies in the same embrace. By the time that the Arts & Entertainment Biography series ran a special on Bardot for her sixtieth birthday in 1994, the seals and the beasts were comfortably integrated into her biographical narrative, right next to the numerous men who have shared her life. Even her famous memoirs published in two volumes in 1997 and 1999 are organized along the two loves of her life: men (*Initiales B.B.* 1997) and beasts (*Le Carré de Pluton* 1999).

BB et moi

I owe my own sensual feelings towards fur to Bardot's baby seal adventures on the Canadian land, and my "natural" longing for beaver fur to my childhood memories of the star. It was 1973 – one of those freezing days when winter refuses to capitulate. All my life, I felt I was this little girl, lost in a little town honorably named after Queen Victoria, raised to believe, like all snow queens, that Canada and fur were two poles of the same problem. I was about ten years old and knew nothing about the libidinal properties of fur, with the exception of the cat's performances in our backyard. As far as I was concerned, "fur" meant that beaver hat and coat ensemble that my mom desperately wanted me to wear when it was –30°C, an outfit "styled" with glamorous, genuine sealskin boots. Picturing myself at that time, I probably resembled a local version of Nanook of the North: i.e., a sexless furred thing. Innocently exempt from blissful memories of beaver tales, fur to me was a stinky, hairy, too-hot second skin, not exotic, not yet erotic – in other words the Canadian trademark par excellence.

While the beaver was not part of my "coterie," my awareness of Brigitte Bardot confusingly corresponded with my understanding of feminine beauty and girlish exhibitionism. My mother had been an avid follower of Bardot for many years, compulsively reading all the gossip about the star that was disseminated in those French-from-France magazines available in the rural land outside Montréal: *Paris-Match, Jour de France, Elle*. But Bardot was not *the* object of my mother's fandom – she preferred Jackie O. and her fabulous sunglasses, or even Queen Elizabeth II, despite the worst hat collection ever exhibited by a monarch. Bardot represented a torturous object of feminine fascination and Roman Catholic condemnation, hence her power over women like my mom for whom Bardot's hair color was as mysteriously unpredictable as the combination formula for Toni hair die and the Holy Trinity mixed together.

Because of the scandalous aspects of her private life, we knew more about Bardot the glossy magazine star than Bardot the French film diva. Her films, more erotically loaded than romantically inclined, were not at all popular among the girls. However, BB the paparazzi star definitely was the ticket: my friends and I were rather fond of her wild hair and her even wilder lips. That was before we all heard about BB and her beasts.

Four years later, in March 1977, what was supposed to be a dream come true turned out to be a national nightmare. The province of Québec had just elected its first sovereignist government, and BB the French star came to town to protest against the annual seal hunt in Newfoundland and the Îles de la Madeleine. Suddenly, Canada was in the media, a white, unified and cold country that retained such barbarian habits as clubbing baby seals for a national sport. Thanks to BB we were finally on the map, and thanks to the media, the quaint image of Canada and Québec as a fur country was well-maintained. During the well-publicized Canadian Assassins campaign (Bourget 1977: 2), BB propagated a uniform image of Canada (no room for French roots) that made a beast – the baby seal – an exotic commodity of the snow and the cold. Perhaps because of all those furs hanging around, this commodification of the Other opened up the erotic properties of the national territory for me. The encounter between BB the sex kitten and the hunted sealskin still provides a powerful conjuncture in which to interrogate how the contact between fur and skin is necessarily highly sexualized.

As someone caught in a Roman Catholic legacy and the hybrid history of French and British colonization, the chance to occupy the position of barbarian was something quite exciting, wild and – why not? – productive. Looking back at this event, beyond the fact that I was intimidated by the vividness of the seal controversy, I became overwhelmed by unusual and exotic fantasies of fur. My knowledge of barbarians and *"assassins"* (murderers) was informed by Hollywood films depicting hordes of hairless, yet *furry* Mongolians, all Yul Brynner lookalikes. Certainly, it never crossed my mind to picture the Canadian landscape as exotic. On the contrary, by constantly attacking Canadians as organized hordes of barbarians and murderers of seals, Brigitte Bardot contributed to a repositioning of issues of Canadian national identity in terms of marginality, gender and colonialism.

Meanwhile, BB's crusade, commonly referred to as "Bardot's war against Canada,"[15] had convinced my mother that it was better to withdraw fur from the public scene and quietly wear the beast in the discreet charm of the home. While Canadian television networks were reporting extensively on the best performance of Bardot's life, my mom was helping to change the face of the country by mercilessly attacking the hairy beast known as the emblem of Canada. With a lot of skill and a pair of scissors, she artfully cut pieces from my beaver coat to make – fur slippers. To this day, I still do not know my mom's motivation: endorsing BB's fury, performing an act of domestic economy through fur recycling, or erasing three hundred years of colonial folklore. Of one thing I am sure, this was my very first experience of the erogenous and rebellious properties of furs.

BB's anti-fur campaigns against the baby seal hunt in Canada offer an ironic twist to colonial history for what was once considered the major source of revenue for the king of France: fur. In a very interesting way, Bardot would go on to create an internationally renowned national business out of this anti-fur outrage, gaining financial and political support all over the world, creating a new trajectory and a new function to the circulation of capital related to the beast economy. Her limited, yet constant collaboration with anti-fur advocate professional organizations such as The Society for the Protection of Animals (SPA), the International Fund for Animal Welfare and Greenpeace[16] also contributed to making the BB Foundation a legitimate player among the animal rights groups.[17]

The creation of the Brigitte Bardot Foundation reveals the extent to which Bardot's so-called humanitarian campaigns already espoused an omni-present animal rights intervention on the global scene. Bardot's campaigns in Canada not only followed the path of other animal rights groups, but were also rooted in a very complex discourse interweaving issues of race, reproduction, preservation and purity, a discourse not far from the eugenics tradition and its actualization in pro-life campaigns. Many points of convergence between anti-fur rhetoric and eugenic consciousness are entrenched in the articulations between science and nature. Implicit to both is the idea that progress and technology – nature considered as a technology (Haraway 1989) – have rendered life such that animals should not suffer primitive barbaric practices, and should be granted human benevolence. Without asserting that anti-fur movements are entirely embedded in eugenic consciousness, both anti-fur and eugenic rhetoric's foresee moralistic preservation in relation to sexuality, gender and race (the purpose of rational and superior white Western technology being to overcome barbarism) as well as nationalist xenophobia – in the fabrication of a domestic response to a global/transnational conspiracy to eliminate the animal kingdom, the primary resource of the wealth of the nation. This demonstrates the extent to which the articulation between reproduction and women's bodies has been central to the development and organization of animal rights politics.

In this sense, Bardot's discourse about the survival of the species cannot be isolated from consideration of the intertwined relations of women, domestic order, economic stability, social purity and the growth of the nation. While historically the eugenics ideology of surpopulation, national property, and cleanliness offered the grounds for a state intervention regarding reproduction and upbringing, in the case of animal rights activism, it is the pursuit of a white colonial supremacy over environmental management and the preservation of the species – all kinds considered – that has led to the most exalted anti-fur interventions. In both cases, contradictory but nevertheless powerful discourses about race and ethnicity, nationalist economic policies, and the implementation of reproductive technologies are central. In the case of Bardot, this would prove to be all the more accurate, since the star also became famous in the 1990s for her outraged declarations on the "problem" of illegal immigrants in France, as well as her publicly xenophobic interpretation of Muslim customs.[18] Her association with the *Front National* and its white supremacist leader Jean Marie Le Pen adds complexity in terms of the tight links between regulating the population, nurturing the nation, and preserving what is considered to be God's gift to the nation: animals.

Curiously enough, and in spite of the extraordinarily abundant literature that exists on Bardot's career, her star image has never been challenged in terms of the sexual economy and racial, colonial power. Nonetheless, throughout her career, Bardot has symbolized sexual freedom and irreverent pleasure, wonderfully embodying the seduction of white (imperial) femininity for the (French) national economy. Her sexual excesses, though highly mediated and often severely condemned by the French media, ironically increased her value as an exotic delight for the international market, and at the same time as an important agent of French culture in a moment of frantic French decolonization. It is this very position of being both a national emblem and the perfect ambassador of French colonial culture that made her interventions so powerfully effective and controversial. Ironically, while her anti-fur vendettas exacerbated the double construction of sex and colony, as a French star she embodied the difficult passage from tradition to so-called modernity (Vincendeau 1992): Bardot was no doubt a star of great stature in the context of the Francophone diaspora. As a French-speaking pop cultural icon, Bardot represented for a lot of women in Québec an element of recognition, even identification, while her sassy sexuality in a still conservative society was framed as belonging to the other/European culture. In other words, in relation to a society where the French language was the passport to power, economy, culture and heaven, sexuality was considered less threatening as long as Frenchness was displayed. Bardot, in various and not always coherent ways, represented the awakening Québec society of the 1960s, offering a Francophone corporate image.

Bardot's media profile strongly echoed the contradictions that Québec was facing in the 1960s: a period known as the Quiet Revolution, which marked a political rupture from the familial discourse and the supremacy of the Church. In the midst of the emergence of the Québec independence movement, Canada was still a British colony. Struggling between puritan Anglophone culture and traditionalist Roman Catholic power, the sixties and seventies marked a very unstable period in Québec, a period of transition from traditional family values, a homogeneous ethnic demographic, and new political concerns. After the end of Québec Premier Maurice Duplessis's despotic twenty-year governance, the 1960s heralded the rise of the Québec independence movement which, historically, had always romanticized France as its natural ally. The French-Québec intelligentsia, who led the separatist movement, were devotees of French "*grande culture*" (high culture). The French pop culture personified by BB was heavily digested through the mass proliferation and distribution of French magazines – including the landmark of good-taste in tabloid journalism, *Paris-Match*, an all-time favorite among female readers.

The same could be argued about the relationship between Bardot the film star and female spectators. Bardot has a long history of controversy in Québec. As Vadim's muse, Bardot saw some of her first films banned by the Catholic Church under the rubric of sexually offensive and morally depraved material. Her most famous film, . . . *Et Dieu créa la Femme* (1956), was released after the board of censors agreed that the film's ending reestablished the monogamous family order. Amazingly, in all of Canada and across the American northeast only Québec showed the film uncut.[19] People from Ontario and Vermont drove regularly to Montréal to see the film in its "original/originel" version.

My point here is less to record and retrace the history of censorship of BB's images in Québec than to challenge the preconceived idea that women were the most virulent opponents of the distribution and screening of Bardot's films in America, as well as the most prominent agents of conservative family values. One cannot ignore the fact that in Québec the censor establishments were entirely controlled by men from all-powerful institutions such as the State, the Church and the Francophone petit bourgeois, mostly Catholic. If women effectively were present and active within pro-censorship groups (mostly affiliated with Catholic authorities),[20] one cannot ignore that they were also the most faithful consumers of movies and a range of derivative products created by and for the star industry. This latter element is crucial for an understanding of the extreme media and popular attention that the BB anti-seal hunt campaigns received in Canada. It is because BB's persona was able to attract both women and men that most of the animal rights activist campaigns designed by and for the star in the 1970s had her playing the dual role of sex kitten and loving godmother. I would even argue that it is because Bardot was sexy for women that the campaigns were able to play the godmother dimension in such a convincing fashion. Bardot's troubled position as aging sex-symbol and caring guardian of the endangered species provided the ultimate conditions to create a spectacle out of the intimate relations between beasts and humans. Bardot's attractiveness to women with environmental concerns was a key asset for the pro-animal advocacy politics, and so eventually were her positions towards protectionist and nationalist policies. "And God Created an Animal Lover."[21]

BB and "le Castor," alias de Beauvoir

Brigitte Bardot's image has often been analyzed in terms of the heterosexualized nymph and sex goddess, but never in relation to national representations of sexuality, which I insist includes questions of female fandom. Simone de Beauvoir (1959) and Mandy Merck (1993) have both raised the issue of the ambiguity of Bardot as a star and *French* sexual bombshell for a male heterosexual audience, but hardly anything has been said about women's response to Bardot's public persona and performance in terms of sexuality and nationalist rhetoric.

For example, in their fine analyses of the star neither de Beauvoir nor Merck have questioned Bardot's sexual construction in relation to the political and national construction of sexuality. What does it mean to see BB as the simultaneous expression of the tensions between sexuality, nation and colonialism? In fact, star theory rarely questions how sexuality and national values intertwine in the circulation and regulation of star images. If the nationality of the star is put at the forefront, it is to better flesh out a folkloric cultural pathology, in order to play out the otherness of sexual desire. For example, it is common to assert that Bardot is more open sexually because she is French. What remains unquestioned is how the commodification of national identity is mediated through the sexualization of the star persona, i.e., Bardot. Worse: such a framework maintains a tight separation between the national as a male space and the sexual as a heterosexual feminine individual surface, a body remote from the economic constituencies of national reproduction.

Simone de Beauvoir's intimate portrait of Bardot's sexual capital in "Brigitte Bardot and the Lolita Syndrome" (1959) offers a poignant and vivid example of a dichotomized analysis between the nation as production site and nation as sex-symbol. First written for the trendy, high-class American intellectual male readership of *Esquire* in 1959, de Beauvoir's article may at first appear to offer a legitimate view of the wildest of French delights, but it nevertheless consolidates a gendered, nationalist and pathological diagnosis of the controversial reception of Bardot in France in the late 1950s. De Beauvoir asserts unequivocally that BB's fame is owed to the fact that she is, as a woman, the victim of "the peculiar French hostility" and as a sex-kitten she is an icon of American adoration. Her charm and value are built upon these tensions between hatred and love, between adult and child, and between exoticness and familiarity. In opposition to the recurrent image of the little girl trapped in a sex-symbol body found in the popular press, de Beauvoir unfolds for the American readers an emancipated, independent, Don Juanesque portrait of Bardot, that of a woman whose sexuality is not a façade but an intrinsic dimension of her fame and attraction, hence her threat to conservative moral values, conveniently channeled through French women, the mothers of the nation.

Apart from the fact that this convincing celebration of Bardot's sex capital by the famous French feminist betrays a hint of lesbian voyeuristic desire (Merck 1993), de Beauvoir's study also maintains a heterosexist analysis of the star industry and popular culture in a national context. According to de Beauvoir's careful argument, the national space is solely constructed and visible through heterosexual male desire, and the performative embodiment of national and exotic markers that emanated from Bardot and in response to Bardot's excess of sexuality is totally silenced. De Beauvoir's subjective and engaged portrait of Bardot, in its defence of Bardot-the-natural-born-sexual-hunter, is rich and troubling on many levels and still stands today as a powerful means of resistance to understanding sex, money and ethnicity as a contradictory terrain for national production and international circulation. De Beauvoir's article, lavished with more than thirty-one close-ups of BB, elides the historical and ideological context within which the Bardot myth has been created and incessantly reinforced: a period of transition of social and cultural transition in a still stiff Gaullist France. Grounding her analysis in a psychosocial portrait of the ideal woman fantasy "that distinguishes North American men from French men," de Beauvoir opposes the so-called egalitarian spirit of the men in the US – "coincidentally," Beauvoir was involved at the time with American writer Nelson Algren[22] – to the macho superiority of their French counterparts to explain why Bardot was welcomed more in the US than in France. In doing so, she confines her analysis of Bardot's commodified sexuality to the limits of a male and heterosexual national space: an object traded between French men and American men, leaving no room for women to mediate that space.

Reproducing the traditional division between the nymph goddess and the wife-mother in her analysis, de Beauvoir never addresses sexuality as a complex articulation between national economy, gendered agency and desire. The historical context within which the *Esquire* piece was written (the late 1950s) does not excuse the fact the de Beauvoir's reading of Bardot's body vibrates only within a male social space. While her portrait of Bardot may betray a feminist sympathy for the BB erotic and cultural phenomenon, "the most perfect specimen of these ambiguous nymphs" (de Beauvoir 1959: 11), her analysis of women's response to the sex-kitten craze betrays an elitist, masculinist and bourgeois spin on women's position and women's fandom that curiously share similarities with Vadim's reckless observations of the Bardot years and the hysterical gender. By suggesting that the popular (sic!) animosity towards Bardot in France was principally motivated by a feeling of male superiority with which many female viewers are "accomplices"[23] de Beauvoir objectifies women, and celebrates the Bardot-made-Woman as the muse of new freedom. Such analysis not only ignores the participation of women in the national production as principal consumers of stars, but it also firmly reinforces the belief that Bardot was necessarily an avant garde symbol of sexual emancipation, without questioning the conservative remainders of Bardot's representation and representability as sex symbol.[24] In other words, de Beauvoir silences women in the creation of the Bardot myth and denies the fundamental yet contradictory role that women have played and still play as consumers of stars and fashion products in the development of the national economy.[25]

As I pointed out earlier, the recognition of women's participation in the circulation of star images is fundamental to my analysis of the Bardot seal crusades in Canada and in Québec. Contrary to what has been asserted by feminist theorists such as *le Castor* (Beauvoir) about the gendered popularity of Bardot, I argue that BB was enjoying an incredible and controversial attraction among women, hence her fantastic and successful output in the early stages of her activist career. For instance, the anti-fur campaigns designed by and for the star addressed both the fans of BB and those considered the majority consumers of fur: women. Bardot, once a fur criminal, redeemed herself before the eyes of millions of consumers, demonstrating that "conversion" to fake fur was possible and still a hot thing for women. This was a major move given that Bardot had a guilty fur past as one of the "fur legends" for the Blackglama campaign sponsored by the Great Lakes Mink Association and conceptualized by New York-based advertiser Jane Tracey. Launched in 1968 with Lauren Bacall, Melina Mercouri, Bette Davis, Barbra Streisand and Judy Garland, the campaign signed Bardot for the 1970 collection, next to other divas such as Leontyne Price, Rita Hayworth, Maria Callas and Barbara Stanwyck. The concept for the campaign was skillfully developed around the idea of making fur unique – and legendary. As I discuss in chapter 6, in order to thwart the anti-fur movement in the United States, Tracey and photographer Richard Avedon emphasized the high-class dimension of fur, over and against the popular conception of anti-fur advocates. Like all the other legends, Bardot posed unclothed for the classy, expensive, pristine mink coat, in order to "create recognition for the fur itself" (Rogers 1979: 8). Thanks to America-wide distribution of the ads to furriers, it is still possible to admire Bardot as a fur legend in Montréal's Labelle Fourrures store today. No other trace of Bardot's association with the Blackglama fur campaign exists – the trade catalogue for the campaign offering a black window in lieu of Bardot in furs – and the star made no allusion to her Fur Legend Life in her memoirs (see Figure 5.1).

In this sense, Bardot's media image in the seal campaign offers a powerful contrast to her fur trade sponsorship. The star circuit was and is still today a key element of attraction for the design of the anti-fur actions, and Bardot herself was fully aware of the power of her name to gather media attention, if not money. Actually, as much as fashion is a trade led by stars, the anti-seal and other animal welfare movements also owe their visibility and power to prominent stars of the animal rights/liberation culture, a curious mixture of professional star advocates (Brian Davies from IFAW, Paul Watson from the Sea Shepherd Conservation Society, and Ingrid Newkirk from PETA) and entertainment pop figures such as Kim Basinger or Sigourney Weaver. Nevertheless, the beauty of the BB early anti-sealing campaigns was its ability to convene a mixed audience: on one hand, a popular one composed of fans with a cultural knowledge of BB; and on the other, a more middle-class, educated one that corresponded more closely with the usual profile of environmental activists[26] and for whom Bardot's name was vaguely associated with the brunette (bewigged) muse of the pope of new cinema, Jean-Luc Godard in Le Mépris (1961). Such a strategy set out in the context of the late 1970s was timely in relation to the growing importance of environmental issues, and certainly the fact that Bardot retired early made the encounter between star and nature a true cannonball. When Bardot stepped into the public for first baby seals

Figure 5.1 Labelle, the fur iron lady as Bardot. *La Fourrure* cover (1978). Print courtesy of Sogides/Editions de l'Homme, Montréal.

and later horses, etc. she was no longer the Venus of the "What Becomes a Legend Most" campaign, but a self-professed mature, grown-up woman. The new revamped post-kitten BB was a down-to-earth woman, close to nature, a genuine beast lover – in other words, the anti-star par excellence.

The main targets of the BB seal campaigns ranged from conservative women wearing traditional fur coats to hipsters and youth embracing environmentalist discourse and fancying fun fur. In this sense, Bardot represents a primary example of the involvement and "use" of stars in contemporary anti-fur activism, and animal rights and animal welfare movements in relation to female consumers and producers. The 1980s and the 1990s have witnessed a growing parade of stars eager to have their names attached to the most high profile animal rights groups, from the former British-based Lynx[27] to the European-based International Fund for Animal Welfare (IFAW), and to the US based media-star savvy People for the Ethical Treatment of Animals (PETA). The latter has without a doubt been the champion of star gazing in the 1990s, successfully "signing" a variety of prominent Hollywood, television and fashion stars, including the 1990s plastic surgery reincarnation of the early Bardot, the all-Canadian beach babe Pamela Anderson Lee, in the smashing and breezy PETA campaign "Give Fur the Cold Shoulder."[28]

However, Bardot's close association with the baby seal crusades defied any other strategy of coupling stars and beasts in animal rights/welfare campaigns and marked a unique trend in pro-animal advocacy, one that came close to an eco-feminist tradition. While the stars of today involved in such campaigns as "I would rather go naked than wear fur" (PETA) trade fur for more skin, Bardot made motherhood and nurturing, not her skin, the core of her campaign. Against Pamela's bare shoulders displayed in magazine ads and billboards across North America and Great Britain twenty years earlier BB adopted the respectable, conservative body of a midwife, caretaker and mother to the nation of animals. Far from being a marginal case, Bardot perfectly blended with the structure and organization of anti-fur and animal welfare culture, making the necessary links between women, the land and the animal rights economy even more obvious.

Bardot's paradoxical position as French national symbol – her beauty immortalized as Marianne, the bountiful symbol of the Republic – and as one of the most lucrative human commodities of her time, reveals how female sexuality is indissociable from the national market of trades and goods. Bardot has embodied the French national trademark like no one else before, displaying an image of the national as a sexual and commercialized space that has historically been at the very basis of colonial and postcolonial relationships. Considered in the 1960s of greater value for the French economy than car manufacturers Renault and Citroen combined,[29] Bardot's transnational mobility as celebrity skin was informed by a tight articulation between sex/uality and national property. In this sense, if identificatory practices are also informed by "intimacy between femininities" (Stacey 1994: 172), Bardot's crusades provoke tantalizing questions about the articulation between sexuality, economy and nation. With these contextual elements in mind, I shall turn to a close examination of the BB seal campaigns in relation to national/colonial representations.

The Empress has no clothes: the 1977–8 campaign

In 1977, a forty-three-year-old Bardot, still considered a new retiree from the world of men (her last film was *Don Juan*, R. Vadim, 1973), joined the rank of full-time animal lovers. Totally devoted to the animal kingdom and the cause of her life, a naïve Bardot was making her way through the business of professional activism. In her memoirs, Bardot describes this initiation period as a frustrating, thankless one, where her true love for animals was constantly diminished by the nitty-gritty of national politics and corporate animal enterprise turf fights. Nevertheless, the star was strongly committed to spending her time and her money for animals. The various alliances she would contract with the animal rights movement in the following years, as well as the carefully scripted media interventions and public performances she would personally sign, need to be understood in the broader context of global marketing of the environment and local/national preservation of resources.

Bardot's involvement in the baby seal hunt war in 1977 was not an impromptu gesture, but should be contextualized as a powerful expression of tabloid animal activism where discourses about national preservation, female mothering and life advocacy all intertwined to produce a contemporary animal fairy tale. Ironically, the baby seal's dreadful fate succeeded in bringing Bardot on a diplomatic trip to Canada, a land that the star had avoided visiting on many occasions, which only added to the media circus around the event. From the outset, Bardot's dramatic landing on the icy land of Labrador (territory of Newfoundland) was orchestrated by Greenpeace guru Franz Weber and gave the entire adventure a sensational and melodramatic cachet with dream elements: an innocent anthropomorphic victim, a dramatic rescue, and a tearful image of the beauty and the beast in each other's arms.

The 1977–8 campaign and the specific representations that inform it, reveals the articulations between Bardot's bodily associations with the white baby seals and the national and colonial formations implied through such constructions. Framed as mature, authentic (no make-up but a not-so "discreet" eyeliner, no plastic surgery – unlike her lifetime rival Sophia Loren), responsible, but still incredibly desirable, Bardot turned with a vengeance to the respectable and dignified image of the middle-aged woman devoted to a humanitarian cause. Her conversion to the world of animals was denounced by many journalists and critics as just a publicity stunt for the aging star.[30] But Bardot ignored the critics and worked to have her advocate image mark her "transformation" from love beast to beast lover. As she succinctly puts it: "I gave my youth to men, I am now giving my wisdom to animals."[31]

Although within the star system and star economy endorsements are recognized as an intrinsic part of the lucrative cultural and fan capital (as the PETA campaigns have shown over the past decade), in the case of Bardot, this culture of sudden concern is more troubling and certainly politically charged. In fact, the short-circuited equation of "Bardot-and-the-seals equals fame and money" minimizes the ways that Bardot's animal advocacy is deeply rooted in the rhetorics of life/family politics, immigration, and women's roles in reproduction and preservation of the nation, a convergence that would reach its apogee during the last seal stunt in 1994. The reassuring image of the woman with a cause echoes on many levels the colonial and liberal traditions of the so-called women's societies and clubs that proliferated during colonization, and afterwards in nationalist movements, notably in Europe but also in North America. In other words, Bardot's seal escapade embraces the three nodal roles of women in the preservation of national culture/land: guardian, bearer and nurturer, in an economy dominated by corporate colonial nationalism.

The anti-seal hunt interventions led by Bardot responded to the nationalist condemnation of the exploitative globalizing economy over the development of the national/local economy. In fact, this has always been a strategy espoused by anti-fur groups. Even Yourcenar in 1968 made it clear in her letter to Brigitte Bardot, that the "filthy lucre" made out of the killing of baby seals served the ends of multinational companies over the development of regional economies. In other words, the fur business was a transnational economy, an economy of death, that represented a constant threat to the survival of nations, an economy of life. As the most likely of Yourcenar's heirs, Bardot adopted a similar discourse by building on this antagonistic link between national resources and international exploitation, showing in fact that international furriers (very often identified as "immigrants") were the real murderers, and the true threat to national interests.[32]

> In fact, the beneficiaries of these hunts are first and foremost those companies (mostly Norwegian) organized around the fur trade, the usual intermediaries, and the Canadian government's balance of trade. The majority of the hunt is carried out by icebreakers and helicopters belonging to subsidiaries of these companies.
>
> (Yourcenar 1995: 282)

However, as I discuss in chapter 6, the core of the fur renaissance rhetoric in the 1990s has been about demystifying such clean boundaries while troubling the traditional polarization suggested by anti-fur groups between nationalistic national/regional economies that are seen as ecologically sensitive, and global economic exploitation of local and national resources, seen as a menace to the welfare of the environment of the nation.

The success of Bardot's campaigns cannot be dissociated from the fact that the star and her friends provided a representation of Canada that elided complex questions of ethnicity and gender in favour of a predominant scenario where the colony is a homogeneous, sexually-objectified space. Reappropriating late nineteenth-century discourses of women as the true daughters and mothers of the national land, the BB campaign clearly shared some common ground with a conservative and traditionalist vision of women as reproductive dolls. In many ways, the BB campaign can be seen as a response to the women's liberation movement initiated in the 1960s around the question of women's sexual subjectivity. By reframing women's agency around issues of preservation and reproduction, the anti-fur movement plays on female sexuality as a valuable trading good, stressing how politically worthless and culturally exploitative fur was for women.

Considering the highly controversial nature of Bardot's history with motherhood and sexuality,[33] Bardot's interventions reinforced the already political relationship between women's sexuality, ethnic regulation and national formation in the context of Québec and Francophone Catholic communities. In the context of tremendous change related to sexual liberation and the women's movement in the 1970s, the rhetoric of animal rights activists and the anti-fur lobby, particularly regarding issues of preserving and nurturing the motherland for the protection of the national heritage, flirted ambiguously with conservative discourses (including debates about abortion) asking women to respect acts of God and not interfere with nature, and to procreate for the future of the national environment.[34]

As I have already pointed out, if Bardot's raids took place with a climate of social revolution in Québec, it was also a moment of political instability and national affirmation in the context of Canadian federalist politics, where the ethnic factor (too often contained within the model of Francophone minority) was a delicate issue and manifested itself as a constant concern for survival vis-à-vis the threat from outside. As both the object of identification for a generation of women raised in the shadow of the women's lib movement and of condemnation as the symbol of the rejection of family values, Bardot better than anyone embodied the competing paternalist narrative of the value of women for the nation and maternalist call for survival. Furthermore, considering that "identifications do not take place exclusively within the imagination, but also occur at the level of cultural activity" (Stacey 1994: 171), the real cultural activity addressed through Bardot's call for a ban on seal hunting concerned the translation of a paternalist narrative into a maternalist representation of women's position as the guardians of the nation. This identity of the nation's gatekeepers was ironically mobilized against competing narratives between a marginalization of the place of women in the birth of the nation (i.e., the fur trade dominated by men) and a social necessity to make the family unit the backbone of a strong economic nation. Bardot's extreme position as both a threat to family values due to her excessive capital and curious vehicle of conservative colonial values, is reconciled through the nationalist and maternalist dimension of anti-fur advocacy for women; and Bardot as the mother of the seals will leave a legacy to the children: passing on tales and stories of love between animals and humans.

La fée des animaux, or Noonoah's mother

> The little book Noonoah had been released and was selling well, with all profits going to Greenpeace. We hoped that it would be a hit with kids at Christmas.
>
> (Bardot 1999: 121)[35]

Fifteen years before Bardot capitalized on her animal activism by having her foundation registered as non-profit making in 1992, one of the most spectacular campaigns led by Bardot and her friends portrayed her as a snow-white seal lover, tearfully condemning the unnatural, unmotherly dimensions of baby seal killings. A mixture of naturalist cliché, celebrity redemption and motherly camp, the campaign has to be understood as probably one of the most effective in uniting transnational animal rights advocates and a celebrity. The fact that even today the picture of Bardot hugging a white baby seal dominates the BB-and-the-beasts years speaks for itself: despite the fact that Greenpeace and IFAW were the masterminds behind the Canadian crusade, Bardot is still the central figure of the crusade. The fairy tale of Bardot flying from France to hug a Canadian whitecoat baby would become a legend – as well as *the* success-story of animal rights advertising, which included T-shirts, posters, postcards, films, buttons, candy bars, etc., featuring the crying baby seal.

The famous and dramatic photo showing a live-from-Canada Bardot lying in the snow, a baby seal in her arms, courageously defying the eye of the camera, hugging the beast to keep it safe from looming hunters made the rounds of the front pages as often as the star's famous *moue*. Documented by the French agency Sygma, who have been granted the exclusive rights to the Bardot animal advocacy performances, the photo of the star mother with the baby seal was taken from a longer film sequence made and staged for the Brigitte Bardot Foundation, broadcast and distributed worldwide through the IFAW network in close association with Greenpeace International.

Ironically, Bardot and her acolytes picked up where *Paris-Match* left off in 1969 in one of the most graphic and outrageous of Western media reports on the commercial seal hunt of "white babies," redeploying the maternal melo-drama of whiteness and civilization. With a full color cover featuring a tearful (so it says) white baby seal, *Paris-Match* created a piece of tabloid intervention in two special issues devoted to the outrageous massacre, intermingling the voices of the innocent victims with that of thousands of readers who wrote to voice their shock, dismay and distress before such barbarian acts. A gem of sensational narrative, the *Paris-Match* cover would become an emblem, an icon of the baby seals crusaders, and is still copiously reproduced today on a range of activist commodities: from IFAW's latest direct-to-public "educational" video special report *Canada's Seal Hunt*, to the engraved nickel-bonded steel collector coins of endangered species, to the Endangered Species Chocolate Co. (The Harp Seal series), to Grasset's graphic design that reproduced the photo of Bardot and her "baby" on her second volume of her memoirs, *Le Carré de Pluton*.

Behind the corporate activism of BB and the seal campaign lies an incredibly effective commodification of motherhood. The Bardot picture is only one of the many financial and affective bonds that link women and the anti-fur groups. The myriad of intertwined tactics and strategies used by anti-fur corporations such as IFAW and the Brigitte Bardot Foundation speak directly to the gendered organization of the campaigns and the politics of visibility deployed by animal rights advocates. For example, the Bardot expedition to Canada in March 1977 was not a lone gesture, but was carefully prepared and staged by the two prominent figures of animal rights corporations, the all-star founder of IFAW, Brian Davies and Greenpeace brain Franz Weber. Davies' agenda was to ban the whitecoat hunt (something Davies finally succeeded in pressuring the Canadian government to do in 1987) and to formally prohibit any Canadian sealskin export products within the European Economic Community (EEC). Organized by Weber and starring Bardot, the expedition was partly funded by Bardot herself, and some logistical assistance was provided by IFAW, i.e., Davies. As a condition to Bardot's presence was the guarantee that Davies would invite more than fifty journalists in March 1977 to join the animal rights crew on the ice floes in the Gulf of St. Lawrence. No matter that the loving baby seal/Bardot embrace was tainted later by rumors that mocked the event as being about Beauty and the stuffed baby seal: the international mediascape happily circulated the image of the blonde Goddess, redeemed as the Joan of Arc of the white baby seal people.

The 1977 seal campaign built its political and commercial strategy on a series of highly emotional narratives emphasizing two elements central to any sensational reality show story: that the hunted was an innocent three-week-old baby, and that the story, though dramatically illustrated, was true, with real people savagely killing real babies. The "true life" dimension of Bardot's poignant escapade was artfully documented by the camera and film crew invited to capture this historic moment. In a full sequence rerun in the A&E (TV programme) biography of Bardot, the camera follows Bardot walking on the icy land, her hair down, wearing her famous blue jeans, boots and hip-cut white coat, literally coming to save the baby seal in what would become a wonderful piece of animal rights activist ideology – the baby seal is a baby after all and must be saved at any cost. When BB finally gets down on her knees, lies down next to the baby seal, kisses it, and whispers tenderly (staring at the camera): "N'aie pas peur on les aura va" (Don't worry, we'll get them), the national boundaries between the beauty and the beast vanish: the French Snow White's lavish gaze and the baby seal's pleading eyes commune in one tender embrace before the world. The fairy tale aspects of this publicity did not escape the eyes of the Canadian press, who renamed this melodramatic embrace of fur and skin: the "Bambi Syndrome" (Francoeur 1995), emphasizing the Disney-like narrative of the tale.

This thin line between fiction and true story would finally be crossed two years later when this mother/child discovery moment found a new expression in the publication of *Noonoah: le petit phoque blanc*. Written by Bardot and issued by prominent French publisher Grasset in 1979, the story not only offered a contemporary reenactment of *Nanook of the North*,[36] but also targeted children and their mothers as readers. Typical of children's literature but also of animal rights morality, the story is a pristine example of anthropomorphism, in which animals are portrayed with human feelings and emotions. Essentially a fictional account of the baby seal-hunt trauma, the story stars Noonoah the baby seal and its/his best friend, Inouk the little Eskimo, who saves Noonoah and his fellow seals from being clubbed by the adult hunters.

The book, emphatically introduced by Bardot as a true story, is part of the "Sauvons les animaux" (Save the animals) series, which was aimed at raising children's consciousness (through a double identification with the baby seal and Nanook/Inouk) against the atrocities lying just beneath any little boy or girl's mommy's "joli manteau blanc" (mummy's cute white coat). *Noonoah le petit phoque blanc* is only one of many other books written in the spirit of animal rights advocacy and in the name of the animal rights economy (a portion of the profits from sales of the book was donated to the Brigitte Bardot Foundation, while most of it was donated to Greenpeace).[37] While the book is typical of Westernized iconography, notably regarding the sexualization of gendered patterns – the story features a Mama Seal sporting pearls and a bosom that would make Jayne Mansfield jealous – the fact that the story was written by Bardot emphasizes the colonial texture and eurocentric flavor of the book where a whitened Inouk comes to the rescue of the seal colony. Although directed at children, Noonoah's story offers an excellent example of the way that anti-fur advocate strategies operate on a broader, if not a more mature market. Like so many events staged in popular media sprees, the distinction between babies and beasts coalesces to constitute a powerful and effective emotional rhetoric device, a nodal element in any further intervention/action. Since Bardot, like her spiritual animal welfare mother Yourcenar, had always had mixed feelings about motherhood – a sin exploited ceaselessly by the French tabloid press, and an assertion that Bardot would fully endorse in her own autobiography – the seal campaign and her animal rights activities allowed her to redeem her lack of love for human babies with her natural love for animals. Just like in a fairy tale, Bardot adopted a baby seal renamed "Chouchou," completing the cycle of activist motherhood. Bardot, portrayed as a failed mother for her only son Nicholas, would become the mother of an international colony of seals, horses and other animals, her name and photo hugging furry things featured on the cover of the same magazines that, not so long before, tracked her as the ultimate sex kitten. Bardot's animal godmother and madonna role[38] was clearly informed by a long tradition inaugurated by Victorian women, whose actions of preservation were orchestrated both locally and outside the country. Like a true daughter of the order of the animal kingdom, her crusades led her to travel around Europe and America, rescuing and protecting endangered species, telling stories to the children of the world about men's atrocities. While herself a prey of the paparazzi, Bardot succeeded in exploiting tabloid representational strategies to capture and address female agency as part of national and postcolonial formations, first as a star, then as an animal activist, and finally as a (trans)national godmother.

In this sense, despite the apparent individualist touch of her intervention, Bardot's activities can be understood within the context of the rise of international environmental movements in the 1970s, traditionally associated with the Left. Bardot's media interventions were definitely synchronized with environmentalist politics, but they also illustrated how celebrity culture inflated these movements and was crucial to their economical survival. Her collaboration with other stars of the animal rights movement, including Davies, Weber, Watson and even Peter Singer of the Animal Liberation Front (ALF) is framed in that context of the economy of animal welfare and protection. However, without denying conflicting values between the discourses of liberation and preservation of animals, what I wish to question here is how these political "life cultures," naturally associated with ecology and leftist politics, share rhetorical strategies with those of right-wing politics, particularly regarding questions of the role of mothers as vessels/agents for living/human beings. For instance, right-wing politics constantly target women as the main perpetuators and consumers of low-moral practices while making the success of their campaigns and politics dependant on women (the famous conservative vote long associated with women in Western democracies). The same can be argued about the BB campaign: women were both the sinners (as principal wearers of furs) and the saviors (as mothers of the species). This fine balance between morality, racial and ethnic markers, as well as the nationalization of sexuality for the humanist's/ animalist's sake was at the core of the 1977 seal episode and vital to its success. But its ambiguous resonance with right-wing cultural and scientific movements, such as anti-abortion groups and eugenics advocates, would eventually consolidate Bardot's intervention as a powerful maternal economy of the nation.[39]

Human or animal? It doesn't matter, they are all babies

The analogy between animals and human babies is a constant of animal rights activist groups. Although this might be explained by the close connections between public-health advocacy and animal rights interventions, it is first a question of thinking of animal welfare as human welfare. A recent joint campaign orchestrated by the National Easter Seals Society, the Association of Birth Defect Children, the Child Health Foundation and the Heimlich

Foundation, offers a vivid example of a strategy that indifferently substitutes babies/kids and beasts. A leaflet produced and distributed by the Physician's Committee for Responsible Medicine denounces the hypocritical politics of fund-raising campaigns like the March of Dimes.[40] It targets such institutions for accepting endorsements from corporations guilty of performing animal testing and experiments without any significant scientific results but participation in animal cruelty. Featuring a photo of British pop icons Paul and the late Linda McCartney in a direct address to "the people," the message warns consumers and parents against the animal experiments conducted by international corporations and pharmaceutical companies (mostly North American-based such as The Wolfson Foundation and Quest Cancer Test), accusing them of harm against the human population in general and to babies, more specifically. In bold characters, the "If You Really Want to Help Babies" message states specific facts about animal testing in the design and development of new drugs and vaccines. "Birth defect breakthroughs depend on understanding how genetic and environmental factors affect human beings. Animal experiments are unnecessary and often misleading," insists the message. Under the subheading, "The Wrong Kind of Research," the pamphlet, anchored in a strong moralistic condemnation of abuse of innocent victims – here babies and animals – vehemently advocates for direct-to-human testing as strategy number one in drug design and testing. Outing the complicit alliance between a charity display and corporations that conduct animal experiments, the group argues:

> The March of Dimes should be putting all its resources into human population studies to track down the causes of birth defects and into prenatal education and care to prevent them. But, in fact, the March of Dimes has given millions of dollars to experimenters who gave nicotine, cocaine, or alcohol to animals, even though we already know from human clinical experience that these substances can harm a developing baby.[41]

What is interesting in the Physicians' campaign is not only the conflation of babies/animals but also the ambiguous but nevertheless powerful address to mothers and parents as pro-life advocates. In this sense, there is a disturbing relation to pro-life discourses, notably concerning the obsession with making babies a public property and denying women any kind of agency in relation to their reproductive function. In other words, in "nature," mothers and babies are one.

This is precisely the rhetorical agenda of "life" discourses. The success of pro-life movements over the last two decades in making the personhood of the fetus the real focus of debate has had direct consequences for the erasure of the figure of the mother as an agent both of life and the preservation of nature, and a subject distinct from the baby. As Carol Stabile rightly points out:

In terms of the traditional maternal environment, female interests have been historically subsumed beneath the interests of the family, but this more recent erasure has little do with martyrdom or self-sacrifice. Instead, representation of "fetal personhood" depends upon the erasure of female bodies and the reduction of women to passive, reproductive machines.

(Stabile 1992: 180)

In the case of animal rights causes, the reproductive role allotted to women has been the position of protective and commercial agents of the anti-fur business, ranging from chameleon performances as beasts in cages during demonstrations, to models of the naked truth, to entrepreneur crusaders à la BB.

The BB seal crusades were committed to restoring the generic figure of motherhood and its nurturing mode for the nation. Ultimately it was not mothers per se who were on display, but the social functions of a maternal economy. In this sense, in an efficient anthropomorphic strategy, the baby seals became the real subjects of the tragedy and the real heroes of the story. Located in Bardot's activities against the baby seal hunt in Canada is a significant echo of this collusion between pro-life discourse and animal welfare protection. No wonder that BB found the role of her life in the baby seal episode: BB, the unfit mother, who spoke of motherhood and birth as a female curse, would seek revenge by triumphantly eclipsing herself through the rescue of white baby seals. In this way, BB abdicated her lead role to the baby seals, and later to other animals. The obviously racialized anthropomorphic representation of "white baby seals" as true stars of the anti-fur war – not to mention how 'bébé phoques' sounds in English: 'BB fucks' and 'baby fucks' – brought even more authority and authenticity to the crusade. As the 1969 issue of *Paris-Match* shows, the success of the campaign stems from the capacity to mobilize action around two cultural markers vital to the stability of colonial enterprise and postcolonial societies: whiteness and reproduction (babies).

Along the same lines that pro-lifers advocate for the individuality of the fetus, anti-fur activists advocate for the rights and welfare of animals, and even in some instances for the liberation of animals – and more specifically "babies" – a line encapsulated in the bible of pro-animal groups, Peter Singer's *Animal Liberation* (1975). As Olson and Goodnight suggest in their analysis of the social controversy over pro and anti-fur rhetorics, "More radical anti-fur advocates accept Peter Singer's perspective that even beings that cannot speak and are not the intellectual equals of adult humans can think, know fear, suffer foreboding, and feel pain much as a human infant can" (Olson and Goodnight 1994: 259). This association of babies–animals provides a performative articulation between the right to life and the condemnation of murder, within which the babies and animals are the true subjects. As Stabile puts it:

> The maternal space has, in effect, disappeared and what has emerged
> in its place is an environment that the fetus alone occupies . . . [and]
> In order for the embryo/fetus to emerge as autonomous – as a person,
> patient, or individual in its own right – all traces of a female body
> . . . must disappear.
>
> (Stabile 1992: 180)

In the case of the baby seals, all the gore and horror is captured in the
representation of the baby seals as the innocent victims of the hunt. Images of
watery-eyed bleeding baby seals – always presented as newborns – were in many
ways tantalized by pro-life iconography of the fetus, a reminder of the cruelty
involved in the disposal of a baby's life. Infanticide was certainly the most
powerful discursive paradigm used to rally world wide opinion against the
massacre. The ice floes were constantly depicted as an imagined nursery, hence
the condemnation and moral opprobrium towards the slaughter of the "nursing
marine infants on the breeding ground." Greenpeace and IFAW have been
incredibly active in the construction of a family narrative around the hunt,
recycling highly contentious conservative and traditionalist politics around the
"family," babies and mothers in their campaigns. What is even more disturbing
here is the fact that the strategy betrays a clear similarity with pro-life discourses
about the preservation and conservation of life. Nature shall triumph over
culture, and the enforcement of such natural law is a matter of maternal
morality.

This correspondence betrays an interplay of economic nationalist interests
and racial politics, as well as issues over technological control, that permeate
both pro-life and anti-fur discourses. It is far from my intention to unproblem-
atically suggest that all anti-fur movements are connected to the white religious
right for example, and the multiplicity of political identities is also intrinsically
part of the anti-fur culture. I criticize such a monolithic and erasing construction, knowing the racial, gender and sexual politics clearly displayed
within pro-fur advocacy groups notably around the question of distribution of
resources between white and native trappers, furriers and retailers, crafters
and designers, women and men, so-called immigrants and Québécois/Canadien
de souche. However, there is a troubling convergence between the racial and the
sexual in both rhetorics that sometimes cannot escape the economic structure
of the fur trade.[42]

Such racialized and gendered fur politics would find their ultimate expression
in the second campaign led by BB in 1994. Through this campaign, abundantly
anchored yet again in multiple layers of star mediation, what in 1977 had
been addressed in terms of a humanist, essentialist care for the survival of baby
seals and mother earth, became, in light of the growing visibility and activity
of right-wing groups in Europe and in America, an explosive terrain for
xenophobic and racist politics of all kinds. This last episode demonstrates that
the fragile boundaries between left and right politics in relation to women,

bodies and nation are deeply intertwined over issues of reproduction and the survival of species.

Unlike the 1970s campaign, the 1995 anti-seal hunt campaign witnessed a spectacular reversal of fortune where the traditionally conservative pro-fur world suddenly "became" racially and genderly inclusive, "native conscious", and nationally protective. The most unbelievable and often most unpredictable alliances were created between native crafters and artists, women designers and fur retailers against what was conceived as white-dominated anti-fur groups. As I discuss in more detail later, fur suddenly became ecological, sensitive to the pioneer native role in the fur trade, and the most natural way for women's entrepreneurship to shape and sign the new national economy. In some circles, to wear fur, to think fur became politically anti-colonial, a gesture of national pride, a feminist statement, and a concrete intervention in nature management.

B.B. Phoque™: celebrity skin and the 1994–5 campaign

I learned with immense sorrow that the Canadians had ended the eight-year ban on the killing of helpless baby seals, which meant that their terrifying massacre would resume this year [1994]. I immediately organised a press conference with Frank [Franz Weber] . . . I could not believe my eyes or ears. After having expended so much energy for so many years to abolish this monstrous massacre, here it was once again, as though I had done nothing, as if it was completely normal. All this despite the fact that the whole world was disgusted and revolted, pointing the finger at Canadians for this unacceptable and cruel hunt. But since other revolts and other dramas have taken over the headlines, people had forgotten the white baby seals and their bloody bodies tormented on Canadian snow banks. And the killers were making up for lost time . . .

In the Middle-Ages, we burned witches . . .
In 1995, we massacre baby seals.
                    (Bardot 1999: 619–20; emphasis mine)[43]

I wish to contextualize the Bardot 1994–5 campaign in relation within two fundamentally disparate yet interrelated elements. First, over the past twenty years, the growing presence of female stars and celebrities in the campaigns designed by such animal rights groups as PETA, CATCSH (Canadians Against the Commercial Seal Hunt) and IFAW[44] in America has made the survival of the species a constant advertising battle. Second, the involvement of national agencies in support of the fur trade has increased the political and cultural manifestations of economic nationalisms, and led to the production of institutional literatures destined to sensitize the good consumer to the "Fur Facts," to quote the Fur Council of Canada.

The ways that the media and pro-fur groups have polarized the representation of the debate between pro and anti fur advocates along the lines of fur versus skin enhances the sexual nature of the links between women/fur/skin/animal. As I will discuss further in chapter 6, the fashion scene has been a privileged site for the advocacy of anti-fur positions, denouncing fur consumption as a death gesture and bringing shame to catwalks across the globe. PETA's campaigns with slogans such as "Fur is Dead" or "Buy a Fur and Slip into Something Dead" were a publicity coup during the late 1980s and early 1990s, successfully discouraging prominent designers from using fur in their collections, at least for a while.[45]

The public shaming associated with these campaigns, aside from the fact that it was clearly part of a moral battle regarding the human side of animals, also served another purpose: humanizing stars and top models, themselves too often considered as zoo animals. "The celebrities' role in anti-fur advocacy is to not only publicize the negative associations of fur, but also to make fur consumption unfashionable by showing fashion-setters rejecting fur publicly" (Olson and Goodnight 1994: 262). The stars' presence is a vital part of a direct public shaming strategy that primarily targets "ordinary" female consumers, at the same time that it promotes the ethical image of the stars who agree to lend their skin to the anti-fur campaigns. For Olson and Goodnight, shaming is a public performance that confronts if not "inverts" the relation between shame and status (Olson and Goodnight 1994: 263).

One has only to recall the PETA naked poster campaign in the early 1990s that featured stars proudly displaying their furless apparel on behalf of the animal rights group. From actress Kim Basinger to models Cindy Crawford, Christy Turlington and Naomi Campbell, to rock star Melissa Ethridge with her former girlfriend Julie Cypher, to Nancy Reagan's daughter Patti Davis cuddling Playboy founder Hugh Hefner's dog, the stars lined up to pose under the famous banner: "I'd rather go naked than wear fur."[46] But no matter who's showing off her skin here, or which spot, this profusion of flesh politics is a prime illustration of the circulation of skin as the new ecological and sensitive issue. In a new spin on nature and sexuality, the beaver ladies are becoming the natural substitute for fur coats. See this great example of naked skin as fur, in this report by Reuter, *La marquise et la fourrure*. The story reads:

> An Italian marchioness who posed naked a year ago for a billboard campaign against the use of fur coats asked her husband, the former European Environmental commissioner Carlo Ripa di Meana, to join the fight. The latest advertisement released by the Italian division of the International Fund for Animal Welfare (IFAW) shows the naked couple snuggling in bed with the slogan: "Poor little things, they buy fur because they have no one to keep them warm." Carlo Ripa,

the former leader of the late Green Party, agreed to participate in the campaign in order to remind men that they too must assume their share of the guilt in the sale of fur. "Too often, men, or lovers offer fur to their partner because they are incapable of offering love, warmth and affection", explains Ripa in a press release. Marina, his wife, confessed that in the past she had worn fur, but renounced it once she found "peace" with her husband. Last year, the marchioness posed nude, her pubic hair well-exposed, with the slogan: "The only fur I'm not ashamed of".[47]

I would argue that shaming strategies in the fur battle are informed by a sense of display of the previously pro-fur self that overshadows the necessarily sexualized and racialized cultural formations of the agency of the female subject. In the context of anti-fur tactics, shaming as a performative act only makes sense for those who make a spectacle of themselves (i.e., pro-fur advocates) for those whose skin speaks for the dead animals. In this scenario, the fur consumer is completely excluded, reduced to an absent subjectivity, no identity, no agency, no trace, only a raw materiality, barely a body; in other words the fur consumer/wearer is reduced to a dead fur coat. This process of disembodying the fur consumer to commodify her as a fur coat on one hand, and on the other to favor a politics of anthropomorphism in which animals suffer as humans, must be articulated in the politics of the postcolonial subject. This is exactly what happened with Bardot when her final public performance in 1995 led to the most incredible colonial and national resentment from both sides of the fur divide. And once again, faithful to her reputation, Bardot's relation to the female body remained ambivalent, while the relation to race and nation was addressed and marketed in an unproblematized fashion.

With Bardot, the separation between skin and fur has not been entirely consummated, contrary to most of the American stars who have participated in anti-fur advocacy. While the star's skin, from Pamela Anderson Lee to Melissa Ethridge, was used to obscure the fashion industry as the ultimate fur dispensary, Bardot's bodily position on the contrary reinforced the strong association between skin and fur as the true locus of national economies and politics. One of the trademarks of Bardot's campaigns was to contextualize fur as part of an international mega-complex where fashion is only one tiny element of a global movement facilitating the hybridization/spoiling of species, both human and animal.

In this sense, the 1994–5 campaign focussed on two important targets: women and "strangers." On one hand, Bardot's interventions exacerbated two fundamental remainders of colonial culture in the postcolonial space. First, the commodification and fetishization of women through the association fur equals skin, and second, the dramatization of a national loss through the permeability of national frontiers. This is why a significant part of the Brigitte Bardot Foundation's actions, once limited to a series of dramatic rescues, now stress the necessity of intervention into the politics and national regulations concerning immigration, export and circulation of both goods and people. Bardot's anti-fur interventions go beyond the sole motif and highly trendy scene of fashion – despite numerous fights with models and stars who displayed their furs like cemeteries, two of the most famous being Italian diva Sophia Loren and French fashion darling Jean Paul Gaultier[48] – to address the globalization of an international plot to destroy the true nature of the nation. Herein, her pro-animal position and anti-fur politics are inseparable from her growing condemnation of inadequate immigration regulations in France, and her serious concerns for the future of 'la nation française' as imagined by her idol General de Gaulle and now promoted by *Front National* leader Jean Marie Le Pen.

Her last crusade in 1995, a media and political failure, generated a level of xenophobia rarely reached on either side of the fur divide, adding ethnic and racial polemics to existing layers of gender and sexual targeting. While the 1977 campaign was designed as a tearjerker featuring all the mothers of the land first, despite some colonialist overtones the 1995 campaign adopted a quite different, if not radical, tone. At the forefront were a series of attacks against the ethnicization of the fur market, but above all against savage ethnic (vs. cultural) practices aiming at killing animals.

Alongside attacks condemning the traffic of seal penises to the Asian aphrodisiac market,[49] are the constant charges by the star about the laxness of immigration laws in France. The sadly famous episode when the star wrote to *Le Figaro* to protest against the Muslim's Aïd-el-Kébir, denouncing the disgrace that such a heretic ritual represented for France as the surrogate mother of these "immigrants", found a powerful echo in the context of the political situation in France at the time. Le Pen was flirting with 10 percent of the voters – not since the postwar period has right-wing discourse been so popular. Bardot's "indirect" link with Le Pen through her new husband Bernard d'Ormale, a close advisor to Le Pen, was also a matter of political puzzling, and despite constant denial by Bardot of any connection to *Le Front National's* agenda, it was public knowledge that the star was a fierce admirer of the flamboyant leader.[50] In this context, Bardot's attacks against the Canadian government were actually de-centered to not only include Canadians/barbarians as in 1977, but to also denounce the external forces who would benefit from the hunt, hence her targeting of Asian men as impotent perverts.

While any smart marketing person would have profited from such politically incorrect faux pas, the Canadian government, followed by a range of pro-fur advocates, contributed to bringing the debate to an even more racist and ethnocentrist context. Some Canadian public agencies – including state-funded television networks such as Radio-Canada – as well as representatives of the fur industries launched a counter attack intended to show how "hypocritical" were the European countries who signed the ban on animal trapping. One of the sharpest replies came in a one-hour documentary produced by Radio-Canada entitled *L'Europe veut notre peau* (1997).[51] Broadcast coast to coast one Sunday night on Francophone prime-time television, this amazingly pro-fur documentary condemned the European anti-fur lobby for its dubious tactics and for not denouncing questionable European trapping practices. For sixty minutes the television crew attacked Dutch practices of eliminating muskrats, a hunt entirely subsidized by the government, and exposed fur ranch conditions beyond bestiality, etc. What the documentary clearly states is that all things being equal, the Europeans had no right to vote for EEC economic sanctions against Canada while guilty of similar sins.

Meanwhile Bardot, despite her recent sixtieth birthday, was still the queen of the media, and though less darling and less popular, her famous initials alone were enough to secure space in the media. In this sense, nothing really matched the Bardot frenzy. First called to the rescue by the Canadian Society for the Prevention of Cruelty to Animals (SPCA), who on the eve of their 125th anniversary were confronting serious financial problems, (Arpin 1994) Bardot reappeared on the Canadian map – from her quarters in Paris. At the same time, and in light of a federal governmental reevaluation of the seal hunt, Bardot reiterated her position concerning the necessity of maintaining the 1987 ban on the baby seal and the quota on the harp seal hunt. Playing the diplomatic godmother, Bardot harped harder than ever on the atrocities of the baby seal hunt in Newfoundland (though officially banned), accusing Canadian Prime Minister Jean Chrétien of being a murderer, requesting meetings with the Canadian ambassador in Paris – who twice refused – and threatening sabotage of all the parties involved.[52]

Faded was the charm of the 1977 campaign and the Disneyesque Noonoah fairy tale. This time, an ageing Bardot found no mercy: the Canadian government as well as the press totally ridiculed the French actress, using stunning ageist, racist and sexist tactics to discredit Bardot's latest coup d'éclat. Television networks and commercial radio stations did not miss a beat, emphatically trapping the star in pranks to demonstrate to an indifferent crowd how Bardot knew nothing about Québec's political specificities, and was thus devoid of authority and legitimacy to intervene in a national affair.[53] Bardot was French and the effigy of the Republic, but no queen of the Confederation.

Bardot was sixty in 1994 and benefited from a celebratory exposure, in Québec as elsewhere. However, despite the artifacts of Bardotmania and the media rush to commemorate the sexiest French star to ever invade the mediascape and the marketplace, a more favorable conjuncture in the fur economy was articulated in an extremely aggressive campaign led by the Fur Council of Canada (FCC) to reestablish the glamour of a national industry. Launching its fur renaissance with a witty slogan: "Fur: the Fabric of a Nation," the FCC, subsidized by the Heritage Ministry and various government and industry agencies, fought back from the very position for which they have been condemned: fur became natural and ecological (see chapter 6).

The FCC campaign hit hard at Bardot and her Foundation. The shaming campaign, teamed with the baby seal maternal melodrama so effective twenty years previously, didn't bite this time. The star was mocked in public campaigns, her body becoming the repeated source of political grotesque. In brief, Bardot the hunter became the hunted. As illustrated in this sketch by political cartoonist Serge Chapleau, "B.B. phoque" (Figure 5.2), the anti-fur/pro-fur campaign was embedded in a definitive individualization of the debate through the potential that Bardot offered, to sexualize the politics and diminish the impact of her discourse. Portrayed as a fish (in an obvious reference to the female sex, but also to the term "poisson" meaning someone naive), BB is chewed on by a seal – the predator. The cartoon convincingly summarizes the issues at work in the 1994–5 campaign. Faced with a fragile seasonal economy and a significant decrease in fish stocks in Atlantic Canada, fishermen and seal hunters, supported by the Canadian Sealers Association, asked the Canadian government to revise the 1987 agreement and raise the annual quotas. Arguing that seals were depleting fish stocks, the Association urged the government to reestablish a fair situation that respected the traditions of the people of the Atlantic region.[54]

Figure 5.2 "BB Phoque", *Le Devoir*, 22 March 1995. Serge Chapleau, print courtesy of the artist.

Figure 5.3 "Tobin augmente les quotas de la chasse aux phoques," *Le Devoir*, 20 December 1995, B2. Serge Chapleau, print courtesy of the artist.

The B.B. Phoque caption is a witty bilingual double entendre for "fuck" and "phoque" (seal in French). BB the phoque (seal) hence became a good to be consumed as well, downplaying Bardot herself as an agent of pro-fur advocacy. Moreover, Chapleau's cartoon offers a powerful visual materiality for the ways that BB and the baby beasts/seals campaign succeeded in capitalizing on the blurred boundaries between the female body, male politics and anthropomorphism. In a second drawing (Figure 5.3), Chapleau portrays a fierce argument for a pro-fur position: the living seal, now the king of the sea, is a luxury that the nation cannot afford to "waste" anymore. With the blessing of the government and the seal premier of Newfoundland, Brian Tobin,[55] the seal has been declared a national treasure. No matter how many BB's and baby phoques visit the icy land, the nation needs its economy back (fish and fur). Reversing the fate of their fairy godmother, BB's baby seals, once the hunted, innocent victims of savage international profit, now become the hunters, the ones responsible for a shaky regional economy.

What is most telling in this latest BB-and-the-beast episode is how quickly the pro-fur lobby adjusted to the 1980s anti-fur commandos, notably in regard to ways of screening and mediating women's bodies and resources to tie them to the preservation of the nation. An international sex-kitten in 1977, by 1995 Bardot was portrayed as a xenophobic, French and (I insist) old star whose position and dubious declarations about immigration and other cultures did not help her to consolidate her public credentials. Bardot's groups, like other animal rights lobbies that have built their success on giving a woman's face to their organizations (despite notorious and charismatic male leaders) were completely overwhelmed by the arrival of a platoon of PR commandos and the presence of female figures in key functions in various pro-fur advocate groups and hunter associations across North America. In this context, not only did the figure of the pro-fur lobby change, but so did the political discourse. While anti-fur movements maintain a right-wing strategy of targeting women as guilty of the death of animals, incessantly playing on the image of women in bloody fur coats, pro-fur advocacy in Canada is making room for women, too long excluded from the politics of fur production and fabrication. In a spectacular reversal of fortune, women would become the highest profile agents of the fur comeback in the 1990s, the new entrepreneurs of the fabric of a nation. Interestingly enough, the pro-fur discourse in Canada and North America has rearticulated the most effective anti-fur arguments ("fur is death") to present the contemporary fur industry as a more humane, ethical, responsible, and ecological one, and a gem of traditional national economy. Following the spirit of the "Fur is For Life" group initiated in the 1980s by American fur retailers to thwart the effects of anti-fur protests on the fur market, most of the Canadian fur retailers have completely reshaped the fur landscape, recycling pro-Canadian discourses to promote fur as a natural and renewable resource.[56] And once again, women – white, but also native crafters and designers – are central to the building of a new bodily stockmarket around the fur trade.

6

VENUS FOREVER

The next fur generation

> In the postcolony, magnificence and the desire to shine are not
> the prerogative of only those who command. The people also
> want to be honoured, to shine, and to take part in celebrations.
>
> (Mbembe 1992: 26)

Beaver power

In 1996, Disney Studios produced a live flesh-and-skin version of its landmark
animation film: *101 Dalmatians* (Stephen Herek, 1996). Starring Glenn Close
as the Machiavellian fur crazed, meat-eating, chain-smoking fashion house
diva Cruella DeVil, the film evokes the quintessential fur revenge fantasy
of the 1990s. Cruella's ferocious appetite to get the little dogs as her second
skin reads as a burlesque, yet provocative piece of pro-fur rhetoric. When the
fabulous dyky Close, draped in a "real" Siberian tiger skin (an endangered
species, indeed) whispers to her mirror: "Mirror, mirror, who's the furriest of
them all?" one can almost see Anna Wintour and Joan Rivers on Fifth Avenue,
provocatively turning their back to the PETA people, with all the attitude the
magnificence of their fur coats commands. Far from being a moment of
fetishistic self-indulgence for luxury fur digressions, I want to offer Cruella's
words as a way to look at how the fur industry has reemerged from the dead
after disastrous years. No matter that *101 Dalmatians* is a feel-good-for-animals
film, it does express the sensational, spectacular and yes, ironic response of the
fashion and fur industries to years of bare skins.

In Canada, the comeback of Cruella has coincided with the resurrection of
the beaver. Long considered dead meat by the industry, as well as the consumer
and anti-fur advocates, the beaver has been refashioned as the queen of fur glitter
in North American collections. Since 1993, the Canadian beaver has been a
favorite on the spring catwalks, reaching the summit of its fame by appearing
in more than 50 percent of the fur garments presented at the 1999 Montréal
North American Fur and Fashion Exposition (NAFFEM), one of the most
important markets for fur retailers and designers in the world. The authentic

Canadian beaver has been elected the No. 1 fur in numerous works produced by female and male Canadian designers in recent years, from Irma Paytler, Paula Lishman, Véronique Miljkovitch, Hilary Rayner and d'Arcy-Moses, to the all-star of transnational fur, Zuki. What seems a renaissance is actually a lifting, a trimming. The beaver had never completely vanished, nor had fur. What was gone was the traditional way to portray women in fur, to think fur, to think beaver fur, to think fur ladies. Not everybody has Cruella's genes, but pro-fur certainly has a strong sense of business.

The 1990s fur trade owes its "renaissance" to an ensemble of discourses, practices and policies that have totally reshaped and reoriented the visibility and popularity of fur among both consumers and designers, reinstalling fur and women as the essential fabric of the nation. As paradoxical as it might sound, without the anti-fur campaigns and the powerful discourse about environment preservation and ecological discourse, the comeback of the beaver would not have been so glamorous. As I discussed in chapter 5, the success of anti-fur movements during the late 1970s through to the early 1990s at the popular, media and governmental levels was significant and hit the industry hard. After reaching a peak in 1986, fur sales were inconsistent with some dramatic plunges in 1987–9. Montréal saw the historic HBC Fur House close, the fur district was virtually "moribund" and empty,[1] and the popularity of fur was in serious decline. In addition to various European bans on wild furs that directly affected overseas exports, a struggling national economy and the arrival of the Third World–manufactured fur on the international market contributed to the slow-down in the Canadian fur industry. Produced in-factory, with the help of technology rather than crafters, Korea or Dominican Republic fur offered consumers an alternative to the high-quality, high-priced Canadian fur garment. Seasonal employment became more common in an industry that had been fairly stable, fur retailers struggled with excess of inventory, and major fur houses had to shut down, transfer or reduce their payroll to a minimum.[2]

Across the industry (from traders to retailers), the price of pelts dropped, cutting into the profits generated by the sales. The beaver coat, pride of the nation, was an endangered species and a poor trader. Having for centuries been the king – and queen – of colonial and national diplomatic relations, on many occasions making a better host for the nation than the prime minister himself (the beaver welcomed the athletes and tourists to the Montréal Olympics in 1976), the beaver became a national shame, provoking a national scream.[3]

But the beaver tale was not forgotten. If the traditional industry, depressingly conservative in its configuration and devoid of any creativity in its marketing, was a pure waste, another generation of fur designers was emerging, slowly but surely. The next fur generation, the one that grew up in the anti-fur period of the 1980s and 1990s, is contributing to a reversal of fortune for the beaver. A generation as eager as Cruella to cut up granny's tired beaver coat, but smarter than Disney's despotic fur lady in knowing how to capitalize on ecological/environmental discourses to make the new image of fur "look smart," and the fur ladies look like sensitive citizens. A loose pool of designers and people of the industry, supported by a succession of fur politics and policies where fur ladies was the motif, managed to crown the beaver queen of the country after years of disgrace. The next generation is ageless, full of contradictions, with an edge for the transformative qualities of skins, human and animal.

In this sense, because of the romantic narrative tied to the beaver and the formation of the nation, the Canadian fur industry occupies a special place of its own. Beaver furs and women powerfully embody the visible labor of the fur renaissance, as well as the creative force of the modern fur trade. Moreover, the impressive list of female designers "doing" fur, is eclectic, multi-ethnic, multilingual, as if the beaver trade was reclaiming its colonial origins. As a tribute to the creativity of the female designers, the beaver is also going through a major face-lift. Sheared, dyed, knitted, recycled, recut – the beaver stands amazingly young after 400 years. To the annoyance of the anti-fur lobby, the *Castor Canadensis* shows a surprising (re)productive vitality: according to the last Fur Facts provided by the Fur Council of Canada (1999), there are as many beavers in Canada today as there were at the beginning of French and British colonization.[4] In light of such contributions to the vigor of the national emblem and the fertility of the land, the presence of women next to the proud beaver offers a unique conjuncture in which to interrogate the interplay of the beaver economy and national enterprise. While the beaver and nation are too often reduced to questions of heritage and tradition, in this chapter I demonstrate how the numerous beaver trails that shape the national fur economy today are more than ever distinctively marked by the imprints of the fur ladies.

The fur renaissance, while readily apparent in such a small market as Canada, is also happening at a global level. According to the Fur Information Commission (US), whereas the sale of fur coats generated revenues of approximately $1.8 billion annually twelve years ago, followed by a crash that brought the sales down to $1 billion in 1991, fur is slowly coming back, reaching $1.27 billion in 1997.[5] The allure of fur is on the rise as well: while only 42 designers used fur in their collection in 1985, it was estimated that in 1997 more than 160 designers were using fur, ranging from the traditional haute-couture houses such as Dior, Yves St-Laurent and Fendi, to star designers and the hipster kings of fashion design such as Isaac Mizrahi, Jean Paul Gaultier, and Galliano.[6]

But there are a few exceptions to these political and economic flurries. The Fendi house, led by the five Fendi sisters, never stopped designing fur collections, even at the peak of the cold shoulder era (Luksic 1986). For three generations (all directed by women), the Fendi sisters Alda, Franca, Paola, Anna, and Carla have been among the most important producers of fur fashion in Italy and Europe, having established an empire of skins and furs around the world (according to conservative figures, Fendi has over 300 sales points in the entire world and 2,000 employees at its Tuscany factories). Every year Fendi brings its collections – eternally designed by Karl Lagerfeld – devoutly to the catwalk – cold or hot. Fendi is the famous name that wrapped Gudrun Langrebe in furs in Liliana Cavani's *The Berlin Affair* (1985), and more recently Madonna/Evita Peron's skin in *Evita* – a notorious "F" for fur, as opponents of fashion and fascism would say, as both films chronicled two major fascist moments in history.

Vivienne Westwood is another who stood by her pelts over the years – fake and real – a provocation in the context of the well-organized and efficient English anti-fur movement (Mulvagh 1998). Westwood's renowned taste for fake fur trims and extravagant puffy garments, though often self-parodic have been typical of the diva's punk edge that defies categories, especially political correctness and artistic moralism. While Westwood's eccentric furs read affront and waste all over, and accentuate the distance between fur and skin, most designers embrace a nature-friendly approach to fur fashion, making ecological awareness a question of bodily fitness. Accordingly, fur is not a garment anymore, fur is skin. In this sense, the early 1990s, though dreadful for the fur business and fur economy, witnessed the burgeoning of a new ethics of fur in which women designers and female entrepreneurs have brought the very act of touching fur closer to the borders of the skin. In Canada, the renaissance market has been marked by Véronique Miljkovitch, Angela Buccaro, Paula Lishman, Mariouche Gagné and Wendi Ricci who "with their modern style, add the plus-value of fur, and really contribute to the distinction of Canadian products from what is produced at less cost by China, Russia, Greece, Hong-Kong and Taiwan."[7] Paradoxically, this national "emergence" has been only possible through a transnational circulation of labor and resources. Many of the new kids of fur industry went to Europe to train with Saga, the star Danish producer and European leader of fur design and retail, to "specialize" in fur design and to encounter European species pelts, in order to cheer up the image of the poor little beaver.

Like a busy Canadian beaver, the next generation of female designers is contributing to the reinvention of the mobility of fur as a powerful device for the production and promotion of a fur geography, that redefines the contours of the sexual economy of the nation. What is striking about the pseudo-fur renaissance has less to do with the culture of the obvious, i.e., the increasing visibility of fur in fashion magazines and retail store windows, than with the erasure of the difference between skin and fur. In other words, the new economy of the beaver is entangled in discourses of the female body as a complex site revealing the specifics of capital, commerce, culture and national enterprise, as it emerges within this new market of skins. The contemporary fur trade is about women in furs, both as commodities and producers, in all sectors of activity. White or native, women designers, trappers, and spokespersons shine as the new stars of the business. This growing positioning of women as agents marks a significant shift within the institution, organization and commercialization of a fur trade dominated and controlled by white men for centuries.

In the 1990s beaver tales, women are literally (re)presented as the angels of the nation and commerce. The 1998 FCC campaign "You'll feel comfortable in fur," consisting of a series of three print ads featuring a designer, a fur trapper and a fur farmer encompasses this mixture of *art de faire, art de vivre* and the everyday quality as the true nature and value of fur.[8] With headings such as "For me, fur has always been a natural choice" (Wendi Ricci), "We were eco-friendly way before our time" and "I'm your eyes and ears on the land," the campaign enlists a gleaming feeling of national belonging. It accords firmly with the power of the legitimacy of the real (i.e. Canadian) skinners over the tourists and dilettantes (i.e. the European and American) represented by the stars of the anti-fur movements. The real stars of the fur trade are those who are actually close to fur, who have fur tattooed on their skin, unlike the glamour stars of People for the Ethical Treatment of Animals (PETA) who are estranged from the business and who display their skin as a professional gesture, a performance, instead of an "*art de faire*" (arts of doing) and "*art de vivre*" (arts of living).

Against the sensational tableaux vivants of famous flesh and skin signed by PETA in their shaming campaigns, the fur industry replies with the creation of a reshaped beaver tale: each of the 85,000 Canadians who makes fur their livelihood.[9] Ricci's advertisement, for one, embraces the various levels of articulation involved in the construction of women's agency in relation to the trade: motherhood, entrepreneurship and conservation. "Meet Wendi Ricci, a mother of two who's been in the fur trade for more than 20 years," reads the first line of the ad. Intermingling the demands of the fashion market with concern for ecological renewal, the ad carefully presents Ricci – or "Wendi" – as a sensitive and responsible caretaker. "Fur also offers many ecological benefits. As Wendi says 'a well made fur garment will last for years and if you ever feel the need for a change, no problem: take it apart and re-style it.'" The "feel comfortable" campaign thereby fleshes out crucial elements of the next fur generation discourse: the articulation between preservation and national care. Clearly, at the same time that the transnational character of the fur trade is valued, its national/local/domestic nature is reinforced.

With a sense of historical irony, the pride campaign tells us that the beaver stands again as the champion of the nation, but this time as the best expression of female and native national enterprise in relation to design and trading. The discourse put forward here flinches at the various intimacies at work between skin and fur, between female skin and animal skins. This gendered, sexualized, and anthropomorphic management of the colonial heritage find its most sophisticated expression in the transformation of the materiality of the beaver as fur and pelts into beaver as a natural fabric. As fashion designer and producer Paula Lishman, one of the leaders of fur renaissance, explains, "it [fur] is the ultimate natural fibre."[10] The naturalness of fur here becomes central to the marketing and cultural circulation of the trade. Interestingly enough, the naturalness plays the double function of acknowledging the cultural specificities of both native and white women at the same time that this naturalness mediates a traditional industry and a modern conception of fur collections.

In this sense, I want to reformulate what I suggested earlier in this book in the following terms: that despite the zillions of ways of transforming beaver fur, the basic argument for the fur renaissance is that fur is the quintessential ecological fibre. Fur is what fits and defines female skin best as the fabric of the nation. If according to Buck-Morss: "In fashion, the phantasmagoria of commodities presses closest to the skin" (Buck-Morss 1989: 97), the skin and fashion geographies here are entrenched in a complex articulation of popular references, from culturally paradigmatic representations of sexuality to national identity traditionalism. In other words, the materiality of beaver is not limited to the contours of the body, but finds an extremely challenging expression in what I have been referring to as the sexual economy of the fur. It is the natural-ness of the fiber, human and animal, that reaches the epitome of the sexual economy of fur, and it is remarkably captured by the new strategies of producing and representing fur on the skin(s) market.

The next fur generation "wave" has learned a great deal from the anti-fur movement. Most of the anti-fur rhetoric stems from polemics around female bodies and babies and reproductive sexuality in the eco-politics survival of the land. The "nature" of female agency in relation to fur is presented as exclusively encompassed by the anti-fur position, and women's participation in the fur economy is mapped by the natural bounds between female bodies and babies. This is exactly what fed Brigittte Bardot's "save the baby seals campaign" in 1977 and 1995: the articulation between nationhood, motherhood and the survival of the species (see chapter 5). The means by which the anti-fur movement built on women, stars, activists and sponsors to stop the killing of animals finds some echo in the actual configuration and representation of the new fur fashion scene. Moreover, in the new fur trade the words "pro" and "anti" no longer exist: what dominates is a cultural and economic rationale that situates women and native communities as the backbone of a traditional, yet renewed, hip and creative industry. In other words, in response to the public shaming and gore tactics employed by anti-fur groups to discredit women wearing fur, the new fur trade stresses pride in its association of women and fur. Proud entrepreneurs, proud designers, proud trappers all stand for the proud nation. The public mediations of the beaver become the ultimate gesture of national embodiment for the next generation.

Accused of producing and making capital out of an economy of death, the fur trade has developed tremendous strategies to give a human, i.e., female, face to the business. To the crying baby seals and suffering animals of the sensational anti-fur lobby, the next generation offers images of women involved in the various stages of the business, giving voice to the traders, designers, trappers, etc. The "Canadianness" and domestic quality of fur ladies, para-doxically represented as "transethnic" and "transclass" are strategically used and remain central to this next fur image opposing the "international" and anti-national references of anti-fur advocacy groups such as PETA, IFAW and the Brigitte Bardot Foundation. If anthropomorphism was a key tactic of anti-fur groups, here, on the contrary, the humans are humanized, with names, a face, a culture of their own and no longer just a corporate logo. The industry continually introduces its new stars, its everyday stars, the ones who by their labor contribute to the national economy, building a significant portrait gallery of fur ladies.

In other words, the strategy behind this humanizing campaign that really kicked off in 1994 has been less to sell fur[11] than to sell names and faces to clearly thwart the image of fur as an economy of death.[12] The idea was to personalize, individualize, humanize the purchase of fur. If you buy a Paula Lishman, you buy not only a wacky, crazy, original fur knitted garment, but you also support a woman who, throughout her career, has styled herself as a nature lover, a dedicated mother, a responsible creator, but also a fierce female entrepreneur. Conservative and liberal values intertwine in this new portrait of the fur lady. The same is true for Zuki Balaila and his wife Betty, who run the hottest international fur fashion company in Canada: Zuki Furs. One of the most popular fur designers on the American market, the Jewish designer is well known for his extravagant cuts and designs of beaver furs.[13] Consumers do not simply acquire a beaver coat with traditional aboriginal patterns, they get a "Zuki," a team-creation, an imprint, a recognizable figure. Ditto with Véronique Miljkovitch and Mariouche Gagné (Harricana). Queens of recycled furs, both young designers incorporate aboriginal influences into their work to stress the natural, ecological association of fur – and the tradition of aboriginal women's transformation of pelts into fur clothes and accessories. In other words, behind each fur design there is a face, a profile, a beaver tale, a story where women act as narrators.

In this way, the new marketing strategies put forward by the designers and agencies have created a totally different scope to the relationship between women and fur. Against the bimbo image of female consumers so predominant in many anti-fur activities and fictional accounts, the modern fur trade constructs narratives within which women are the agents of the fur nation. Tales of the fur trade are now filled with portraits of young women, designers and fur makers, whose sheer commitment to the land and to national economic survival is to wear fur and to "make fur." Each tale is built to educate the consumers that the era of petroleum fur has been more damaging to the environment than the "recycling" of beaver fur. The sensationalism that has marked the public commandos of anti-fur advocacy are countered here by the rational and responsible discourses of female entrepreneurs for whom the recyclable quality of fur says it all for the sake of the nation. The rhetoric is that nothing beats natural fiber, and fur is the ultimate natural, ecological fabric. To put it bluntly: the next fur generation is about the redefinition of the authentic as traditionally tied to women in furs, doing furs, literally being furs.

Indeed, these dramatic changes in the representation and manufacturing of fur and, to an extent, fur ladies, have totally recast the production of Canadian fur culture. The entire trade – both corporate and independent – benefits from the next fur generation's ways of taming the beaver. While the comeback of fur delights the old-timers of the retail business such as Holt Renfrew, Ogilvy and The Bay,[14] it also means new retail possibilities for companies and shops that emerged from the trend of the 1980s ecological economy. For instance in Montréal, C.A.L.I.C.O., the pioneer of chic recycling/natural fiber promoting earth consciousness as a smart buy was the first to carry Harricana's recycled fur accessories (Gagné's fashion line) displaying bags, mittens and belts next to hemp and linen garments. Targeting mostly hipsters and youngsters sensitive to environmentalist/nationalist concerns,[15] C.A.L.I.C.O. reached a niche market of sophisticated consumers who would not normally buy their fur accessories at any of the local landmarks of the glorious years of colonialism in furs, such as Holt Renfrew and The Bay, but who would not have any ethical problems getting their fur patch at environmental retail outlets, if not vintage stores.[16]

Actually, the place of recycling and vintage economy in the fur continuum cannot be neglected on many fronts. Recycled fur is often assumed to be a new post-fur animal rights activist strategy of economic survival and ecological awareness. However, historically recycling has been a common technique in the fabrication of fur garments, a technique where class, race and economic markers operate quite strongly. For instance, at the peak of the beaver trade across North America and the trendiness of beaver hats in Europe in the seventeenth and eighteenth centuries, the beaver pelts that had the most value were those first worn by Aboriginal peoples – and later by Black-African slaves. The sweat and grease mixture produced by the intimate contact, the touch between the native and skin and animal fur (the hair was worn inside) pre-treated the beaver pelts for the chemical processes involved in the fabrication of beaver hats, adding value to the primary resources. Worn as a second skin by native and african people, the beaver pelts were then traded, transformed, and transfigured into a new "fur-skin" this time designed for a white colonial market.

In a more contemporary context, two strategies of recycled fur management coexist: the commercial strategy, à la Mariouche Gagné, in which old-new items are created; and the vintage strategy, a market of "as is," alterations, and creations that constitute a significant portion of the fur sales realized on the fringe circuit. Led for years by Marjolaine Thibault, the vintage economy in Montréal is a significant factor in the fur renaissance, and I argue that the recycled retail business and the fur vintage and recycling trade, in appearance parallel economies can be analyzed as a necessary economic continuum of the commercial fur fashion scene. While people get fur-with-style downtown in the fur district, they are more likely to get a touch of fur on the Mont-Royal vintage road, whether real or fake. This is important in terms of what I earlier hinted at in this chapter: that in a context of resistance to fur, it is crucial to maintain the cultural visibility and momentum of the idea of fur, even if it means parodying it or totally blurring the boundaries between mock and real. In this context, as a form of "micro-economies" (McRobbie 1998), the vintage and recycling trade have been key agents of preservation of fur, playfully creating beasty patterns (the vintage trail of 1996–7) or disembodying fur to offer accessories as a fur lady imprint. Over the past four years for instance, faithful to the blurring of value between fake and real fur, the vintage patch displayed fur items real and fake on an equal footing, very often displacing the highest value to the fake fur items. By treating real and fake as belonging to the same cultural referent, the vintages stores clarified that the item for sale was the idea, the concept, the cultural fabric of fur, not fur itself. The economic discrepancies between fake and real fur can be explained by the excess of real fur versus the acquisition of fake fur fabric. In order to sell fake fur, most of the subcontracted designers had to buy new fabric, which contributed to the inflation of fake fur prices, contrary to the amazing stock of real fur available in thrift stores, church sales, garage sales and estate sales, all privileged stock rooms for vintage designers.

In her article "Second-hand dresses and the rag market," Angela McRobbie (1989) insists on the crucial roles played by subcultural entrepreneurs in the development of what is considered a marginal, but still integrated economy: vintage culture, to which I would add the recycling business. McRobbie ends her analysis by calling attention to the importance of subcultural entrepreneurship in the development of London vintage culture (McRobbie 1989: 23–49). Picking up where McRobbie left off in her article, I wish to pause here and consider how this new wave of fur fashion economy in Montréal – which includes second-hand and first-hand recycled products – is among the best wardens of the nation. This trade and its gallery of national Venuses (entrepreneurs and models) is seen not only as a site of reconceptualizing traditional ways of producing fur ladies; it also constitutes a powerful site of colonial continuum.[17] This is why in this specific context I am critical of invoking the notion of the subcultural entrepreneur to describe the commercial practices of women designers in the fur trade. Instead, I suggest describing them as a hyphenated sexual economy of fur that confuses the traditional premises of feminine displays of racialized and sexualized Venuses, while proposing a production of fur ladies on the edge: not quite in, not quite out. Building on a sort of "residual economy" (Williams 1983) and hyphenated trading space, the next Fur Generation asserts the value of fur through the commodification of national identity, no matter whether fur is real or fake, natural or dyed, recycled or brand new.

Vintage stores are not only second-hand businesses, but constitute a true culture of enterprise, where the local, national and transnational circulation of style and goods are central to its functioning. Vintage and recycled fur are not to be taken as outside the fur trade but as necessary sites that allow the absorption and fulfillment of the excesses and inconsistencies of the more traditional fur business. Recycling and vintage economies could be framed around the following cultural markers: first as a mean of producing the commercialization and display of domestic management; and second as

175

the articulation of various representations of female agencies in relation to the nation and race. In such a fluctuating environment, the distinction between macro and micro becomes obsolete: the fur trade is actually constructed of multiple hyphenated economies.

One interesting way to think about the various localities of production and circulation of fur fashion and style is to analyze the exchange and circulation of social and economical strategies between them. For instance, the vintage and recycling businesses have played the same role as the anti-fur movement for the traditional fur trade: i.e., that the traditional trade has learned, and sometimes freely copied some of the specifics of the recycling/vintage cultures and marketing to rejuvenate its image, its production, as well as its collections. How else could one explain, for instance, that Mizrahi, after his celebration of faux fur in drag in 1993, used recycled real fur in his 1994 collection? What does it reveal about the multiple uses of a fabric by multiple designers and creators? And what does recycling as a process of domestic management tell us about the contribution of women to the politics of fur survival?

If some entrepreneurs such as Harricana (Mariouche Gagné)[18] have made recycling the central process of their fur design and collections, many designers have played the game of trimming old furs to make new skins. With various methods of dying, cutting and shaving the beaver – still the top seller in terms of numbers of pelts from the wild animal trapping supply in Canada – these new collections have embraced the ecological twist, while at once developing and increasing the areas of fur production on the national scale. In selling the articulation between recycled fur and women as a gesture of rational utilization of waste, the trade and the media recuperate the sensitive, motherly image of the caring businesswoman. Also, on the basis that fur is no longer reducible to one life, one shape, one form, but on the contrary is materialized as a commodity that challenges the concepts of value and waste under the skills of women's agency, the modern fur trade is promoted by agencies as well as by its own agents as an open field, a creative, opportunistic laboratory for women who care for the local and national economy. Paradoxically, in a still male dominated field, the next Fur Generation of female entrepreneurs are heavily dependent of the subsidies of various national and local bodies.[19] At first a completely marginalized and local phenomenon, the vintage patch is now billed as one of the main tourist attractions of the city for hipster tourism. Concentrated mostly on the Plateau (Mont-Royal, Rachel and St-Denis, and St-Laurent), the trend for vintage and fringes really kicked off with Scarlett O'Hara, the first store to not only offer "as is," but also to create a fashion trade for young designers. The development of the vintage business in Montréal was not a spontaneous gesture or a rebellious one, but was initiated by young graduate designers, notably from Lasalle College in Montréal, an Americanized and more commercial version of the Royal Academy of Art and Design.[20] At the crossroads of the twentieth and twenty-first centuries, as fur styles keep changing and the price of mink skyrockets, even the traditional fur trade is making between 30 and 40 percent of its gross income on recycled fur, i.e., coats that have been redesigned, recut, reshaped, dyed, remodeled, etc. If such practices of "recycled fur" were considered a national secret during the golden years of fur retail – mostly the 1950s and 1960s – this specificity of the business is now commercialized as an expression of ecological awareness. Major fur houses and retailers offer this second-life economy to their customers, and fur coats are regularly transformed as remodeled, restyled coats, or as accessories (mostly hats, gloves and belts).[21] Though not the main source of income for retailers, the recycled market has significantly contributed to the incomes of the traditional business.

In this sense, in terms of marketing strategies and the production of ecological economy, the fur renaissance owes its success to the fact that it draws its strengths from the simultaneity of identity politics impinging on hipster culture, capitalizing on the fact that the same consumers who would buy Harricana's recycled latest mouton pilot hat would not flinch from wearing Diesel jeans, the international Italian company known for having capitalized on highly trendy and graphic anti-fur campaigns.[22] This is the productive paradox of the next fur generation: absorbing the contradictions and aberrations of anti-fur discourses and ecological consciousness and making them human. Public shaming is marginal, even tired; individual pride is the new motto. The next generation has undertaken one of the most effective campaigns in the rehabilitation of national pride: fur as the pride fabric of the nation.

I can't believe it's beaver

"The Thrill is Back!" 1998 *Vogue*'s cover screamed, with Canadian supermodel Linda Evangelista draped in a blue fluffy mongolian lamb coat shining her beaver teeth to the camera. Fur flies again and for the past five years any magazine or newspaper with a flair for fur monies, has caught the mood. If it is true, as Angela McRobbie argues in her study on British fashion design, that "the market is heavily mediated by the fashion press" in the double articulation of being imaged and imagined (McRobbie 1998: 130), it is also true that over the past fifteen years fur was never erased from the national story. The recent so-called "comeback" of fur seems to be first a question of economics over media exposure, given that during the worst decade of fur fashion and the fur business, magazines made a point of covering every single fur patch still alive on the international fashion scene. This was all the more true of the most prestigious fashion magazines such as *Vogue*, *Elle*, *Women's Wear Daily* and *Harper's Bazaar*. The transnational circulation of fur advertising in these publications kept an open window for the hard-heads of fur design during the 1980s and early 1990s, documenting the last fur splash produced by the hair balls of Fendi, St-Laurent, Dior, Chanel, as well as Saga Furs in Scandinavia, to name a few.

In Québec and Canada, even during the cruel anti-fur decade of 1983–93, *Elle-Québec*, *Marie-Claire*, *Chatelaine*, and *Clin d'Oeil* stubbornly fur trimmed their glossy images with the latest fur collections, zealously tracking down hundreds of beaver trails, not missing a beat of the anti- and pro-fur rages that have shaken the fur country. In other words, fur never vanished from the national media scene: even at the peak of anti-fur activism, when women with a touch of mink were perceived as dreadful collaborators in the slaughterhouse economy, women in furs were still the pride of the oldest national industry. For instance, at the same time that local and national newspapers ran public awareness campaigns sponsored by anti-fur coalitions, fashion magazines were surfing on anti-fur discourses, defiantly offering the next lady in furs as the next exquisite delight for the holiday season. Ironically, right next to the nth version of the death of the Montréal fur patch (i.e., the fur district), could be found an ad by Alexandre Furs or Labelle Fourrures.[23]

In reviewing over twenty years of fashion magazine coverage for this research, the extent to which fur and its close embodiment to women has been vividly mediated is striking. Ultimately, the "quality" split between authentic and faux fur was not the question: the crucial strategy was to infiltrate the media-scape with hair references and iconography, whether fake, real, recycled, dead or alive. Magazines devoted special advertising sections to fake-fur collections ("Trop Belles pour être vraies," "Le Grand Frisson," "Vive la Fausse Fourrure," "Chic Synthétique"),[24] often followed by classic ads for real furs.[25] Suddenly, (female) consumers were asked to discover the flip side of the beaver business: the fake-fur industry was also a fur affair. While the 1980s and 1990s have seen the blooming of fake fur and teddy-bearish garments as high-fashion, historically, mock fur has commercially circulated since 1929 when it was introduced either as an economical alternative to the real thing, or as a practical, urban and "domestic" solution to natural fiber (Vincent-Ricard 1989).[26]

Until the 1980s anti-fur campaigns, synthetic fur was perceived by the industry and designers – and the consumers – as the poor woman's skin, the bastard beast, worse – the castrated image of the fur trade.[27] Reminiscent of the 1960s and *Barbarella*'s boudoir (R. Vadim, 1968), faux fur was a curious amalgam of teddy-bear market, psychedelic entourage, and fluffy hair culture. Yet at the peak of anti-fur shaming, some fur designers did not hesitate to discreetly insert mock fur in their collections.[28] Furred mirage of the motherly bond between fur and national space, synthetic furs continued to evoke the cold and snow that have made real fur a Canadian trademark. Paradoxically, while most of the advertising campaigns for fake fur are shot in natural settings, emphasizing the traditional romantic link between the cold and women in furs, others have dared to challenge this link between nature and reproduction, choosing to present a modern version of the fur lady from the snow: the urban fake fur flies with an attitude (Isaac Mizrahi). Campaigns were also designed to appeal to a fragmented market of women whose relationship to their bodies was more technologized, denaturalized than their fur lady ancestors, but who nevertheless represent a significant value to the trade.

As a premonition of the so-called fur renaissance of the 1990s, fake and real furs cohabited together in a kind of crazy mishmash, revealing the extent to which the fashion retail industry was struggling with a divided, fragile, dispersed and shifting market, traditionally associated with middle-aged white women.[29] It is also during those cursed years that, in light of the treatment of fur coats as a domestic good, fashion columns discussing the virtue of fur as an eternal fabric proliferated, and female consumers were given an array of advice on the preservation and storage of their furs. In other words, no matter how bad the conjuncture for fur sales was, the industry was busy developing strategies destined to keep the spirit of fur high on the consumer market.

In the meantime, the faux was simply not the real beaver. Snubbing the anti-fur trend in the fashion business, Anna Wintour, the PETA's hag-fur lady of *Vogue*, urged designers to bring back fur on the international catwalk. Wintour eclipsed her own fur-fan moment in her appearance in the fur celebration documentary *Unzipped* (D. Reeves, 1994), proudly strolling through New York wizard Isaac Mizrhari's fake fur cavern, savoring every second of her fur glam moment, while the designer frantically immersed himself in Hollywoodish, Nanookish fur glitter in preparation for his Fall 1993 collection. Even if the film has been described as the quintessential 1990s fake fur moment (Maslin 1995), Mizrahi's adoration for the true sense of fur inspired his colorful spin on the hairy petroleum fabric, hence the glittering presence of the all-time goddess of fur fashion. Mizrahi's splendid and outrageous anti-PC Nanook Look collection marked an important moment in the return of fur from fashion industry disgrace. With the unwanted help of Jean Paul Gaultier of France, who scooped Mizrahi with his Eskimo "Le Grand Voyage" true fur collection featured on the cover of *Women's Wear Daily* (*WWD*), Mizrahi and his pink fake/real garments would make fur hip again.[30]

As if it was not enough to play Mizrahi's godfairy/mother, Wintour, putting on her best Cruella drag, got her public revenge with the publication of her "Letter from the Editor" in the September 1997 edition of *Vogue*. Wintour triumphantly announced the resurrection of fur for the season

> Here's a prediction that some people won't like: Fur will be everywhere this Fall. Not just in coats of every style, shape, and length, but as lux accents on collars, cuffs, and linings. In fact, as I write (. . .), Steven Meisel is at an estate in New Jersey shooting supermodels swathed in fur in 100-degree heat.
>
> (Wintour 1997: 48)

Wintour's words were more than prediction: they actually marked one of the most frantic fur production blitzes of the decade. Conscious of the economic resonance of such a statement, The Fur Council of Canada, through Northern

179

Supreme, would include an eight-page full color fashion spread of eight prominent Canadian fur designers, among them the new guard of Miljkovitch, Lishman, Paytler and native designer d'Arcy Moses in the 1997 November edition of *Vogue*. In fact, it was only a matter of weeks for other editors, designers, supermodels and stars to follow the call, some sheepishly repentant – and money savvy – like Naomi Campbell, others saintly and committed to the cause, like Kim Basinger.[31] As a strategic yet tacky 1997 Jim Goff advertisement for a scarlet fur pant garment (for men and women) declares: "Fur Anytime, Fur Anyplace, Fur Anymore, Fur Anyone, Fur you . . ."[32]

Nevertheless, to welcome the beaver back home, the fashion and retail fur industry unsurprisingly has received its biggest support from government agencies (federal, provincial and municipal) – fur is a cultural industry after all. One need only look at how federal, provincial and local agencies have invested in various campaigns and programs in the past years to rebuild the fur economy around women and native communities to realize the extent to which the industry has responded to anti-fur strategies. The "revival" of the Fur Council of Canada in 1986 might have been seen as central to the revitalization of the fur trade following the post-1970s/1980s anti-fur backlash. As the most important fur agency in the country, The Fur Council of Canada has played a visible role in this "second nature" of the fur business. Since its creation the FCC, in concert with other agencies and various governemental bodies, has launched a series of public awareness campaigns (the "respect" campaigns), ranging from educational videos and games to fashion design contests, to the restoration of such fur fairs as NAFFEM, vital and central components of the dynamism of the industry.[33]

These promotional campaigns have coincided with a series of economic measures and policies "imagined" by the federal government to revitalize the symbols of Canadian federalism and its corporate history. So long absent from the contemporary history of the nation, the re-modeled darling of the catwalk, the fur lady, has once again at the dawn of the new millennium become the perfect symbol of national unity and economic strength. And if, according to Ministry of Heritage officials, fur still seems less politically profitable than fish in the popular telling of the origins of Canada – as amazingly illustrated in one of the CRB Foundation Heritage Project vignettes[34] – other agencies have made sure that fur will again become a flag for the nation.

Transforming from inside the claustrophobic motherly and colonialist rhetoric so prominent with Bardot for instance, the new fur economy discourse addresses the management of ecology and national waste as a proactive strategy of conservation. Pro-fur agencies such as the FCC have played on the themes of future of species, guardianships and protection – areas which were central to Bardot and her foundation – in reclaiming the multiple faces and racialized and gendered identities that have informed the fur trade as a purely Canadian phenomenon.[35] The allusions to colonial heritage and postcolonial struggles have vanished or are screened discreetly: what dominates is a strong sense of panCanadian/panfederal nationalism inspired by decades of a federal politics of multiculturalism. A "transethnic" representational map of the fur trade in which a nation struggles to promote and preserve the foundational fabric of the Canadian economy: fur, is welcolmed. Here, in this context of ecological economy, tradition and modernity mingle rather than appeasing their classic constructions. Collections inspired by traditional native influences have received a great deal of attention in the media, constituting not only a promotional vehicle for the fur renaissance, but also naturalizing the historical seizure between civilization and wilderness.

While for Bardot the question of colonialist authority has always constituted an obstacle in her Canadian campaigns, the representativeness of local people, local artisans, craftspeople and entrepreneurs of the fur trade has brought an incredible legitimacy to the next fur generation. To the public shaming attached to fur, the industry responded with the proud *Castor Canadensis*. With the next Fur Generation, the trade is no longer selling fur coats: it is selling the Pride of a Nation, a new beaver story with thousands of beautiful Cinderellas and Pocahontas made in Canada. In the context of a transnational economy, the FCC offers the image of a strong national and local product capable of crossing borders: a new generation of designers, savvy, creative, multilingual, who are committed to market the beaver under all forms and textures imaginable.

Moreover, considering that women have historically been at the forefront of pro-fur campaigns, one cannot help but notice the central role in this association of the added-value between female skin and fur for the recent fur resurgence on the market. As a reenactment of the tradition that has marked the golden years of the postwar fur industry, the many tender ties that stitch female skin and beaver fur are central to the next fur generation. As if, for all those years that the seal was the centerfold of pro- and anti-fur advocacy, the beaver was preparing its dashing entrance. And this despite having recently been disgraced by Queen Elizabeth II as a colonial relic – the Queen no longer buys fur coats, having converted to fake fur fashion, and only indulges in a touch of beaver when opening Parliament or to please people from Canada.[36] After having been in the shadow of other wild and farmed beasts of the trade, the wildest symbol of Canadian nationalism is getting the marquee as the champion and star of the new fur trade. Beaver power is certainly the hot trend of the Canadian fashion scene, and most designers have their beaver handy for the newest collections.

The new fur trade has also managed to design campaigns and fur garments to address an important shift in the contemporary market: now more than ever before women are the ones who buy and pay for their furs. If men still buy fur for their ladies – or themselves, as a recent increase in men's fur collections illustrates – the trade has changed significantly over the last two decades and is now considered a growing female market.[37] The classic image of Elizabeth Taylor in *Butterfield 8* (D. Mann, 1960) swooning to swap a piece of her flesh for a touch of mink is passé, the modern fur trade is targeting women's capital as the new niche market. This adjustment in the marketplace has to be analyzed in the context of the tactics developed by the fur trade to give a female and native face to the business. Against the rhetoric of the survival of the species that dominated the glamorous Brigitte Bardot seal campaign era, a new generation of Québec fur designers regenerates the links between skin, fur and the female body as the essence of the nation. By restoring the faded image of the Venus in furs as a responsible nature lover and fierce natural resource manager, the next generation not only recycles clichés of Canada as the world fur capital, but also repositions the relationship between women, sexuality and re-production in the formation of national identity.

If the pro-environmental discourse of the 1980s and 1990s changed the marketing tactics of the fur trade – notably in emphasizing the recycled value of fur and the value of recycled fur – the return of fur consolidates more than ever the collusion between nation and sexuality. In the rest of this chapter, I will focus on the story of three central tactics that have been developed by the Canadian fur industry to rejuvenate the moribund beaver: pride, creativity and natural fiber. These strategies have been used by the modern fur trade to link notions of survival, recycling and reshaping as the essential elements of the next fur generation.

Strategies for the fabric of a nation:
beaver weaver

A fruitful way to think through the "Fabric of a Nation" campaign launched by the Fur Council of Canada in the early 1990s is to link it to the "What Becomes a Legend Most?" Blackglama campaign introduced by the Seattle Fur Exchange group in 1968. As I briefly discussed in chapter 5, the American campaign was all about the glamour of fur and the sophisticated identity of women wearing mink, hence the electrifying roster of stars signed by the fur producer. The idea was to portray mink as "la fourrure du jour" and as the perfect star's second skin. Over a period of twenty-six years (1968–94), the "What Becomes a Legend Most?" campaign paraded the legends of Hollywood's most glorious years (mostly women), as well as the newcomers of the popular culture scene. One of the most efficient promotional devices suggested by the creator of the campaign was to conflate skin and fur into one single fabric, hence the name of the legend. As one of the creators explains:

> The major challenge was to create recognition for the fur itself. Blackgama . . . is not a designer but the producer of the pelts itself. The format was simple: a portrait with a few lines of copy . . . Because the ladies lived up to the sobriquet "legend," no captions revealed their names. The effect was immediate and powerful – a mere two years later, Blackglama was considered the most prestigious black ranch mink in the world. . . . Very few other luxury items – with the possible

exception of Keepsake Diamonds – enjoy this measure of recognition for their raw materials.

(Rogers 1979: 8)

The Blackglama discourse was permeated by a traditional representation of fur and women in which women were more "Venus in Furs" than agents of the fur economy. The audience for the advertisements was clearly made up of upper-class female or male consumers whose conception of femininity was rather classic, if not conservative, filled with romantic and blissful visions of women's sexual success measured at the length of a mink coat, a woman such as Doris Day in *That Touch of Mink* (D. Mann, 1962). In other words, Blackglama reinforced the unique quality of fur as a privileged fabric for privileged people (i.e. rich white women, or people with the right stuff to become a legend – hence the inclusion of a few black Blackglama girls in the campaign (Leontyne Price, Pearl Bailey, Diana Ross and Jessye Norman, and three Blackglama boys: Rudolph Nureyev, Luciano Pavarotti and Ray Charles).

Though labeled as a pure American product, Blackglama fur was all about the international jet-set wearing a mink coat, hence the association embodied in such so-called international stars as Greek goddess Melina Mercouri, French sex kitten Brigitte Bardot and Italian *venere* Sophia Loren. When BB signed as one of the six Blackglama girls for the 1970 season,[38] the campaign was entering its third year and was already enjoying a great deal of international popularity. The tantalizing and electrifying encounter between Bardot's skin and the mink-farmed pelt is immortalized with sensuality and boldness by photographer Richard Avedon. No need to mention that Bardot-in-furs cuts a priceless image for pro-fur advocates.

More appropriate to the Canadian wilderness, yet less classy than the elegant ranched mink Blackglama, the *Fur: the Fabric of a Nation* campaign stars the stocky, rough, wild, queer and hunky beaver. The *Fabric of a Nation*'s message is straightforward: fur is everywhere, get used to it. In addition, the campaign has been designed to hit anti-fur discourses from as many rhetorical and nationalist angles as possible (Figure 6.1). And its artisans have relied on a very efficient strategy: to articulate fur as a popular woman-made product par excellence in such a way that it totally reinvents the relationships with the racial, economic and sexual boundaries suggested by the anti-fur campaigns. To assure and consolidate both the traditional and more creative aspects of the trade, the FCC campaign establishes fur as a powerful emblem of domestic management of national resources where women are the key agents of preservation. Because it was women-made for women and family, fur reentered the popular space. In other words, for the FCC, fur is popular because it is a matter of fur ladies. Though still a symbol of social mobility for many, the strategy put forward by the FCC and its partners has been to bring back the national pride of fur, this time not as a luxury item, but as a concrete and definite gesture towards environmental and ecological consciousness.

Figure 6.1 Fur the Fabric of a Nation, Fur Council of Canada. Print courtesy of the Fur
Council of Canada.

By arguing that fur is popular, the fur trade is making a statement against a traditional representation of fur as a luxury product, an image clearly associated with the European and American market (i.e. Blackglama and Saga Scandinavia). The Fabric of Nation rhetoric is quite straightforward: fur is presented as a popular fabric of Canadian culture, and while not everybody can afford a $100,000 sable coat, for instance, everybody today can have a touch of fur. The "everyday" of fur is the idea, and this approach has completely challenged the usual assumptions about fur as an inaccessible, unaffordable good. One of the best examples is Paula Lishman's knit beaver fur garments, which have been sold and marketed as the ultimate tactile fiber experience. With sales peaking at $10 million a year, Paula Lishman International is today one of the most important producers and exporters of fur fabric in Canada. Lishman, who sees herself a textile artist, was the first to develop the unique technique of weaving and knitting beaver fur, bringing a sense of warmth, coziness, and domestic technology to fur. Using "full, dressed fur pelts, a natural resource," to create what she called a double-sided washable fur fabric, Lishman stands as a pioneer of a culture of fur trade where domestic concerns dominate the production and the marketing strategies. A long-time environmentalist yet an anti-fur target, Lishman, the Beaver Weaver,[39] carefully defends her furs as humane and "for life" (lasting a lifetime). On her Web site, Lishman, whose collection is labeled "A Touch of Fur," insists that "the mink and fox are ranch-raised in accordance with humane standards. The beaver and muskrat are harvested in the wild by trappers who choose to live on the land. Trapping in Canada is well regulated to ensure a healthy ratio of population to habitat."[40]

More than a simple textile, Lishman's craft popularizes the use and wearing of fur as an everyday practice accessible to the general public. As part of this "banalization" of the luxury of fur and the defetishization of the fur lady, the yarn,[41] once an exclusive Lishman product, is advertised and sold by the company's consumer department as a resource for do-it-yourself adventurers, artists and crafters of the ready-to-wear industry. The Web site offers a complete guide to the technical steps involved in the knitting, crocheting, and weaving of the fabric. In the spirit of recycling and domestic economy, the yarn can also be used as trim. In other words, the promotional approach centers on the facility, versatility and the saleability of the easy beaver (or mink, muskrat, or sable):

> All crafters, including knitters, weavers, rug hookers and sewers alike are in wonder of the simplicity of this novel, tactile fibre experience. Whether it be a beaded necklace with mink, a cashmere cape with a sheared beaver design on the hem, or a floor-length negligee trimmed in sable, a crochet hook or a darning needle can transform an ordinary garment into a one-of-a-kind creation. By simply adding the fur yarn with a zigzag couching technique on the sewing machine, or by weaving the yarn with a large needle through a knit, the possibilities are endless![42]

Lishman's tactile experience has to be framed within the context of fur production, where skin and fur fuse to create the sexual economy of the nation. Thanks to Lishman, now everyone can care for her/his beaver, wash it and groom it, from the safety of her/his home (Lishman's knitted accessories and sweaters are washable). More than a question of technique and marketing skill, I believe that Lishman's tactile moment fits perfectly into the spirit of the fur resurgence and renaissance where the fusion of skin and fur constitutes *le fil d'Ariane* of the new trade. And if Lishman is the Beaver Weaver of the industry, there are also many other designers – new and old – who have turned to the beaver as the easiest fabric of the fur renaissance.

Beaver skinners

This fusion between skin and fur has been vividly translated into and embodied by the exotic interest in native culture and native iconography, as well as its importance in the essentialist construction of the fur trade as the natural expression of the link between the female body and the land.

The Fur Council of Canada, too, was aware of the political importance of addressing the historic role of native communities, particularly native women in the development of the fur trade. Parallel to movements and interventions orchestrated by various aboriginal associations for the defence and promotion of the fur trade and fur trapping as a vital component of local economies, the FCC has capitalized on the growing interest by the commercial trade for native authenticity and native heritage in the conception and marketing of Canadian fur design. For instance, in 1991 the FCC made a coup in signing d'Arcy Moses as the beaver designer of the new generation. Moses, renowned for his beaver patterns and colorful designs, represented the perfect image that the trade wanted to sell: that of a business capable of mixing tradition and modernity, a business made up of cultural differences in which the aboriginal *art de faire* was seen as a key factor in a business still dominated by white capital. Four years later, the corporate agency hit again, this time choosing to capitalize on the memory, tradition and identity of native culture, in which women are the makers of the garments. Under its sponsorship, the native Design Co-op in Toronto was invited to the International Fur Fair Trade Exhibition in Montréal (NAFFEM) in 1995. Six female native designers, Nazanni Bell, Stephania Bitti, Rhonda Dickemous, Eunice Kennedy, Angela de Montigny and Suzanne Smoke were supplied with free furs by the Majestic Fur Association and the Wildfur Council (i.e., Fur Council of Canada) to design collections using fur.

The event received significant media attention, and *The Montréal Gazette* gave the designers the top story of their Style section, with color photographs and a titillating title that says it all: "Fur on The Fringe: Native Indian [sic!] Designers are expressing their heritage through the use of fur" (Monahan 1995). The front page of the report shows two of the members of the co-op modeling their creations: Angela de Montigny in a deerskin jacket with muskrat yoke, and Stephania Bitti in a cape of twelve fox tails. The report can be read as a means of interrogating the crossings of positionalities that native female agency signifies in this context of circulating native memory, nation and sexuality. It shows how the construction of native heritage is entangled in a representation of native women as a national fabric: all the facets of skin and fur converge to "create" the perfect fur lady. The reappropriation by native women fur designers of their traditions – healthy trapping, ecological awareness, chemical-free methods of tanning – are in tune with the interests of the fur business and the FCC. More specifically, these collections offer a strong sense of cultural and national belonging. This happens to have even more cultural and political capital, given that the historical relation between native women and fur/nature has been recently at the forefront of a style where "ecological awareness" and recycled value are the ticket to the new marketing of the fur ladies.

The trend of initiatives deployed to capture the native moment range from the colonialist and taxidermist touch so prominent in commercial international fashion design à la Gaultier, and to a certain extent Mizrahi, to tactics of mediation of national authenticities by white designers (Buccaro and Miljkovitch), to popular reappropriation of cultural differences by native designers such as Reggie Largo,[43] to the staging of events such as *Sanajavut: Our Creations*, at the Museum of Civilization in Hull, Québec in 1996, featuring the works of seven Inuit women designers.[44] Though specific and distinct in their address to a fragmented market, these style and clothing practices or interventions are similar in the ways that they each according to their own position respond to political imperatives in which the nation is spectacularized and the historic body is sensationalized. Rather than seeing them as competing economic and cultural markers on the market of skin and fur tales, I want to disarticulate the discursive and cultural boundaries that all these practices seek to embrace.

I argue that these practices or events, rather than simply offering straightforward representations and reenactments of commercial racism or cultural subalternity, simultaneously produce a mixed-media portrait of fur ladies that challenges unproblematized relations between female agency and the construction of identity around race, sexuality and class. In fact, these images/portraits of fur ladies produced through a national and transnational market stand as sexualized performances that interrogate the tradition and the modernity of associating women and fur. The positionalities of the fur ladies in both cases generates a troubled relation to the monumentalization of history and the colonial legacy as at once informed by modes of representation and self-representation of the beaver as the quintessential fur lady representation.

Two recent beaver fur tales provide a critical way to interrogate the production of the trans/national from a contradictory interplay of identities, sexualities, economies and performances. Mizrahi's irreverent *Nanook Look* collection and Lori Blondeau's hilarious "The Lonely Surfer Squaw" Web-babe family portraits provide critical tools for understanding and questioning how transnational formations – here defined around the ties between women and fur – can be inhabited by memories of national tales and colonial visions. Both "artist/ performers" used self-representational processes to unfix the interactions between economies, cultures and politics in popular discourses around/on fur.

Douglas Keeve's 1995 documentary *Unzipped* follows American fashion wizard Isaac Mizrahi during the months preceding the presentation of his new Fall/Winter 1994 collection. For ninety-one minutes, the witty designer conveys the spectator to his temple of creativity, sharing his not so secretive longings for popular culture icons, his love for his mom, and his satirical imaginary to imagine fur all over. Mizrahi's frenzy about his new *Nanook Look* collection is contagious: it will be fur from head to toe, fake and real fabric sharing the highlights in one single embrace. Mizrahi's *Nanook Look* speaks to a colonial and romantic representation of fur as the ultimate "primitive" fabric, and of fur ladies as the classic, yet most critical embodiment of the artifice of fur. The film opens with a landmark of ready-to-fur: Flaherty's *Nanook of the North*, which is introduced by the designer as the quintessential beauty of the fur market. Mizrahi's creative process, far from being led by authenticity, quickly becomes a tapestry of cultural and sexual references in which his fandom for Mary Tyler Moore, his mother and Nanook all cohabit. The puffy-fluffy Mizrahi collection carries a racialized and sexualized ready-to-wear edge entangled in popular interpretations of "Eskimo" subaltern identity, juxtaposed with his own identity as a gay Jewish bear boy who dreams of Mary Tyler Moore – who happens to be a fierce anti-fur figure.[45] The constant movement between sexuality and race in the movie creates important discursive and representational ruptures. For Mizrahi, the Eskimos of Flaherty's *Nanook* are not simply an ethnographic delight, but a sensual interpretation of the encounter between fur and skin, and this encounter is necessarily nationalized and sexualized through the intimate contact between pelts and skin.

Mizrahi's collection travels between various articulations of fur culture and fur display, in which racial, sexual and class references are constantly challenged. For instance, "his" fur ladies belong to different historical, national and cultural contexts and his inspiration does not discriminate between the nineteenth century fake-fur coat at the Musée des arts, de la mode et du textile (Paris), Nanook's sealskins, Loretta Young's frozen image in the *Call of the Wild* (W. Wellman, 1935), Eartha Kitt's exotic fur reverie, Canadian-born top model Shalom's little linguistic lesson on the ties between fish and Inuit, and his white poodle. These fur travels literally transform static representations of women and fur into a matter of movement between the real and the faux, between the wild and the urban. Mizrahi constantly reasserts his belief that skin and fur are seamless, that beneath the fur there is the skin and the skin is only a premature fur. The fur collection becomes then an evanescent, quasi bodiless moment: textures, skin fabrics of all kind dominate both the aesthetics and materiality of his eccentric collection. However, unlike Gaultier's creation of *Eskimo Chic*, which betrays a quest for authenticity and pastiche eloquently captured on the *WWD* cover showing a model fixed in a virginal, plastic Eskimo girl pose, Mizrahi's fur ladies have a definitively troubled relationship to identity, sexuality and nationhood. What transfigures fur for Mizrahi is its iconographic raw material tie to the snow land. In the world according to Mizrahi's furry visions, fur exists only because it is translated through his Hollywoodish and Americanized version of the "out there", the land of furs. Women died elegantly in the snow, faded sexual icons wrapped in furs; the real is captured in the mummified *Nanook*; and the present is a pastiche where skin and fur generates a troublesome moment where sexuality is actually seen on stage, on the catwalk, between the backdrops, beneath the camera lenses.

Hence, the emphasis in Mizrahi's collection is not on the nature or status of fur, but rather on the transformation of the fabric into a tactile and sexual experience. The reinterpretation of the relations between fur and women is one of sexual economy that might emerge as a masquerade (for his models) of a drag performance (for himself). In this sense, more than just a gesture of the clash of cultural difference, Mizrahi's provocative way of indulging himself in fur bliss is all about artifice: the artifice of race – as revealed through tourist imagery and ethnography taxidermy – the artifice of the authenticity of the fur lady as symbolized either by Hollywood culture or by anti-fur imagery (which explain his craze and fascination for playing with the real and the faux). Mizrahi's fur ladies are located in the transnational movement of the fur trade, where soundbites of racial cliches and sexual artifacts add to the value of the product. Unlike Julia Emberley (1998), who analyzes Mizrahi's fake/real-fur extravaganza as a site of sexual wildness,[46] what I find compelling about Mizrahi's knitting of fur, sexuality and race are the ways that he reasserts the power of the encounter between skin and fur as the sensual, sexual economy of fur performance. For Mizrahi, fur is by essence queer, and the encounter between fur and female skin more so. The challenge of Mizrahi's collection is less about the confusion between animality and humanity – and the politics of cultural "differences" – than about the designer's ability to *expause* in Derridian terms (Derrida 2000), i.e., to skin off over and over the sexual and economic intimacies of the trade, and that also means posing literally as a Prince, as a fur merchant and trader who uncovers the double-skin of fur in which women are wrapped.

The final scene of the documentary *Unzipped*, "Mizrahi – The Show," reveals the full dimensions of what I have been arguing throughout this book: that without skin, there is no fur. For his fur show, the high point of the documentary, Mizrahi sets a screen, a gauze backdrop that acts as the model's closet and changing room. Between the various tableaux, the audience attending the show can see the models changing on stage behind the screen in a mish mash of skin and fur. The *mise en scène* is stunning and the contrast between the catwalk and the backdrop disturbing: for each fur lady who parades on the catwalk there are a dozen behind the screen skinning their fur. Suddenly the tactile quality of fur is revealed in this naked image: that of female skin. The artifice of the furs – dyed, sheared, cut, miscut, fake, real – is doubly emphasized vis-à-vis

the naked display of white and black skin, along with the silky screen that
ostensibly filters the model's skin. When Naomi Campbell, Cindy Crawford
or Linda Evangelista hits the catwalk wrapped in pink, blue or beige fur fussy
things, there is zero degree of separation between the fur garment and the
model: it is all about fur ladies, the distinction between skin and fur becomes
absolutely obsolete.

While in Mizrahi's collection identity and sexuality are about the
transformative movement between the fake and the real as informed by popular
references between/on women in furs, Lori Blondeau's *The Lonely Surfer Squaw*
internet *tableaux vivants* navigate the relation between identity and sexuality
as foremost a matter of intermediation between tradition and modernity.
Photographed by Bradlee Larocque, Blondeau's twelve Web card Squaw series
is driven by disruptive ways of conceptualizing the relation between
authenticity, memory and the sexualization of the nation space. While located
and positioned in a different technological culture/space/setting than the fashion show, i.e., the Web, Blondeau's Surfer, Betty Daybird, ironically stands
as a quasi-classic pin-up, a barbiesque version of the native babe. Posing for an
internet "audience," the portraits show Blondeau at the beach flaunting a fur
bikini and fur boots, ready to entertain herself with beach toys and beach games
(Figure 6.2). Created in May 1997, the series of twelve vignettes, part of the
collaborative project Cosmosquaw, plays on variations of the 1950s pin-up:
whether hugging a pink surfboard or running to the water, Blondeau/Betty
Daybird poses for the surfer gaze, "taking idealized images of women in popular
culture and putting herself into the picture."[47] "Born from a life-long dream
of surfing the warm waves of the Pacific Ocean,"[48] Betty offers a romantic and
fantastic counter-vision of the white pin-up and the white fur lady.

What does Blondeau's Surfer Squaw bring to the debate about the modern
fur trade and its inclusive strategies of addressing native women's agency as
part of fur culture? Part of the response lies in the sensitive way that Blondeau
playfully captures the articulations between identity and nation through the
reappropriation of a western imagery of the racialized, exotic, "other" pin-up
as the fur lady. A Saskatoon-based aboriginal performance/theater artist,
Blondeau is not a fashion designer, but her spooky self-portrait as the ultimate
fur lady, *The Lonely Surfer Squaw*,[49] stands as a participatory performance that
addresses the legitimizing agency of native women in relation to popular and
spectacular designations of female bodies and fur. This translates most notably
into a revaluation of what constitutes national dress for native women.

Blondeau's *Lonely Surfer Squaw* disrupted the fixity of the postcard in the way
that she marks herself as part of a sexual icon, an amalgam of pelts and skin,
in which native women's traditional national dress is redesigned through
a reappropriation of the artifacts of the market of skin and Western tourist
imagery. Through this representation, in which the *Sports Illustrated* bikini
babe meets the traditional fur crafter[50] – native women being the ones
who traditionally design garments – Blondeau suggests a provocative way of

Figure 6.2 "The Lonely Surfer Squaw," artist Lori Blondeau. Credits: Bradlee Larocque, print courtesy of the artist.

remembering the commercial, popular, economic and identity markers that inform the troubled relationship between female skin and fur. Blondeau's self-portraits speak to commercial and sensational representations of women in furs as they regularly appear in fashion magazines or international fashion events. This finds a peculiar echo as the bikini Venus in fur is a long time classic of the othering of sexuality and the sensational in white culture, from Bardot as the Leopard Goddess in *Boulevard du Rhum/Rum Runner* (Robert Enrico, 1971) to the heroine of the 1963 pulp fiction *Devils Dance in Me*, to June Sauer's 1970s portrait of a lady in white rabbit fur.[51]

In a more contemporary version and as part of this native fur fair culture, the fancy dress ball reenactment of the Exotic Aboriginal in the fashion industry reappears regularly in the collections of the most important fur retailers and fur producers. Véronique Miljkovitch's *Ethnic Light* collection, for instance, created for and sponsored by Saga Furs of Scandinavia in 1994, directly recycled and refashioned the visual concept of native dress as national dress. Made out of Pearl SAGA mink, *Ethnic Light* is introduced to the market by the furrier as a "unique, visual concept of native dress by Véronique Miljkovitch. Her design reflects the soft, loose construction of the indigenous tradition."[52] As Melissa Sones puts it: "Miljkovitch specializes in furs with a primitive edge. Think Nanook of the North meets the sleek ski crowd" (Sones 1998: 52). And considering the ways that Galliano's Dior and Alexander McQueen's 1998 Givenchy collections launched a Pocahontas extravaganza (Blanchard 1998), the association between style, race and the skin market is a prolific trademark.

In this sense, Blondeau's *Lonely Surfer Squaw* playfully challenges the ethnographic gaze on the Inuit woman constructed for centuries by the obsessive white Western fascination for a Nanook wilderness aesthetics. Moreover, by posing in a bikini/boot ensemble, Blondeau winks at the contemporary commercial and fashion representation of exotic fur sex delights continually offered by popular magazines, as the *Wallpaper* November/December 1998 cover featuring Adam and Eve wearing Fendi fur muff, hat, mittens and boots splendidly remind us. There is nothing romanticized or authentic in Blondeau's surfer, but she is definitely sexy: wearing a fur bikini as a close-fitting second skin, she troubles a nostalgic colonial imagery of native women full dressed in furs. The fur bikini acts as a white imprint on the native surfer's skin, as an archive in process in which fur translates as the trading value of the surfer squaw. On the same level that Mizrahi's Nanook fur ladies and Lishman's beaver-lady weavers intersect with popularized forms of cultural production, Blondeau's *Lonely Surfer Squaw* accounts for the articulation between the native body/ sexuality and fur. The fact that Blondeau is not immortalized at the Museum of Civilization, on a coatrack in a so-called national costume, but on a popular ephemeral Web site, also functions as a critical way of representing female subjectivities and histories outside/inside the traditional national culture. Here, the bikini fur lady, in a reference to *My Fur Lady*, comes to mediate the nation through her native skin, thereby making a distinctive contribution to her revised transracial beaver economy.

On an other scheme, what *The Lonely Surfer Squaw* reminds us is that the division of labor within the various levels of the modern trade is tightly structured around the crossings between gender and race. Hair/fur is still the fabric of the nation, and women are tightly stitching a tradition of white economy. For instance, Gagné prides herself on using buttons and other "little things" (sic!) made by native peoples in her creation. In other words, Gagné, like Miljkovitch and Lishman, subcontracts native crafters to complete and polish their collections while keeping a close control of the flow of capital that comes from the sales and retails. In this sense, the native "touch" (or flair, to use a French expression) claimed by so many designers of the Next Generation is re/produced through a racialized and ethnicized fragmentation of the modalities of fabrication. The authenticity or the memory of tradition and identity is not carried by the motif, the pattern ON the fabric (see Gaultier and Lagerfeld for instance), but through the process of capitalizing on the cultural value of aboriginal *art de faire* as part of the recycling process so crucial in the works of designers such as Gagné, but also Lishman. Recycling becomes then a process of translating movements between cultures and genders, in addition of marking trading moment between the producer and the consumer. What is particularly challenging – and troubling – about the vintage and recycling business as translated by the fashion industry is the way that the traditional politics around women, fur and the nation are reshaped to address new concerns about economy and access to resources. The trading circuit also becomes part of the process of recycling itself, hence its extreme possibilities for the fur nation.

* * *

As an example of the way access is part of this hyphenated sexual economy, I do not think that it is a pure accident that during the winter of 1996–7, at the same time that fur was making a huge comeback in the windows of first-hand retailers such as of The Bay, and Holt Renfrew, Mont-Royal, the nest of the vintage scene in Montréal, was all dressed up in fur. On a *flâneur* stroll on Avenue Mont-Royal I captured some fascinating images of colonial sites revisited through fake, real and recycled fur. It came as no surprise that most of the vintage racks endorsed the same exchange value for real and fake fur. Ironically and to my great pleasure, women were the definitive queens of the fur extravaganza – as designers, entrepreneurs, consumers and models. The simultaneous all-star display of fur and fur ladies in both vintage and major retail stores shows that fur is not informed by a purely conjectural or romantic allure, rather, it is deeply embedded in the fashioning of identificatory formation where the nation is sexualized. In part, this rearticulation between identity, nation, gender and sexuality is informed by the popularization of the points of contact between fur and female skin. Popular in the sense of rechanneling fashion and style, popular as a way to interject economic practices through moments of domestic management and conservation, popular as a practice of access and mediation of the sexualized nation.

If the fur trade is designated as a communicational device for the history of Canada, allowing the settling of many fur posts and fur sites from coast to coast, the fur ladies are the communicational personas, the perfect mediating landscapes through which exchange and trade took place. Henceforth, the images of fur ladies moving throughout the fur territories is not only seductive, but troubling: the crossing of borders between skin and pelts, between the tactility of fur and the economic materiality of female bodies convey not only towards modalities of thinking fur through sexual economy, but also to considering the nation as a sensual fabrication.

NOTES

1 *MY FUR LADIES*

1 *The Softest Touch: What Every Woman Should Know about Fur*, produced by the Fur Information and Fashion Council, New York in the 1960s (p. 1).
2 My translation. "Suis-je complice d'assassinat en effleurant de mes doigts la douceur animale? Je n'éprouve aucun remords et je refuse de renoncer à ce frisson d'un corps que l'on enveloppe doucement dans la fourrure, à cette émotion d'un instant, lorsque la soirée s'achève sur les promesses de la nuit" (Konopnicki 1995: 9).
3 Despite the importance of the beaver to the history of Canada, and its long-standing public acceptance as a national symbol, it was only in 1975 that the beaver was formally adopted as Canada's official animal by Parliament (Bill C-373).
4 Beaver hats in vogue in the seventeenth and eighteenth centuries were made not of fur but felt. "The true beaver hat was made not from the glossy long-haired pelt but from the fine thick underhair, shaved and sheared from the skin" (Newman 1998: 41).
5 Innis explains: "Early French writers (that would be Samuel de Champlain, first governor of Québec City) agree that the colour variation is largely the result of climate and that the fur becomes darker in more northerly latitudes. North of the St. Lawrence the fur was regarded as being much better and the skin much thinner than in more southerly and warmer areas" (Innis 1956: 3). Actually this introductory chapter by Innis is one of the most graphic and descriptive accounts of beaver fur. Voyagers and colonizers showed a great deal of precision and enthusiasm in depicting the precious fur. Innis reports that Lahontan, among others, emphatically explains that "a beaver has two layers of hair; one is long and of a shining black color, with a grain as big as that of Man's Hair; the other is fine and smooth, and in Winter fifteen lines long. In a word, the last is the finest down in the world." L. A. Lahontan, *New Voyages to North-America*, Chicago, R.G. Thwaites, vol. 1, 1905; quoted in Innis 1956: 4.
6 *Canadian Fur Review*, 1950–51, vol. IV, p. 86. This event was actually the first full-fledged convention in the entire history of the fur industry to unite all the major furriers, exhibitors and manufacturers in Canada at the same time. Two fashion shows were put together under the supervision of Mrs. Kate Aitken, "unquestionably Canada's busiest woman" (p. 83). After being praised for her volunteer contributions to the convention, Mrs. Aitken was flatteringly described

as "Women's Editor of the *Montreal Standard* [one of the most important dailies in the 1950s] Women's Director of the Canadian National Exhibition, lecturer, author of cooking books, etiquette books, and a regular contributor on radio for two food companies" (p. 84).

7 During her career as a "chanteuse," Bardot recorded a song suggestively entitled "Mon Léopard et moi."

8 See for instance Lewis (1996); McClintock (1995); Solomon-Godeau (1996); Yuval-Davis (1997). I am not trying to diminish the incredible and insightful contribution of these texts, but rather to point out the peripheral dimension of the economy of the female subject in their approaches.

9 In addition to Van Kirk, many texts have addressed the politics of the interracial economy in critical terms and in the context of feminist studies in the 1980s and 1990s. However, in the spirit of the 1950s, I was able to track down a fair number of "journalistic" accounts produced by women for the HBC magazine *The Beaver*, always eager, even today to make room for ladies' travel narratives praising beaver culture. See for instance, A. L. Johnson, "Ambassadress of Peace," *The Beaver*, December 1952, pp. 42–5; and M. Wilkins Campbell, "Her Ladyship, My Squaw," *The Beaver*, September 1954, pp. 14–17.

10 For a succinct analysis of the impact of Les Filles du roy on the new colony's economy, see *L'histoire des femmes au Québec depuis quatre siècles* (1982) by Le Collectif Clio, especially chapter 2: "Heroïnes sans le savoir," pp. 60–3. It is still hard to estimate the numbers of women/girls sent but according to the authors from 1634 to 1673 1,034 "filles" [girls] were recruited by religious orders and the Cent Associés Companie to be sent to Nouvelle-France. Also, National Film Board filmmaker Anne Claire Poirier directed a dramatization of the story of those women and girls sent to Canada, *Les Filles du roy*, in 1975.

11 See also Spivak's response to some of the critiques and debates around her important argument in "Subaltern Talk: Interview with the Editors (1993–94)," Spivak (1998).

12 De Certeau has a nice way of explaining the two orders of representativity as "prendre la parole" and "prendre les affaires en main" (de Certeau 1968: 203). If Spivak's conclusion seems to lead towards a mute/speechless subaltern colonial female subject, her decision to call attention to the economic rationale and structure of the imperial/colonial order that eludes the subaltern female subject illustrates the contradictory if not tangential nature of subalternity. In fact, Spivak's controversial reading of sati calls attention to the fact that the subaltern woman's materiality is mediated by her self-representation. For Spivak, the subaltern female subject is speechless because she cannot be heard, which does not mean that she does not have a materiality. Hence, a position of enunciation is denied under very specific conditions of (non)existence, but it does not mean that the subjectivity of the widow – as subjected to the very "nature" of her body and value in the process – is not a reality.

13 "It is possible to locate (as we did in Anthias and Yuval-Davis 1989) five major (although not exclusive) ways in which women have tended to participate in ethnic and national processes, in relation to state practices. There are: [1] as biological reproducers of members of ethnic collectivities; [2] as reproducers of the boundaries of ethnic and national groups; [3] as participating centrally in the ideological reproduction of the collectivity and as transmitters of its culture; [4] as signifiers

of ethnic or national differences, as a focus and symbol in ideological discourses used in the construction, reproduction and transformation of ethnic and national categories; [5] as participants in national, economic, political and military struggles (1989: 7)" (Yuval-Davis and Anthias 1992: 115).

14 However, in a 10-minute interview with Mary Lou Finlay for *Take One* that aired on CBC Television in November 1975, Anahareo advocated for a more "humane trap as opposed to the traditional traps such as the leg-hold trap." As many are aware, this issue of humane trapping was extremely contentious and decisive in the European Economic Community's ban on fur from Canada in the 1970s and 1980s. This episode of *Take One* reveals the political climate in the 1970s regarding the use of sensational dramatizations by pro-animal groups as a public strategy of shaming and empathy. Intertwining images of fur fashion shows and scenes of animals agonizing mercilessly in different kinds of traps, the interview also provides a rare media glimpse at Anahareo as she talks about survival trapping and her new professional career as an agent of nature. Release/Diffusion: 1975–11–17. Ref: CAVA/AVCA: 1978–0316 (Canadian National Archive audio-visual collection).

15 In *Gendering Orientalism*, Lewis explains that her project addresses "the role of white European women as cultural agents, within an analysis of the constitutive role of culture in the formation of imperial relations" (Lewis 1996: 2). She goes on to say, "One of my arguments is that imperialism played a role in the very construction of professional creative opportunities for European women" (3). Without being as celebratory as Lewis concerning the creative opportunities offered by imperialism for women, her analysis necessarily addresses some of my struggles concerning the manifestations of women's involvement, commitment and activity under colonialism and even in nation-building strategies.

2 PRINCES, BEAR BOYS AND BEAVER MEN

1 In its 10 July 1999 edition, the daily *Ottawa Citizen* published "scientific" evidence that the Canadian beaver, for centuries marketed as a monogendered mammal, was a pseudo-hermaphrodite. See p. A1.

2 For this research, the material was eclectic, ranging from ethno-mystical narratives written by the Jesuits, to the sci-fi tales written by French novelist Jules Verne, to the correspondence and diaries of the fur ladies, wives of the grand seigneurs of the HBC and the NWC. Worth noting, Thwaites's *Jesuits Relations* is being put on-line at URL: http://vc.lemoyne.edu/relations/

3 The mythical journey of the voyageurs offers a good illustration of the hero stories so profusely disseminated in the history of fur. The "voyageurs" sometimes knows as "hired men" and "canoemen", and not to be confused with the *coureur des bois* à la Radisson, were mostly French Canadian and Native. P. C. Newman blesses them with the appellation "The Magnificent River Rats" (an early version of the "rat pack" perhaps), stressing the male bonding intimacies tattooing the life of these heroes of the fur trade. As Newman observes: "No smear of their sweat or echo of their ribaldry reaches out to us, yet in their time they were cockleshell heroes on seas of sweet water. Unsung, unlettered and uncouth, the early fur-trade voyageurs gave substance to the unformed notion of Canada as a transcontinental state. Their eighteen-hour paddling days were more wretched than many men then

and now could survive. They were in effect galley slaves, and their only reward was defiant pride in their own courage and endurance." Newman glorifies their resistance to pain and mutilation in the name of the beaver: "Hired to man the canoes through season after season in the Fur Country, they eagerly signed up for unimaginable toil that cracked their backs and ruptured their intestines but never broke their spirit" (Newman 1998: 288–9). The latest revival story of the voyageurs is an Imax film to be released in 2001. Produced by a Franco-Manitoba company (Les Productions Rivard), shot in Winnipeg (home base of the Hudson's Bay Company headquarters) and tied to the local Francophone St-Boniface Festival des Voyageurs, the film will be available in both a French and an English version, featuring a soundtrack of French songs only.

4 Two of the earliest films commissioned by the HBC are *Call of the North* (1930) and *North of Hudson's Bay* (1936). The first one was part of the HBC's exhibit at the 1930 Leipzig exhibition, the first fur trade market in the world; the second is an edited compilation of "home movies" made by HBC employees in northern posts. HBCA: Ref: RG2/3 97 & 98. Also, in the 1950s and 1960s, HBC retained a production company, Crawley Films Ltd., to make educational and PR films. The HBCA in Winnipeg holds copies of two of them: *A Store is Born* (1974), a behind-the-scenes promo film about the HBC retail organization, and *Merchants in the Changing Land* (1969), about life in the north in a modern setting. HBCA Ref: RG3/ 80 (Hudson's Bay Company Archive).

5 Titles by the NFB of Canada included two so-called anti-corporatist documents: *The Other Side of the Ledger: An Indian View of the Hudson's Bay Company* (Martin Defalco and Willie Dunn, 1972), about the 300th anniversary celebration of the company and the overshadowing of native people in the history of the nation; and the docu-drama *Mistress Madeleine* (Aaron Kim Johnston, 1986), produced in the series *Daughters of the Country*. The story set in the 1850s tells the struggle of Madeleine (French-Québec actress Mireille Deyglun), the common-law wife of an HBC clerk who is divided between her loyalty to her "husband" and her allegiance to her brother, a "free" trader in direct conflict with the monopoly trading policy instilled by the all-powerful company.

6 I am referring to Ann Cvetkovich's re-interpretation of Marx's *Capital* and the body at work as a sensational story. See Cvetkovich (1992: 165–204).

7 In contrast, the presence of French colonizers and of La Compagnie des Cent Associés is often described as a global initiative of the Catholic Church, the King of France and some *influent* French businessmen.

8 Dyer describes in these powerful terms the stereotype of the homosocial in the film noir as the sad young man.

9 Newman has authored three best-sellers on the subject, collaborated on several television series and specials on Hudson's Bay, written countless articles for *MacLean's* – always managing to deliver harmonious and sympathetic if not fan-like narratives on the glory of the HBC for "the making-of" beaver land. Newman's most famous contribution to the HBC saga is contained in his three-volume history of the Company: *Company of Adventurers*, *Caesars of Wilderness* and *Merchant Princes*. In the Fall of 1998, CTV and PBS documentaries series produced a two-hour series based on *The Company of Adventurers* and *Caesars of Wilderness*, retitled *Empire of the Bay*. The original two volumes were republished by Penguin Press under the title of the TV series.

10 See Newman wrapped in a British flag on the back cover of his illustrated history of the HBC, *The Company of Adventurers* (1995).

11 See CBC North's documentary about the history of the fur trade, *Company of Adventurers* (Ref CAVA/AVCA 1985–0594). Newman accounts for the 315 year history of the HBC.

12 Peter Lely's 1644 portrait of Rupert, which is part of the National Portrait Gallery in London, made the cover of the 1820 HBC calendar. The portrait is now featured on the HBC website at: URL: www.hbca.ca

13 See notably A. Municchi's (1988) study of men in furs. The book has been translated in French as *Fourrures pour hommes* and in English as *Men in Furs*. Ewing, in *Fur in Dress* and Toussaint-Samat also have sections discussing fur style in men's fashion and culture.

14 Fashion historian M. Toussaint-Samat devotes an entire section in her book (1990) to what she calls the "castorie," a regulated space and system defining the close links between the beaver trail and the modeling of male European fashion. See the chapter entitled, "La croix et les bannières: sur les chemins de la Castorie," pp. 86–101.

15 Coincidentally, Cregar, who was physically imposing with his 6 ft. 3 in. frame and his 260 pounds was actually recruited because of his stunning interpretation of Oscar Wilde in a theatre production. C. P. Wilson: Memo to Mr. Chester and Mr. Rtab, 29 July 1940 HBCA Ref: RG2/7/511.

16 The reference for material related to *HB* can be found in the following files: HBCA Ref: RG2/7 508–16.

17 MacKay died tragically in a plane crash when the script and the film were yet to be completed. His wife took over the historian's job in Winnipeg. She is also the one responsible for the revised edition of the book in 1949.

18 *Jezebel* (W. Wyler, 1938) starring devil queen Bette Davis and Henry Fonda was produced by Paramount, while *Gone with the Wind* (V. Fleming, 1939), featuring the eternal couple Vivien Leigh and Clark Gable was a 20th Century Fox production.

19 DeMille wrote to P. Chester, HBC Head in Winnipeg to inform him of his decision. "We have not, as yet, been able to get from the subject the story that we believe is the right one to tell about the Honorable Company. The subject is still an intriguing one to me, and I shall not give up of finding the right treatment of it for a motion picture. In the meantime, I feel that you should know of my decision not to make it my next picture in order that, if you so desire, you may place the title elsewhere." Rumors in Hollywood were that DeMille had already started *North West Police Mounted* at the time. DeMille to Chester, 5 March 1938, HBCA Ref: RG2/7/510.

20 To the dismay of the HBC headquarters the media splash around *North West Mounted Police* was quite a scene. *NWMP* was released two months before *HB*, and Paramount made a substantial effort to "cover" the Canadian market by sending three of its stars in a promotional tour across the border: Madeleine Carroll, Preston Foster and Lynne Onerman. See "Captivated Winnipegers Won by Visiting Stars." *Free Press*, 23 October 1940, p. 7. Paulette Goddard, probably the biggest star of the crew, was not part of the extravaganza, but in early January 1941, in the middle of the publicity craze around *HB* and Gene Tierney, the Winnipeg *Free Press* ran a glamour story on the actress in the front page of the Saturday magazine edition entitled: "Goddard's Got'em Going" (by Lucille Nieville, 4 January 1941).

21 The war frenzy was gaining and dividing the Canadians along the ethnic line, with the Anglos pro-royalists, and the Francos fiercely opposed to conscription. Next to Muni, the local soldier and proud subject to the King of England, the famous national resources du jour, the Dionne quintuplets, then aged 6, were patriotically displayed as national Francophone ambassadresses of the Canadian Victory Bonds. While Radisson's main purpose was to boost the local and national economy, the heroines of the national war effort, the quintuplets, brought the national commodity up front through their call for a safe and secure war time. In both cases though, fiction and reality played a part in the movement of capital to reinforce national unity and patriotic commercial practices. The ad featuring the quints was sponsored by General Motors of Canada, and ran in Winnipeg's *Free Press* on 23 December 1940. A week later, Eaton's Canada, an important retail store in Canada, and rival of HBC, sponsored an inside in the *Free Press* featuring the Union Jack, a bombardier and a battleship, with the following caption: "God Who Made Thee Mighty Make Thee Mightier Yet." As for Muni, the plan was to bring him to a well-publicized banquet premiere in Winnipeg with the clear objective to send all the proceeds to the war effort. Subsequently, the quintuplets were commissioned for numerous Canadian Victory Bonds campaigns.

22 Most of the correspondence discussing Nute's expertise on Radisson and Groseilliers and her contribution to fleshing out the authenticity of both characters can be found in HBCA Ref: RG2/7/510. Actually initially Nute, then a Fellow at the Minnesota Historical Society, was approached by Paramount who at the time was looking to use her research on Radisson for drafting a screenplay. HBCA Ref: RG/2/7509.

23 MacPherson seems to have triggered the Paramount's decision to withdraw. She held documents loaned by HBC to Paramount for ages, irritating the HBC people, notably MacKay, about this lack of dialogue. Some of the drama filtered into the correspondence between MacPherson and Mackay. More importantly, some of the correspondence showed to what extent the HBC people had no clue of what was going on in Hollywood. In a three-page document: HBC Film – Report on a visit to Los Angeles (5 January 1937), HBCA Ref: RG2/7/509, Chester, general manager for HBC Winnipeg, offers a quite naïve look at the movie magic. Also, strictly on the legal matter, there are a fair number of letters documenting the company's concern for having the name registered for future use in a feature film by Hollywood (Paramount's working title was actually "Hudson's Bay Company").

24 Wilson and the evil Hollywood saga lasted way after the film was over. The papers revealed that Wilson was most amazed by Trotti and the set decorators' liberties in interpreting historical accuracy, ranging from funny accents and dialogues, to landscape aberration and aestheticization of life in the wilderness. In other words, in the fictionalization of the Honourable Company's environment, including the ongoing debate about Fox's decision to draw an idealized portrait of Radisson and to confine Prince Rupert, the historical star of HBC, to a shadow of the wiggy Charles II. Class and imperial ethical codes were also a delicate subject.

25 The "Alice loves Hollywood" correspondence can be found mostly in MacKay's personal file, HBCA Ref: RG2/7/510.

26 The Canadian five-cent coin (the nickel) features the beaver.

27 Interestingly, 20th Century Fox (with Zanuck leading the project) was apparently pushing for a story on G. Simpson ("Lord Strathcona") rather than one on Radisson, to the great pleasure of the governors. This fact is confirmed by a letter from the

the Governor and Committee, London and the Canadian Committee, Winnipeg (16 May 1939), stating that "Believing this to be a considerably better background for a Company film than the Radisson idea, we have been encouraging this development."

See also A. MacKay letter to MacGowan, 3 March 1939, praising Simpson "as a complete success story," over "the elusive rascal Radisson." HBCA Ref: 2/7/510.

28 Letter from MacPherson to MacGowan, 14 February 1939: HBCA Ref: RG2/7/510. The ceremony was also immortalized on newsreels; see footage CAVA/AVCA 1982–0194.

29 Letter to Miss Jeanie MacPherson by Islay Ramona Sinclair, Winnipeg, 3 August 1937. HBCA Ref: RG2/7 509.

30 Seeing MacPherson's voyeuristic interest in Sinclair as potentially scandalous, D. MacKay responded with cool discretion. In a letter to MacPherson (24 August 1937), MacKay barely touched on the sensitive topic, and only mentioned Sinclair's request in a P.S. "I shall wait to hear from you before going into the matter of Ramona Sinclair's letter." Obviously, MacKay was reluctant to bring racial politics (even in its performative expression) to the show. No other trace on this matter was found in the file. HBCA Ref: RG2/7/509.

31 Letter from Sinclair to MacPherson, HBCA Ref: RG2/7/509.

32 Hall (1997) "The spectacle of the other," see 225–90.

33 Letter from MacPherson to Mackay: HBCA Ref: RG2/7 509.

34 Letter to F. Gianfranchi of Pastene Wine and Spirits Co., Boston, Mass., from Turner, 26 September 1940. HBCA Ref: RG2/7/512.

35 I am clearly indebted here to R. Meyer's analysis of Rock Hudson's body and masculinity. See Meyer (1991: 259–88).

36 Wilson was diligently commenting on Trotti's script aberrations, and Trotti was listening albeit distractedly. Dozens of memos and letters of revisions were exchanged between the two men. More importantly, accuracy was the least of Zanuck's concerns as executive producer: atmosphere was the aim, motivated by the tremendous cut to the film budget due to the decrease in American and European revenues in a context of wartime. Second hand costumes were used, etc. See Wilson's memo to Ryan and Chester, 29 July 1940 HBCA Ref: RG2/7/511.

37 Fifteen-minute script for "Hudson's Bay" (over radio, night before premiere showing at Capitol, 16 January 1941) HBCA Ref: RG2/7/514.

38 A. McClintock, for one, draws a strong racial and sexual analogy between a Lacanian vision of women as unrepresentable and the colonial construction of women as the Dark, unknown continent. McClintock argues that "Lacan shares with imperial discourse the image of woman as riddle. All too often, colonials represented the colonized landscape as feminine, unknowable and unrepresentable. So too in Lacanian theory the feminine is an unrepresentable absence effected by a phallic desire that grounds the signifying economy through exclusion. Women become the Dark continent, the riddle of the Sphynx" (McClintock 1995: 193).

39 See Newman's insight in CBC North's documentary *Company of Adventurers* (op.cit.)

40 A. MacKay to MacGowan, 21 November 1938. HBCA Ref: RG2/7/510.

41 *Mocassin Telegraph*, December 1941.

42 Re Muni's marvelous accent (not!), see Lamar Trotti to C. Wilson, 8 August 1940. Also Nute's letter: 'What pleased me most was that the French was good, and especially the broken English as spoken by a Frenchman. Usually actors talk

something that is a mixture between baby talk and pidgin English, which in no way resembled a cultured Frenchman's beautiful accent.'

43 *Winnipeg Free Press*, 18 January 1941, p. 4.

44 Ironically, while some organizations were pushing the patriotic enthusiasm over the edge, the publicity department, led by J.J. Fitzgibbons, in a memo (date unknown) to movie theater managers gave the following instruction: "any inference that [HB] is purely an educational picture should be avoided. Play up romance and drama at every opportunity." HBCA Ref: RG2/7/512.

45 See Mabel Godwin's letter to Wilson from the Department of Mines and Resources, 16 June 1946. Wilson's response (21 June) was harsh and he advised the museum against purchasing the film as "I hesitate to say it is an educational film. It has very little to teach historically." HBCA Ref: RG2/7/512.

46 In a joint venture of 20th Century Fox and Famous Players Canada, the screening map for the film in Québec was established as followed: Loew's Theatre, Montréal 24–30 January; Capitol, Québec: 1–5 February; Cartier, Hull: 16–18 February; Capitol, Rouyn: 16–18 February; Capitol, Trois-Rivières: 16–18 March; Masha, Ste-Hyacinthe: 16–18 March; Granada, Sherbrooke: 9–11 March. Letter to J.J. Fitzgibbons Jr., FPCC, Winnipeg from J. Casey Booker, 20th Century Fox, 14 January 1941.

47 For an insightful, wild, yet detailed script account of the national publicity campaign monitored by HBC Winnipeg, see files HBCA Ref: RG2/7 512, 513, 514.

48 Wilson in a letter to Lamar (27 December 1940) "I am sorry, too, to see that Gene Tierney has such a small part in the end because what she did was done very well, don't you think? I suppose the chief reason for the rewriting of the first part lay in the fact that you had originally intended Lord Crewe to be the principal actor." Crewe was originally written for Tyrone Power. HBCA Ref: RG2/7/512.

49 The film 'avant-premiered' in Vancouver, B.C.

50 Apparently, the response to the premiere in NYC was quite mild, if not annoying, as noted by the Hollywood people (McGineva to Ryan, 13 January 1941). Reviews documented in the HBC files included: Pelswick, R., "Hudson's Bay Has Premiere at Roxy," *New York Journal and American*, 10 January 1941, p. 10; Cameron, K., "Paul Muni Dominates Picture at the Roxy," Daily News, 10 January 1941, p. 42; Crowther, B., "'Hudson's Bay,' a Ponderous Epic, at the Roxy," *New York Herald*, 10 January 1941; Winsten, A., "Hudson's Bay Opens at the Roxy Theatre," *New York Post*, 10 January 1941; Mortimer, L., "'Hudson's Bay Is Pure Hollywood, Except for Scenery," Daily Mirror, 10 January 1941, p. 23; Creelman, E., "'Hudson's Bay,' a Story of Adventure," *New York Sun*, 10 January 1941; Boehnel, W., "Muni Stars in Hudson's Bay. Picture Tells Story of Trading Company," *New York World-Telegram*, 10 January 1941; Ager, C., "Muni Would Play the Rogue," *PM*, 10 January 1941, p.18). Note: a shot of Tierney and not Muni accompanied the articles. However, the Hollywood movie business was much more receptive and intrigued by this other snow movie. See the note from Harry Brand, 20th Century Fox. HBCA Ref: RG2/7/512.

51 Many polite memos and letters were exchanged between the two bureaus, but it is clear that 20th Century Fox was not keen to see its stars becoming dollies for the HBC blankets. For one, Muni was not a Fox star, and Tierney was arguably said to work on another film. On that legal matter involving the Actors Guild, see

Cooper's letter to Gasston, 4 October 1940 and McCarthy to Gasston, 22 October 1940; HBCA Ref: RG2/7/513. Winnipeg responded by disseminating the national fabric across the continent in one of their most aggressive world-wide campaigns – an "HBC goes to Washington" type of stunt. See HBCA Ref: RG2/7 512–514.

52 A major feature of the promotional campaign was the costume and trading artifacts attached to the film. Moreover, the Actors Guild and 20th Century Fox quickly expressed reluctance about the free use of their "goods," and made no secret of the eventual legal and political problems that would result from any association of the studio stars to such traditional HBC trade goods as alcohol, tobacco, etc. HBC insisted on the unique opportunity offered by the national release of the film to promote British merchandise to American tourists and domestic partners, ranging from Imperial Mixture tobacco to HBC handkerchiefs and Hudson's Bay Scotch. All of this commodity circus was orchestrated through star treatment of the blanket. The letter, addressed to J.C. Atkins, Blanket Division in Winnipeg, was from J.W. Richardson Furniture Department, a North Bay (Ontario) retail story which specialized in hardware, sporting goods, radios, etc. HBCA Ref: RG2/7/14.

53 HBCA Ref: RG2/7/14. Atkins to Dodman, 17 January 1941. This is an interesting document and it shows the extent to which the fur retail and warehouse business in Canada was involved in the promotional success of the film as a transnational niche market for the fur trade.

54 *Dayton's*, a Winnipeg fur retailer, had the following: "Presenting Hollywood Fashions: To Thrill all Women," with a picture of Heidi Lamarr "now playing in 'Boom Town'" at the Metropolitan Theatre. As a reflect of the "democratization/popularization" of fur market with a direct-to-female-consumer approach in the 1930s and 1940s, the ad boldly states: "Charge it at no Extra Cost!"

55 Letter by F. Ryan, Manager, Blanket Division to local store managers, 30 December 1940. HBCA Ref: RG2/7/513. Ryan concluded: "this will stimulate great interest in our Company and its products and which should bring you greatly increased tourist business as a retailer of Hudson's Bay 'Point' Blankets."

56 Even today, the HBC still fetishizes the corporate fabric as its most precious historical marker and commodity. As revealed in a recent report in *The Beaver* devoted to considering how the 330-year-old institution is moving into the new millennium, the "Point" blanket stands as the reliable bridge – although slightly altered from its original design. "Has millennium mania affected even as venerable an institution as the Hudson's Bay Company? Well, not quite. But on the eve of the year 2000, the 330-year old company has taken the radical step of – wait for it – introducing new colours in its point blankets. The blanket, first introduced in 1779 as a highly prized furtrade good, has always been either scarlet, green, or blue, or white with green, red, yellow and blue stripes. (Well, when King George VI was crowned in 1937, a limited edition in a new colour was offered, but we digress.) Now fashion mavens, just in time for Christmas shopping, those famous blankets are available in a more contemporary understated chic, charcoal gray with accenting black stripes, and off-white with stripes ranging from light taupe to chocolate brown. In addition to the blankets, the traditional wool coats as well as linens and bedding products will reflect the new colour selection. However, we're not sure if you can trade beaver pelts for one of them. Seems doubtful." *The Beaver*, March 2000.

57 Both Tierney's and Price's letters are filed in HBCA Ref: RG2/7/513. Price marvels more about the cigars and (bad) scotch that HBC sent along with the blanket to all the male stars and executives involved in the production . . . which says a lot about the "style" of the blanket.

58 Museum of Civilisation, Memories, exhibition catalogue, Spring 1997.

59 Ironically, in its economic globalization, the fur trade has always been a matter of immigration.

60 The Nor'westers were the governors of the North West Company, a Montréal-based company founded in 1783 by French and Scottish fur traders to challenge the monopoly of the Hudson's Bay Company.

61 Consistently, the historical narrative of the fur trade has limited the colonial enterprise to a fight between English Lords and French/Francophone Lords, neglecting not only natives and women, but also the direct implications of Americans such as John Jacob Astor in the mapping of the alliances over American fur territory.

62 Two of the prominent ladies were Liza Frulla Hebert, then Liberal government minister and now TV host, and Ginette Reno, popular singer and "spiritual" grandmother of pop music diva, Céline Dion.

63 This association between the Beaver Club and the fashion and cosmetics business did not stop with Watier. In 1997, in the spirit of the theme night "Tweed & Lace and Fashion's Face," the roster for the night featured, the elite of national fashion design "garbed in 18th-century attire": Michel Robichaud, Jean Claude Poitras, Michel Desjardins, Francoise Bouthilier and Thomas Nacos, then president of the Fur Council of Canada, all surrounded by representatives of the animal population, a definitive highlight of these annual dinners.

64 Falardeau directly quotes French-Québec separatist poet and activist Pierre Vallières's famous essay: *Nègres blancs d'Amérique*. The essay that has reached biblical proportions in the context of the Québec independence movement, compares the French-Québécois' servitude to English-Canadian establishment to that of the colonized Africans.

65 Ardent and colorful advocate for the culture and rights of Amerindians, Max Gros-Louis is a popular figure in Québec. Living on the reservation of Loretteville, in the suburb of Québec City, Gros-Louis has been the leader of the Huron-Wendat Nation for a significant period (from 1964–84, and then from 1994 to today).

3 THE EYES OF JUNE SAUER

1 Although this portrait of the two ladies was first published in 1922, it had a second wind when it was reprinted in *Vanity Fair* in 1923. Hence, my interest in re-contextualizing it within the glittering fashion scene of the famous American style magazine.

2 As E. Wilson puts it: "For fashion is more than language. True, it communicates. It is also tactile, visual, it is about touching, surfaces, colors, shapes. It embodies culture" (Wilson 1993: 14).

3 See J. Mulvagh's (1998) preface.

4 Bon d'Allonne, born in France, immigrated in Canada in 1678 and opened a trading post in Kingston (then Fort Frontenac). She became the first woman to own land in Ontario, and quickly became an important fur trader. Mistress of explorer and

"discoverer" of Louisiana, Cavelier de Lasalle, she was quickly ostracized by the other commercial traders, and had a legal battle with the King of France over control of the trade. TVOntario made a docu-fiction of Bon d'Allonne for its series *Témoins du passé*. Ref: CAVA/AVCA 1988–0154. Jeanne Sirbain, immigrated from France in the 1950s, was the first woman to open a store specializing in only fake fur – the store is still in operation today. Caroline Labelle is certainly in a class of her own. Her grandmother started the family fur business (Labelle Fourrures) in the 1930s, and Labelle took over in the 1960s, after her dad. Labelle is one of the most important fur retailers in Montréal attracting a mostly middle-class white clientele (largely Italian, Greek and Portuguese). Famous for her bloody fights with the Fur Council of Canada *and* Brigitte Bardot, Labelle is the grandmother of the women's fur business circle in contemporary Québec. She modeled for Sauer in the 1960s. Isabel Gunn, an Orcadian, passed herself as a man in order to be with her lover, a factor for the HBC. She shipped from Scotland to Canada in 1803 and worked for HBC until being outed as a woman. See the mythical portrait of Gunn by S. Scobie (1987), and the insights by M. Bolus (1971). Annie Mildlige was a Lebanese widow who established herself as a petty fur trader in northern Québec against the HBC monopoly at the beginning of the nineteenth-century (1996). Finally, Marie-Anne Barbel represents a typical case of how women were doing business under the colonial regime in the nineteenth century. Following the religious sisters who were guardians of the financial interests of the Church of France in the new colony, Barbel created her own company in order to keep the family trading business alive after the death of her husband (from 1749–55). For an analysis of Barbel's commercial intervention, see Plamondon (1977).

5 Excerpt from *Mademoiselle* magazine, New York (1948), obituary (J. Sauer personal papers).

6 Max and June Sauer Studio Collection NAC Ref: DAP/ADP: 1989–001.

7 See "Six Photographs by Max Sauer Jr.," *The Beaver*, December 1933; and "Four Arctic Photographs by Max Sauer Jr.," *The Beaver*, March 1934.

8 Though the two companies were merged into the HBC in the 1930s, the trade name of Révillon was still in use.

9 The two other titles of Verne's trilogy are: *Une île flottante* and *Famille sans-nom*. The first is a naive love story; the second, a fictionalized account of the 1837 Patriot Rebellion in Québec.

10 For a recent feminist analysis of Victorian north as a masculinized environment, see (1993) "Nationalism on Ice: Technology and Masculinity at the North Pole".

11 I borrow here the sweet reference to companions from White (1999).

12 *My translation.* "Comment une femme osait-elle s'aventurer là où tant d'explorateurs avaient péri? Mais l'étrangère, confinée en ce moment au fort Reliance, n'était point une femme: c'était Paulina Barrett, lauréate de la Société royale. On ajoutera que la célèbre voyageuse avait dans sa compagne Madge une servante, mieux qu'une servante, une amie dévouée, courageuse, qui ne vivait que pour elle, une Écossaise des anciens temps, qu'un Caleb eût pu épouser sans déroger. Madge avait quelques années de plus que sa maîtresse, – cinq ans environ. Elle était grande et vigoureusement charpentée. Madge tutoyait Paulina, et Paulina tutoyait Madge. Paulina regardait Madge comme une soeur aînée; Madge traitait Paulina comme sa fille. En somme, ces deux êtres n'en faisaient qu'un."

13 See *Canadian Fur Review*, official publication of the Canadian Fur Industry, 1 June

1950. Although the anniversary publication is tame and conventional in its graphic design and iconography, there are some graphic gems to be found that reveal some of the witty minds behind fur advertising in such a conservative context. See for instance the picture of Natural Beaver in the introduction, featuring Carmen Lister, for Arpin-Gendron Limited.

14 Sauer was commissioned by the city of Montréal for the shoot. Montréal mayor Jean Drapeau was preparing to promote the city beauties as a feature of the World's Fair, Expo '67.

15 National sports events also became a substantial source of income for Sauer's studio. Sauer photographed the Commonwealth Games of 1957, in addition to commissions several sport-tourism campaign for the federal government, featuring notably her top model Carmen Lister.

16 Pierre Elliot Trudeau (1919–2000), father of multiculturalism and official bilingualism and grand rival of the Québec separatist movement, was one of the most popular and controversial Prime Ministers of Canada. Young (only thirty-nine) when first elected PM in 1968, Trudeau's extravagant style and tastes made headlines more than once – tastes that included a shared fondness for furs of all kind – made him an honorary fur lady in Sauer's family album. He retired from public life in 1984.

17 The McCord Museum holding of the Notman's collection represents something like 18,000 photographs. For a better estimate and close analysis of Notman's pictorial influence, see J. Bara's dissertation.

18 See *The seal trapping views*, 1866. Sports 7452 Studio Hunting Trapping. Mccord 21956–1.

19 See the two major studies on the subject by J.L. Bara (1986 and 1991).

20 Ironically, the photographs of Queen Elizabeth II wearing the mink coat "live" were spread around the world. Throughout her career Sauer was never involved in photojournalism, and she never photographed fur on the catwalk or during "live" events.

21 S. G. Triggs describes the composites in the following terms: "These were large group photographs produced entirely in the studio, the individuals being photographed separately and the prints cut out and pasted one by one to a large painted background. The final paste-up or composite, often containing close to 300 figures, was then copied and printed in a variety of sizes to be sold to members of the group and the general public alike." See Triggs (1992).

4 MY FUR LADY, OR CANADA'S LIBERTY

1 For a substantial discussion on this question of white settler postcolonialism and national shaping in a Canadian context, see Tamara H. Vukov (2000), *Imagining Canada, Imagining the Desirable Immigrant: Immigration Spectacle as Settler Postcolonialism*, unpublished M.A. Media Studies thesis, Concordia University, Montréal.

2 For an excellent discussion on morality, impurity and national formation in the Canadian context, see Kinsman (1996) and Valverde (1991).

3 It is only recently with the clear erasure of British nationalism in Canada that the Order has shifted to more domestic/national related interventions, and without erasing the distance from the Anglo-Celtic cultural elitism that has constituted

the spice of their mission. Known as fiercely conservative, the Order shamelessly adopted anti-communist and anti-independence positions, standing for colonialism rather than nationalism.

4 For a thorough and quite original argument linking sexuality and race, see Somerville (2000) *Queering the Color Line.*

5 Mbembe pursues his explanation of the economy of death in terms of what the burlesque, the obscene and the grotesque come to signify for the postcolony. "This also accounts for the baroque character of the postcolony: its eccentric and grotesque art of representation, its taste for the theatrical and its violent pursuit of wrongdoing to the point of shamelessness. Obscenity here resides in a mode of expression that might seem macabre were it not that it is an integral part of the stylistics of power" (Mbembe 1992: 21).

6 For a more substantial discussion on the intersections between miscegenation performances and everyday display, see J. Brody's inspiring study of race and Victorian culture (1998), specifically chapter 1, "Miscegenating Mulattaroons."

7 See Whitlock (1995) "Outlaws of the Text." Whitlock reminds us that "The female body has always been crucial to the reproduction of Empire, and deeply marked by it. On the other hand, it can also be at the bosom of de-scribing Empire" (1995: 349).

8 *My Fur Lady's* track record is impressive: it staged 402 performances in eighty-three centres from Charlottetown, Prince Edward Island to Victoria, British Columbia, was seen by an audience of over 400,000, and realized a gross revenue of $900,000. The final show was performed 3 August 1958. The *My Fur Lady* adventure lasted eighteen months, involving close to 500 people.

9 *My Fur Lady: An Original Musical Comedy* ©1957 Quince Productions. Book of the musical by Donald MacSween, Timothy Porteous and Erik Wang.

10 Quince Productions consisted of five McGill Graduates: Brian MacDonald, James B. Domville, Erik Wang, Donald MacSween and Timothy Porteous.

11 See this collective reminiscence of the five *My Fur Lady* creators, McDonald *et al.* (1975), "The Triumph of *My Fur Lady*," 124.

12 Olivia, a professional ballerina, died tragically in a car accident in 1958. Brian MacDonald is still directing at the National Ballet of Canada today.

13 See Brody's (1996) insightful analysis of the mulattaroon.

14 Such pretensions of square/fair deals with the native trappers were the pride of the Hudson's Bay Company and became part of a corporate legend about the so-called "friendly," if not tender ties between the Company employees and the native traders.

15 "I'm into the World" (Roy Wolvin): Act I, Scene 1; "I'm for Love" (by Timothy Porteous, Galt MacDermott: Act II, Scene 4.

16 It is worth noting that one of the ladies (arguably the wife of one of the Quince creators) in charge of clipping and collecting the material related to the production of *My Fur Lady* also clipped an article from *The Gazette* on Vincent Massey, Canada's Governor General and head of the Massey Commission; see Jefferies and Whealen (1959).

17 The most enthusiastic nationalist article was from the *Montréal Star* with the title "National Flag Flies on Quips in Revue's 'Make Believe'," 31 January 1957.

18 On 20 May 1966, eight years after *My Fur Lady* closed, Anna Stuart, on the behalf of the Mary Court Club of Windsor, Ontario, a local social club, wrote to Jim Domville to request the use of the flag backdrop for the Centennial Follies organized

by her club. In a laconic response, Domville explains to Stuart that actually the flag may have been lost or destroyed, and there went the last trace of the once great flag (15 June 1966).

19 Rex (a reporter for the magazine *True Canadian Romances* who acts as the "tutor" and educator for the naive little Aurora): "Well, although New France was conquered by the English, they soon lost interest in the whole business and let the the Scots, who had nothing better to do, come over to exploit the land. One such hardy Scot, James McGill by name, made so much money in the fur trade that he sunk his fortune into education just to claim tax exemption" (Act I, Scene 2).

20 The list of political and cultural figures who attended the repetitive premieres of the musical is quite impressive and puzzling to say the least, and is far too long to reproduce here. Obviously, given the PR angle that the show represented for the producers and crew, each "official" response was carefully filed and can be consulted in the *My Fur Lady* files.

21 See *Free Press*, 7 June 1958, two photos of the fair ladies entertaining little children (boys) from the Winnipeg Children's Hospital; and *The Province* (Vancouver), 24 July 1958 with a photo of the now-professional female leads with three marines and officers.

22 See *Montréal Star*, 9 February 1957, a photograph of Ann Golden (Aurora) and Nancy Bacal (GG's secretary) with the caption: "Feminine Leads in McGill's Revue."

23 Major features included in S. Handman, "A College Revue is Breaking All Records," *Weekend Magazine*, 18 January 1958; M. Gayn, "A Song and a Dance about Canada," *Star Weekly Magazine*, 10 August 1957; and a fashion layout for a back-to-college special photo-report featuring Ann Golden in *The Globe* magazine, 31 August 1957.

24 The women's pages of local newspapers regularly reported on the fur ladies off stage going to attend *My Fur Lady*. See for instance, the *Windsor Daily Star* for three large photo spreads of fur ladies cramming in the door of the local theatre in its 14 January 1957 edition; or again in the Victoria *Daily Times* of 26 July 1958 that features two shots of female theatergoers happily wearing furs in the middle of the summer for the premiere.

25 "'Lady' Proves Canadiana is Fun," *Sault Daily Star*, 16 May 1958; "Don't Be Highbrow," *Ottawa Citzen*, 2 October 1957.

26 "Audiences Love to Peer Into 'My Fur Lady's' Mirror," *Vancouver Sun*, 5 July 1958; "My Fur Lady Delights Capacity Audiences," *The Sudbury Star*, 14 July 1958; "Fur Lady Finds Furs Hot Here," *The Daily Colonist*, 29 July 1958; "Furred Females," *McGill Daily*, 8 February 1957.

27 I am thinking here about Man Ray's famous fur piece, *Le Déjeuner en fourrure de Meret Oppenheim* (1936). The three-part piece is a dish/bowl/spoon all-made-of-fur composition.

28 The beaver tail – similar to a greasy, sticky, sweet crepe – is actually a Canadian delight that is sold in markets and to ice-skaters in Ottawa, as well as Canadian Football League fans across the nation.

29 The circumstances surrounding this creation of the Stratford Fringe festival are a bit vague, but it seems that *My Fur Lady* was the first ever Fringe production at the Festival and that its spectacular popularity and success led to the institution-alization of Fringe as a regular event. Portheous, one of the fab five who would all end up heads of dominant cultural agencies, even wrote a press release following

My Fur Lady's guest appearance at the Fringe: "Is there a future for the Fringe," 11 August 1957. Funny enough, right after "her" triumph at Stratford, *My Fur Lady* was invited to be the main attraction at the fiftieth anniversary of the Royal Alexandra Theatre (1907–57), a major Toronto theatrical institution.

30 See letter Domville to Gélinas, 10 July 1957. It is worth mentioning here that Gélinas's most famous collection of short plays, *Les Fridolinades* (1938–46) was arguably an inspiration for the writers of *My Fur Lady*. Inspired by French burlesque, *Les Fridolinades* is also a sort of medley of musical numbers, satire and nationalist calls for the French-Canadians to stand up and take their place in the sun in the nation.

31 See H. Menzies, "Technological Systems and Canadian Development: The Case of the Fur Trade," in *Canada: The Global Village*, (course packet, Carleton University, Canada).

32 Van Kirk argues that "country marriages" and "country wives" were common terms for the interracial "intimate arrangements" between HBC or North West Company men and their native mistresses. In addition to Van Kirk, many texts have addressed the politics of the interracial economy in critical terms and in the context of 1980s and 1990s feminist studies. However, in the spirit of the 1950s, I was able to retrace a fair number of "journalistic" accounts produced by women for the HBC magazine, *The Beaver*, always eager, even today, to make room for ladies' travel narratives praising beaver culture. See for instance A. L. Johnson, "Ambassadress of Peace," *The Beaver*, December 1952, pp. 42–45; and M. Wilkins Campbell, "Her Ladyship, My Squaw," *The Beaver*, September 1954, pp. 14–17.

33 I have specifically in mind the debutante ball act where princess Aurora is introduced to chi-chi Ottawa (upper-class) society, as the debutante ball carries very few cultural connotations for French-Canadians.

34 Act I, Scene 3.

35 Advertising featuring a mink with pearl and crown, for Morgan's, "Canada's quality department store." *My Fur Lady* Playbill.

36 Slogan for the musical as it appears on the cover of most *My Fur Lady* playbills and posters.

37 *My Fur Lady* was also granted support from various governmental federal agencies and local socialites who gladly enhanced the ambassador role of *My Fur Lady* by bringing the British ambassador, Russians and Americans to see real Canadiana (see the list of contributors and special guests to the various "premieres" as well as for the twenty-fifth anniversary reunion in 1982).

38 This was a radio ad for the retail chain Eaton's to promote the 1947 Eaton's traveling fur collection. Broadcast in October 1947 on the CBC radio show *Women's Digest*, the announcer reminds the ladies that the traveling fur exhibit now in Edmonton will be on display until 21 October, closing his blurb with "The traveling fur style show: 400 models for 400 coats." National Archives, Ottawa, CAVA/AVCA: 1979–0019.

39 The picture, probably shot by one of the crew members, immortalized four fur ladies on Vancouver's beach with their furs and swimming apparel: Joan Stewart, Anne Collings, Carol Morley and Margaret Walter. McGill archives, Montréal, 1958/07, b/w, PR038200.

40 K. Rowe, "Canada's Most Popular Gal? 'My Fur Lady' of Course!" *Brandon Daily*, 4 June 1958, p. 5.

5 BB AND HER BEASTS

1 Bardot's first public action for animal welfare was in 1962 around slaughtering methods in France. As Robinson comments in his biography of the star, *Bardot: Two Lives* (1994): "As early as 1962, Bardot had publicly protested against the treatment of animals in slaughterhouses, the first celebrity in France to take such a stand. She'd pressured the French government to proscribe the more antiquated killing methods then in use, and after a lengthy campaign, saw an act passed that obliged slaughterhouses to use the faster, less painful electric-shock pistols. That legislation came to be known as the 'the BB Law'" (Robinson 1994: 223).

2 *My translation.* "Je suis persuadée que vous pouvez plus que quiconque persuader le public féminin de boycotter des vêtements ou des accessoires obtenus au prix de tant de douleur et d'agonie de l'animal."

3 Actually, during the 1977 episode Bardot phoned and wrote to Pierre Elliot Trudeau, the Canadian Prime Minister several times; see Bardot (1999), and Robinson (1994), and see Trudeau's response in 1978, following another intervention by Bardot from Strasbourg, France against the opening of the seal hunt in A. Krebs, "Notes on People," *The New York Times*, 25 January 1978, p. 13; and Canadian Press, "Trudeau defends sealers," *The Montréal Star*, 17 March 1978, A12.

4 *My translation.* "J'ose donc vous demander un geste, que ce soit simplement une lettre au premier ministre du Canada . . . soit surtout une protestation à la télévision contre l'emploi de ces tragiques peaux de phoques, si inutiles . . . L'appel que je vous fais est particulièrement de saison, puisque la chasse (qui dure de trois à quatre jours, et s'étend du golfe du Saint-Laurent au Labrador) s'ouvre cette année le 18 mars."

5 *My translation.* "En ce qui me concerne, j'avoue que ce monde, déjà à tant de points de vue atroce, où nous vivons, me paraît plus atroce encore quand je pense qu'au moment où je vous écris plus de cinquante mille jeunes animaux dispersés sur la banquise sont destinés à n'être d'ici un mois que des carcasses sanglantes, que leurs mères, qui en ce moment nourrissent ces petits, viendront essayer de reconnaître en émettant des espèces de gémissements, après avoir essayé de les défendre quand ils étaient encore couverts de fourrure et vivants."

6 *My translation.* "Les intéressés se sont bien entendu beaucoup moqués de ces détails 'sentimentaux,' mais les photographies et les témoignages sont irréfutables."

7 A portion of Yourcenar's papers are sealed until 2037, and rumors that Bardot's letters might be part of the hidden correspondence persist.

8 Bardot casually comments: "Marguerite Yourcenar, cette femme merveilleuse, qui est venue spécialement me voir à La Madrague juste après son élection à l'Académie française, parce qu'elle a envie de me connaître, m'a dit qu'elle aussi était végétarienne parce qu'elle ne voulait pas digérer l'agonie" (Bardot 1999: 163).

9 This is the SPCA motto.

10 Statistics on women's involvement in anti-fur advocacy groups are scarce and difficult to obtain. But it is fair to say that the anti-fur movements have strong roots in the history of women's movements with environmental issues. On these specific interconnections, see Adams and Donovan (1995) and (Adams 1994).

11 In countless interviews for television or print media, Bardot repeatedly insists on this mature, aging wisdom that secures her legitimacy as animal advocate, contrasting with the image of infant that dominated her public life while an actress. Even in her memoirs, Bardot frames her involvement in animal causes as being that of a responsible citizen, of a woman with agency.

12 This association between the women's liberation movement, black liberation, sexual/gay liberation, animal liberation and environmental consciousness has a long history within the liberation debate. For a good example of the intertwined holistic approach of human and environment, see Leahy and Cohn-Sherbok (1996).

13 Twenty years later the same company published *Initiales B.B.* and *Le Carré de Pluton*, BB's two-volume memoirs.

14 *S.O.S. Animaux* aired on TFI and lasted three years (1989–92). The show was produced by Figaro PGD Jean-Louis Rémilleux (Bardot 1999: 379).

15 As Robinson puts it: "It was no longer just Brigitte and the seals, it was Bardot versus Canada" (Robinson 1994: 234).

16 This was before Greenpeace dropped the seal hunt from its priority list in 1985, see Pineau (1995).

17 In 1994, it was estimated that the BB Foundation employed a staff of 10 and 25,000 contributing members, with an annual budget of US$900,000 dollars. See Riding (1994).

18 See BB's own interpretation of her "indirect" association with Le Pen as well as her tempestuous declarations concerning national cleansing in *Le Carré de Pluton*. As for the xenophobic and hostile condemnation of Muslim's Aïd-el-Kébir, the letter entitled "La France est devenue la fille aînée de la religion musulmane" is fully reproduced in her memoirs (Bardot 1999: 554–5), and I include here the opening statement: "Le sang des moutons a inondé lundi la terre de France. Des milliers et des milliers de moutons ont été sacrifiés n'importe où, n'importe comment en ce lundi de Pentecôte qui fut, jadis, une fête catholique détrônée aujourd'hui par l'Aïd-el-Kébir puisque la France est devenue la fille aînée de la religion musulmane" (Bardot 1999: 554).

19 The film was released uncut in Québec in 1957 after a legal battle. For a gossipy and "view from inside" account of the battle with both the censors and the Columbia lawyers (then the distributor for North America), see Desmarais (1982).

20 Vadim, for one, made it a point to target women as the real opponents against the release of *Et Dieu* in America. Vadim suavely and sensationally recalls in his autobiography *Bardot, Deneuve, Fonda: My Life with the Three Most Beautiful Women in the World* (1986), that "Committees for the protection of morals were organized in more than a hundred cities to prevent the film from being shown. Sermons in churches and temples threatened Brigitte and those responsible for the 'satanic' work with eternal fires of hell. Women were the most indignant. They were not defending sexual equality but protecting the traditional institutions of marriage and the weaker sex in society" (Vadim 1986: 113). Interestingly enough, one has to ask here if Vadim's account was more informed by his famous mysogyny than by cultural/historical "accuracy."

21 Title for a feature article in the *New York Times*. See Riding (1994).

22 For a romanticized account of an affair to remember, see de Beauvoir (1956) *The Mandarins*, Cleveland: World Publishing, 1956.

23 De Beauvoir hints at a pathological female jealousy when she asserts: "In France,

many women are accomplices of this feeling of superiority in which men persist. Their men prefer the servility of these adults to the haughty shamelessness of BB" (de Beauvoir 1959: 23).

24 This is something that Vincendeau (1992) clearly acknowledged when making her argument about the tension between the new and the old.

25 Vincendeau (1992) does, at least, acknowledge women's role in the fashion economy developed around Bardot the film star.

26 In the National Film Board documentary *Pelts: Politics of the fur trade* (N. Markham, 1990), the pro-fur lobby sketches the following anti-fur activist profile: 25,000–30,000 committed activists in the US only (these numbers do not include the voluntary contributors, by far outnumbering the actual "professional" protesters); 80 percent of animal–fur activists live in urban areas; 84 percent are university graduates, with 25 percent holding an MA or PhD; a large percentage of women involved are childless, and most are politically left-wing in their "tendencies."

27 For a thorough and recent analysis of the Lynx anti-fur campaigns, see Emberley (1998), especially chapter 1, "Simulated Politics."

28 Lee featured in the "Give Fur The Cold Shoulder" campaign in 1997. The billboard featuring a bigger-than-life Anderson naked from the waist up in a snowstorm and showing a bit of a breast was unveiled in Berlin, London and Paris. The New York version of the snow Venus covered up the breast, judging it too risqué. The billboard never appeared in Canada, after Mediacom refused it. See Fink (1997).

29 This financial information was shared with the readers of *Playboy* magazine in a feature portrait of the star. See Maurois (1964).

30 See particularly Foglia (1995) and Gruda (1995).

31 This moment was redeployed in an episode of A & E Biography, released for the sixtieth birthday of the star in 1994. The candid revelation might also suggest that women of "a (un)certain age," because they cannot be attractive anymore, have "gone to the dogs." While for many commentators, such a candid television moment reinforces the reputation of Bardot as an idiot, for me that statement – besides pointing out the hilarious analogy between pets and men – emphasizes the tremendous control that Bardot now maintains over her private life as a retired star.

32 My translation. "En fait, les bénéficiaires de ces 'bonnes chasses' sont avant tout les compagnies (surtout norvégiennes) organisées en vue de la chasse aux fourrures, les habituels intermédiaires, et la balance commerciale du gouvernement canadien, et la plus grande partie de la chasse se fait par brise-glace et par hélicoptères appatenant aux susdites compagnies" (Yourcenar 1995: 282).

33 Bardot's crude confessions about her traumatic motherhood and disgust for the idea of giving birth and her disdain of marriage in the first tome of her memoirs, was not only well-publicized in the media, but led to a lawsuit by her first husband Jacques Charrier and her own son, Nicholas. See Agence France Presse "Pas si bêtes, l'ex-mari et le fils de BB," *La Presse* 25 January 1997, D16.

34 The similarities between discourses of "life" and anti-fur politics in their targeting of women is troubling, and is linked to the relation between nature and nurture as an essential character and mission of women in the preservation of the race. I intend to explore this further in my new project on beastly politics.

35 *My translation.* "Le petit livre Noonoah était sorti et se vendait bien au profit de Greenpeace. Pour Noël, nous espérions qu'il ferait un tabac auprès des enfants."

36 Nanook was another landmark of French sponsorship as Flaherty's documentary was funded by Paris furriers Revillon Frères, see chapter 2.

37 This is what Bardot maintains in her memoirs (1999).

38 P. Mahe, "Bardot, la madone des bêtes sacrifiées," *Paris-Match*, no 2193, June 1991, pp. 76–83. In this interview, Bardot presents herself has a fierce believer in God, and a repentant sex-symbol who devoted her soul and money to animals.

39 In relation to the eugenics connection, I develop this idea in my new funded SSHRCC (the Social Science and Humanities Research Council of Canada) research project on beastly politics and healthy nations, "The Clean Nation".

40 The March of Dimes is the national not-for-profit organization whose mission is to improve the health of babies by preventing birth defects and infant mortality. Founded in 1938, the March of Dimes funds programs of research, community services, education and advocacy that save babies. Their Web site: www.gatorbabies.org. Their motto: Saving Babies Together.

41 See also "March of Dimes–Funded Animal Experiments: An Overview," Reviewed by Peggy Carlson, MD – "Extent, Cost, and Types of Animals Used." URL: www.charitiesinfo.org

42 The cleavage between immigrants, natives, settlers and so called Québécois *de souche* offers an important locus to think about the nationalist and xenophobic rhetoric that tainted both advocacy poles. Interestingly, the demographics about the commercial fur trade in Montréal reveal that historically the trade has been structured along ethnic divisions of labor and market. While mostly dominated in its whole by Jewish interests – incidentally on the international market as well – the French-Québécois are more in the retail business, and the Greeks in the manufacturing. See Thibault (1987: 117–24).

43 *My translation.* "Apprenant avec une tristesse infinie que les Canadiens avaient mis fin au moratoire de huit ans interdisant la chasse aux pauvres bébés phoques, reprenant cette année (i.e. 1994) leur terrifiant massacre, j'organisai à la hâte avec Frank (Weber), une conférence de presse . . . Je n'en croyais ni mes yeux ni mes oreilles. Après tant d'énergie dépensée depuis des années pour que cesse enfin ce montrueux massacre, voilà que tout recommençait comme si je n'avais rien fait, comme si c'était normal, alors que le monde entier, écoeuré, s'était révolté, montrant du doigt les Canadiens pour cette inadmissible et cruelle chasse. Mais depuis d'autres révoltes et d'autres écoeurements avaient fait la Une des journaux, on avait oublié les petits blanchons et leurs cadavres qui ensanglantaient les banquises canadiennes, et on en profitait pour rattraper le temps perdu. On brûlait les sorcières au Moyen Âge . . . On massacre les bébés phoques en 1995 . . ."

44 IFAW is the strongest international opponent of the commercial seal hunt. Lately, IFAW has revised its position regarding aboriginal hunt, and no longer opposes this traditional native activity.

45 See Stukin (1997). However, now most of the converted ones have traded their skins for furs: Armani, Donna Karan, Christian Lacroix, Calvin Klein, Dolce & Gabbana, and So Sui are now all standing by the wild child and tattooed fur kid: Jean Paul Gaultier. See "Back from Siberia," *New York*, July 1997, p. 20–1.

46 My favorite star endorsement of the PETA naked poster campaign came from Patti Davis. People would remember that in the early 1990s, Patti's mother, former first lady Nancy Reagan, whose taste for furs were as ferocious as her zeal for the White House, was a favorite target of animal-right activists. Davis's photo ran on

the day the Republican-majority Congress opened on 4 January 1994, and was featured in the *Washington Times*. See "Reagan's daughter takes it off for animals," *The Gazette*, 13 December 1994, A-6.

47 *My translation.* "Une marquise italienne qui avait posé nue il y a un an dans une campagne d'affichage contre les manteaux de fourrure a demandé cette année à son mari, l'ancien commissaire européen a l'Environnement Carlo Ripa di Meana, de passer lui aussi à l'acte. La dernière publicité de la filiale italienne du Fonds international pour le bien-être animal montre en effet le couple s'enlaçant nu sous des draps avec le slogan: "Pauvres petites choses. Ils achètent les fourrures car ils n'ont personne pour leur tenir chaud." Carlo Ripa, un ancien dirigeant de l'ancien parti des Verts, a accepté de participer à cette campagne pour rappeler aux hommes qu'ils portaient eux aussi leur responsabilité dans l'achat des fourrures. "Trop souvent, ce sont les maris, ou les amants, qui offrent une fourrure à leur partenaire car ils sont incapables d'offrir de l'amour, de la chaleur et de l'affection", a-t-il expliqué dans un communiqué. Marina, son épouse, a déclaré qu'elle avait porté des fourrures par le passé mais y avait renoncé après avoir trouvé "la paix" avec son mari. L'an dernier, la marquise avait posé nue, les poils pubiens bien en évidence, avec le slogan: "La seule fourrure dont je n'ai pas honte." (*Le Devoir* 1997.)

48 Gaultier's fights with BB have been notorious, and the wild child of French couture is a fierce defender of the use of furs in his collection. In 1997, Bardot wrote an open letter, denouncing Gaultier's use of a red fox bolero in his 1997 July collection, stating that using fur was both "revolting and repugnant." Gaultier's fashion house made a laconic response, reminding the star that the July collection contained not only one bolero, but two: one in red fox, the other in silver fox. (AFP, "Bardot terms Gaultier 'a boorish lout' in fur bolero row," 19 November 1997). As for Loren, Bardot's attack happened in 1994 when the Italian diva signed up an exclusive contract estimated at $1 million with the Italian furrier Annabella. Bardot's open letter to Loren concluded dramatically in these terms: "Don't forget that when you have a fur coat, you're wearing a cemetery on your back." See Neill *et al.* (1994).

49 Seal penises are used in the manufacture of an aphrodisiac. Mostly directed at Asian markets, the sales of seal penises – until recently simply thrown away – represented a profitable business for sealers. See Arcand (1995).

50 Bardot's response to her detractors was to offer camera lenses the happy faces of herself and d'Ormale. See her interview with H. J. Servat (1997) and Bardot (1999).

51 *L'Europe veut notre peau* aired Sunday, 14 September 1997, as a feature of *Le Point* Grands Reportages.

52 Dolbec (1995) and Lacroix (1995). Worth a note: Lacroix was *La Presse*'s fashion columnist.

53 On 22 March 1995, Pierre Brassard, host of an afternoon show on the Montréal-based French-language commercial radio station CKOI-FM and leader of the humorist group "Les Bleu Poudre" managed to trap Bardot in a media prank highlighting her lack of awareness of Canadian and Québécois political scene. For his live show, Brassard telephoned BB at home in France, pretending to be the Premier of Québec and leader of the separatist Parti Québécois, Jacques Parizeau. Passing as Parizeau and pretending to be sympathetic to her cause, Brassard/Parizeau asked BB if she would promote Québec independence from Canada in exchange for a ban on baby seal hunting. BB hastily agreed to such a "fair deal."

The story hits its peak when, two days later, the same Brassard called Bardot again, this time assuming the persona of Prime Minister of Canada, Jean Chrétien. Brassard/Chrétien promised Bardot support from his government if she would stand against the sovereignty of Québec. In an understandably puzzled and confused state, BB tried to kill two birds with one rock and suggested rather to include in the deal both Canada's magnificence and Québec's sovereignty. Curiously, while most of the observers ridiculed Bardot, they downplayed the fact that this is exactly where a lot of Québécois place their political allegiance: at the fringe of the two national borders, in a state of total contradiction between federalism and separatism. See Colpron (1995).

54 The first commercial seal hunt took place in 1754.

55 Tobin, or "Mr. Seal," was the colorful premier of Newfoundland, and one of the most fierce political adversaries of the international protests against the seal hunt on the coast of Labrador (a Newfoundland territory), and against tight federal quotas that restrict the commercial seal hunt. As if his voice were not loud enough, Tobin makes a point of appearing in seal fur gear everywhere there is a camera.

56 While in 1950 Canada had an estimated seal population of 3 million, in 1998, the Newfoundland's Fisheries Minister estimated that the population had reached 5.4 million. This ecological "unbalance" argument has been one of the most aggressive strategies used by the partisans of a complete lift of ban on seal hunts (Canada has gradually loosened up its quotas for the seal hunts since 1994).

6 VENUS FOREVER

1 The fur district consists of twelve warehouses and 725 little shops, regrouped along two tiny streets east of The Bay store. Originally located in the Old Montréal, the fur district moved to its actual location after the crash of 1929. Even today it is estimated that 70 percent of the entire national production of fur is concentrated here.

2 For a portrait of the situation in the late 1980s and early 1990s, see the analyses of M. Tremblay, "La fourrure à rebrousse-poil," *La Presse*, 15 February 1990, D3; and G. St-Jean," La concurrence du tiers-monde coûte cher aux ouvriers montréalais," *La Presse*, 5 September 1990, D9. St-Jean reports that according to the statistics provided by two major fur worker unions, numbers are down from 1,700 members in 1985 to 208 in 1990.

3 The national scream is a wink at the NFB short, *The National Scream* – in French, the sassy title is *La Fièvre du castor* – (Robert Awad, David Verrall, 1980). This 28-minute over-the-top satire of Canadian politics and its obsession with the beaver is probably the most insightful document produced on the odds of the beaver for Canadian culture. Using animation and pseudo-documentary style to investigate Canada's obsession for "national identity," the film ridicules the quest of the beaver as national symbol. The national scream refers to the "intrigue" of the film when the famous muncher escapes Parliament Hill, creating a true "national scream" as Canada loses its symbol, i.e., its identity.

4 Which means 500,000 beavers. See "Fur Facts," a promotional brochure of the FCC. Also, beaver pelts are getting a better price: from $24.50 in 1999, the price for the precious pelt is now back up to $32 (it was $40 in 1986).

5 See B. Luscombe, "Warming Up to Fur," *Time*, 19 October 1998, p. 66–68.

Meanwhile in Canada, according to the FCC exports have increased 67 percent between 1996–99 to reach a total of $269 million (against $400 million in 1986).

6 See J. Christman, "Fur finding favor? Fashion tells us – again – that wearing animal skins is OK. But others say no way," *The Arkansas Democrat-Gazette*, 19 December 1997, E1. According to the last report by the FCC, this number is now up to 200, see their Web site: www.furcouncil.ca

7 *Fur: the fabric of a nation*, a 26-minute "educational" video produced by the FCC in 1999, aimed at ages twelve to adult. As the promo says: "Ideal for social studies, ecology, Canadian history, economics, current affairs, media studies, fashion design".

8 "You'll feel comfortable in Fur" appeared in most newspapers across the nation, as well as in popular entertainment weeklies such as *Voir* and *Mirror*, where the readership (450,000 in the case of Voir) is not usually the fur-lover type.

9 In contrast, PETA claims a half-million followers.

10 *Fur: the Fabric of a Nation*, video produced by the FCC.

11 This conjuncture is no coincidence: 1993 really marked a break for the fur industry. Exports of Canadian fur garments climbed 24 percent over previous years, and mink, beaver and other benchmark fur prices increased between 25 and 50 percent on international fur auctions, the latter acting as the barometer of the industry. See "Fur is Hot Again, export figures show. And brown is the color of choice, fur show participants say," *Toronto Star*, 12 May 1994, J7.

12 As part of its 1992 fur comeback marketing, the FCC bought more than 70 pages of advertising for Canadian fur collections to be splashed in American and Canadian magazines. The FCC did receive government funding for the US campaign in US *Vogue* (a first), and the usual Canadian partners, *Flare*, *Châteleine*, and *Clin d'Oeil*. See L. Binsse, "Relance de la fourrure canadienne," *La Presse*, 20 October 1992, C2.

13 Zuki Furs is basically the backbone of the new fur industry that aims quasi-exclusively at a US market. With exclusive contracts with Nieman-Marcus, Bergdorf Goodman and Bloomingdales, the Zukis are the leaders of haute-couture fur in Canada, and their sales rely on exports. Zuki's sales are estimated at between $4 and $6 million per year (1994), with less than five percent in Canada. See G. McLaughlin , "Fur is Hot: High Fashion and international demand mean Canada's first industry is making a comeback," *The Financial Post*, 1 February 1994, p. 20.

14 The Bay for one, after it abandoned fur for good in 1991, reopened its fur salons in stores in Winnipeg, Toronto and Montréal with grandiloquent publicity in the fall of 1997.

15 C.A.L.I.C.O. closed in 1999 after eleven years in the exclusive design and retail business. The store was also selling in major American markets, such as New York and San Francisco.

16 Ironically, the same accessories could be seen in the fancy windows of Holt Renfrew, or worse, in the street windows of that powerful symbol of colonial grandeur in the core of the fur district: The Bay, the retail face of the Hudson's Bay Company (HBC), as well as at the all-time fur bunkers.

17 For a similar take but in a different context on the participation of women in the national fashion industry during the German occupation in Paris during the World War II, see L. Taylor, "Paris Couture, 1940–44," in *Chic Thrills*, op. cit., pp. 127–44.

18 The Harricana phenomenon (named after the river in Québec used by fur traders in early colonization) is a team of two women designers, Mariouche Gagné and Mylène Laroche. Gagné with her collection Harricana North Pole claims that she basically recycles 2,000 fur coats every year, selecting the pelts and cuts herself, reshaping and redesigning mostly accessories out of them. While Lishman's garments are made out of the best beaver pelts, Gagné is the perfect example of the desacralization of the fur hierarchy: for her, fur is a practical fabric before being chic. Because the fur coats are literally dismantled and ripped apart, her technique is to sell fur by its colour first, then by its species, which results in the production of a very cheap collection for a popular international market – mostly Asian. Customers order by colour (she uses five) rather than by animal.

19 For the record, at the 1996 NAFFEM, out of 95 Canadian retailers or designers represented at the fur salon, only seventeen were women. In comparison, eleven out of fifty-one of the American representatives were women; and six out of seventeen Italian exhibitors were women. As for subsidies, various programs – federal, provincial and municipal – are made available to young entrepreneurs, most of them for promotional budgets, tax breaks and commercial visibility. Gagné, for one, has received the three levels of funding, including a start-up grant from the Montréal Mayor's Foundation.

20 Among them was a graduate of Lasalle College, Thibault, who along with two partners basically launched the vintage market in Montréal and brought it to the level of an extremely lucrative tourist microeconomy in the Plateau–Mont-Royal area of Montréal, before dismantling her little empire three years ago, closing shops and concentrating her commercial activities in fewer venues.

21 For instance, Gagné's 2000 catalogue for her two collections Harricana Sport and Harricana Lux listed fourteen different accessories.

22 For a succinct analysis of Diesel's parodic anti-fur advertisements, see Emberley (1998). Speaking about 1992's Hot to Control Wild Animals and 1994's Pet Shop, Emberley makes this interesting comment: "Diesel Jeans advertisements parody the righteous tone of much of the Lynx and PETA promotional literature, appealing to a consumer perceived as too sophisticated to be taken in by the naive strategies of an increasingly socially conscious 'green' marketplace. Your needn't buy fur coats, but you can still spend a small fortune on designer jeans. Fashionable activism demands fashionable 'active wear'," (Emberley 1998: 13).

23 The volume of reports is overwhelming and far too big to be reproduced here. Nevertheless, in the thousands of documents gathered for this chapter (from five different database search engines – French and English – cataloguing hundreds of fashion magazines, periodicals, trade journals and newspapers across North America and Europe), fur has consistently reappeared at the peak moments of the season: i.e., in the fall (for the Winter retail season); and in the Summer – in a more discreet coverage – while high-fashion designers launched their Fall/Winter collections.

24 As some examples of this fake chic: see "Vive la Fausse Fourrure," *Clin d'Oeil*, no 79 (January 1987); "Le Grand Frisson," Clin d'Oeil, no. 124 (October 1988); "Fausses Fourrures: Trop Belles pour être vraies," *Clin d'Oeil* (December 1989); more recently, "Chic Synthétique," *Clin D'Oeil*, no 140 (February 1992); and finally this amazing article in the very popular Québec consumer advocacy magazine by M. Blinda, "La Simili-Fourrure," *Protegez-Vous* (October 1982): 32–37.

25 Here two typical examples as shown in *Clin d'Oeil*: following the article on "Vive

la Fausse Fourrure" (1987) was a full-page advertisement for an apricot fox fur coat by Laflamme Fourrures. The report "Fausses Fourrures" (1989) was preceded by two "real" fur advertisements from McComber, "Brrr . . . " (fox) and Rosa Mori (mink).

26 For instance, an advertisement in a Québec-French newspaper of the 1930s (*L'Action catholique*) for a children's mock-fur ensemble praised the easy-to-clean, easy-to-wear, easy-to-protect quality of the fake over the real.

27 This image of castration is powerfully associated with the beaver lifestyle. The beaver male, when hunted and feeling the end draw near, cuts off his testicles and literally leaves them to its predator, hoping that its trail won't be followed.

28 As a mark of the merging of the faux and the authentic, Paule Race from Fourrures Georges Pouliot (Québec City), one of the oldest traditional fur houses still in operation (since 1914), used both fake and real fur in her designs.

29 The popularity of fur among middle-aged and elderly women is noticeable through the attention given to consumer awareness articles such as those published regularly in senior's magazines. For instance, see G. Girard, "L'achat d'une fourrure: Une affaire de coeur, mais aussi de raison," *Le Bel Age* 3: 1 (October 1989): 66–9. The article features a woman in her fifties, showing off a coat from Labelle Fourrure (a long time favorite among white middle-class Francophone women in Montréal). See also the "preserving your coat" guideline article by M. J. Lacroix, "Pour mieux protéger vos fourrures," *Le Bel Age*, 9: 6 (March 1996): 80–1.

30 Gaultier's Eskimo girl blessed the cover *Women's Wear Daily* on 4 March 1994.

31 As an indication of the fur craze in fashion magazines, *Marie-Claire* (France), *Clin d'Oeil* (Québec), *Flare* (Toronto), *Elle* (France and Québec), *Chatelaine* (Québec), *Vogue* (US), *Harper's Bazaar* (US), *Fashion Almanac* (US), and *Vanity Fair* (US), all ran special fur advertising sections in their October and November 1997 issues. Interestingly, most of the sections favoured a traditional if not classic representation of women in furs, as the headings suggested "Portraits de femmes avec fourrure" (*Marie-Claire*), "Vénus aux Fourrures" (*Clin d'Oeil*), "That Touch of Mink" (*Vogue*), and the special American Legends campaign, "The Real Thing" (*Vanity Fair*).

32 This is a great advertisement by Goff that actually captures the definite shift in pro-fur agency strategies. With a picture of Goff himself, the ad clearly integrates the new ecological twist with a statement from the designer: "I believe strongly in the use of natural fur that is cultivated through the proper methods of farming and conservation. Nothing compliments the senses more completely than real fur. *Some things you just can't fake!*" (*Fashion Almanac* November/Winter 1997).

33 *Eco-News* is one of the latest of them all. Targeting elementary and high-school students, the series of videos and think-smart games designed by the FCC are funded jointly by Québec, Ontario, and Newfoundland and Labrador Divisions.

34 I am referring here to the 60-second television spot on John Cabot produced by the CRB Foundation Heritage Project: As described in the commemorative video promotional kit: "Voyaging from England to North America in 1497, Captain John Cabot and his sailors encounter the Grand Banks of Newfoundland with cod fish so thick they slow the ship." The CRB Foundation is a private foundation initiated by Charles R. Bronfman, and since 1991 the CRB Heritage minutes have been created as a joint venture between the Ministry of Heritage and the Bronfman's foundation.

35 The FCC, while surrounded by an army of PR women, is closely monitored by Alan

Herscovici, son of a Jewish Hungarian furrier. Spokesperson of the FCC, writer and broadcaster, Herscovici has been a long time pro-fur advocate. Among numerous publicized interventions is *Second Nature: The Animal rights Controversy* (1985), a collection based on a three-part series that aired on CBC Radio Program "Ideas."

36 See "The people's Queen says no to fur," *Evening Standard*, 17 July 1998, p. 10.

37 In fact, as far as the fur industry is concerned, the targeting of female buyers started as early as the late 1930s, as I mentioned in chapter 2.

38 The other 1970 Blackglama girls being Rita Hayworth, Maria Callas, Barbara Stanwyck and Rosalind Russell.

39 Lishman's husband, Bill Lishman is internationally reknowned for his sculptures on wild Canadian birds. His real-life experience as Father Goose has been freely adapted in the 1996 Hollywood production *Fly Away Home* starring Jeff Daniels.

40 See Lishman International's Web site: www.atouchoffur.com

41 The yarn was first launched at the 1998 Creative Needlecraft show in Toronto, and the reaction was "astonishment." "In the 1970s, Paula Lishman developed a process to create a warm and comfortable double-faced fur fabric. This was accomplished by cutting a rabbit pelt from the outside into a narrow strip. The strip was then twisted and used as a yarn that can be knit, crocheted, woven or used as trim. Over the past 25 years, we have developed a strong, washable yarn from beaver, fox, mink and muskrat and reinforced it with a natural fibre core. Combining the luxury of fur with the simplicity of a yarn that can be used to trim or create your own knits, we are now offering this unique product to the general public."

42 Lishman's promo on URL: www.atouchoffur.com

43 See the report on Reggie Largo's 1992 collection in *Clin d'Oeil*, November 1992, p. 73–93, "L'Amérique des Légendes." Largo whose mother was Metis and his dad Italian, hit the fashion trade with a collection reclaiming his native American roots.

44 For an extensive discussion of the event, see Emberley (1998: 174–85).

45 Mary Tyler Moore, a long-time animal lover, publicly gave up her fur coats in the late 1980s.

46 See Emberley's reading of *Unzipped* in the *Cultural Politics of Fur* (1998), pp. 161–68.

47 See Lori's brief bio at URL:
http://www.escape.ca/~mawa/postcards/lorib/bioblb.html

48 Blondeau, artist statement: Betty Daybird Bio (1997).

49 *The Loney Surfer Squaw* is loosely inspired by a portrait of Betty Daybird/Blondeau from her youth (source: Betty Daybird Bio).

50 *Sport Illustrated*'s 1998 swimsuit issue featured two fake-fur bikinis: model Laetitia Casta dresses in a Domani's leopard pattern bikini, and in a brown fake-fur bikini by Montréal store "La Maison de la Fausse Fourrure."

51 My favorite fur bikini lady is actually posing on the cover of a pulp novel by L. Shepard (1963) *Devils Dance in Me*, Chariots Book. The drawing shows a blonde white woman lasciviously posing with a puffy orange bikini with the title in bright red color with the following trailer: "Her body ruled her brain. She lived in a town where female flesh was willing, waiting – and dirt cheap." She, like the Lonely

Surfer Squaw is now a Web card, and can be found on the Web site of Astounding Graphics URL: www.astoundingcards.com ref D-05041.

52 Saga Furs of Scandinavia promotional kit for Miljkovitch's 1994 collection, *Ethnic Light*.

BIBLIOGRAPHY

Adams, C. J. (1994) *Neither Man nor Beast: Feminism and the Defense of Animals*, New York: Continuum.

Adams, C. J. and Donovan, J. (eds) (1995) *Animals and Women: Feminist Theoretical Explorations*, Durham and London: Duke University Press.

Amon, R. (1985) "Saving fashion for posterity", *Newsday*, 4 August 4: 3, 10.

Anderson, B. (1983) *Imagined Communities: Reflections on the Origin and Spread of Nationalism*, London: Verso.

Anthias, F. (1992) *Ethnicity, Class, Gender and Migration: Greek Cypriots in Britain*, Aldershot, Brookfield, VT: Avebury.

Arcand, D. (1995) "Le pénis de phoque, un sujet délicat", *La Presse*, 23 March: A1–7.

Arendt, H. (1958) *The Human Condition*, Chicago: Chicago University Press.

Arpin, C. (1994) "Local SPCA recruits Bardot to aid fundraiser", *The Gazette*, 20 December 20: A 3.

"Back from Siberia", *New York*, July 1997: 20–1.

Bara, J. L. (1986) *Furs in Fashion as Illustrated in the Photo-Portraiture of William Notman in the 1860s*, unpublished M.A. Art History thesis, Concordia University, Montreal.

Bara, J. L. (1991) *The Image of Canada: Iconological Sources of Canadian Popular Symbolism nineteenth-century souvenir photographs*, unpublished Ph.D. dissertation, Concordia University, Montreal.

"Bardot terms Gaultier 'a boorish lout' in fur bolero row", *Reuter News*, 19 November 1997.

Bardot, B. (1978) *Noonoah le petit phoque blanc*, Paris: Grasset & Fasquelles.

Bardot, B. (1997) *Initiales BB. Mémoires*, Paris: Grasset.

Bardot, B. (1999) *Le Carré de Pluton. Mémoires*, Paris: Grasset.

Beauvoir, S. de (1956) *The Mandarins*, Cleveland: World Publishing, 1956.

Beauvoir, S. de (©Esquire 1959; 1972) *Brigitte Bardot and The Lolita Syndrome*, New York: Arno Press and the New York Times.

Berton, P. (1975) *Hollywood's Canada: The Americanization of Our National Image*, Toronto: McClelland and Stewart.

Bertrand J. and Y. B. Morin (1966) *Le guide vestimentaire de la femme: les secrets du chic*, Montréal: L'institut de la féminité.

Binsse, L. (1992), "Relance de la fourrure canadienne", *La Presse*, 20 October: C2.

Blanchard, T. (1998) "The fur flew at the couture collections in Paris", *The Independent* 22 July.

Blinda, M (1982) "La simili-fourrure" *Protegez-Vous*, October 1982: 32–7.

Bloom, L. (1993) *Gender on Ice: American Ideologies of Polar Expedition*, Minneapolis and London: University of Minnesota Press.

Bolus, M. (1971) "The Son of I. Gunn", *The Beaver* (Winter): 23–26.

Bone, J. (1998) "Poaching by 'fur hag' thwarted", *The Times* 25 April.

Bonko, L. (1997) "PETA has won the support of many stars in Hollywood, but not the PETA it wants", *The Virginian-Pilot*, 20 August: E1.

Bougrain-Dubourg, A. (1978) *L'agonie des bébés phoques* (preface by B. Bardot), Paris: Presses de la Cité.

Bougrain-Dubourg, A. (1986) *Et Dieu créa les animaux* (preface by B. Bardot), Paris: Robert Laffont.

Bourget, J.M. (1977) "Feuilleton pour un massacre. Bardot l'injure: 'Canadiens Assassins'", *L'Aurore*, 18 March: 2.

Boyer, P. (2000) "Organon: sur Le Toucher, Jean-Luc Nancy, de Jacques Derrida", *Les Temps Modernes* 609 (July–August): 349–58.

Brody, J. D. (1998) *Impossible Purities: Blackness, Femininity, and Victorian Culture*, Durham and London: Duke University Press.

Brookes, R. (1993) "Fashion photography: the double-page spread: Helmut Newton, Guy Bourdin and Deborah Tuberville", in J. Ash and E. Wilson (eds) *Chick Thrills: A Fashion Reader*, Berkeley and Los Angeles: University of California Press.

Buck-Morss, S. (1989) "Mythic history: fetish." *The Dialectics of Seeing: Walter Benjamin and The Arcades Project*. Cambridge, MA: MIT Press.

Certeau, M. de (1968) *La prise de la parole*. Paris: Desclée Brouwer.

Certeau, M. de (1990; ©1980) *L'invention du quotidien: 1. Arts de faire*, Paris: Gallimard.

"Chelsea Girls [fun furs]", *Harper's Bazaar*, November 1998: 20.

Christman, J. (1997) "Fur finding favor? Fashion tells us – again – that wearing animal skins is OK. But others say no way," *The Arkansas Democrat-Gazette*, 19 December: E1.

Clarke, E. O. (2000) *Virtuous Vice: Homoeroticism and the Public Sphere*, Durham and London: Duke University Press.

Colpron, S. (1995) "Brigitte Bardot mord à nouveau à la ligne des Bleu Poudre", *La Presse* (March 25): B-10.

Coombe. R. J. (1996) "Embodied trademarks: mimesis and alterity on American commercial frontiers", *Cultural Anthropology* 11, 2: 202–24.

Cooper, C. (1997) *Magnificent Entertainments: Fancy Dress Balls of Canada's Governors General 1876–1898*, Fredericton N.B & Hull Qc: Goose Lane Editions and The Canadian Museum of Civilization.

Corriveau, S. (1993) "Les commercants cherchent à rejoindre une plus grande clientèle: Le marché de la fourrure en pleine mutation", *Le Soleil*, 26 October: C3.

Cvetkovich, A. (1992). "Marx's *Capital* and the mystery of the commodity", in *Mixed Feelings: Feminism, Mass Culture and Victorian Sensationalism*, New Brunswick, N J: Rutgers University.

Day, D. (1970) "It has been one giant step for womankind", *Style: The Canadian Women's and Children's Wear Newspaper*, 7 June: 7.

De Lauretis, T. (1990) "Eccentric subjects: feminist theory and historical consciousness" *Feminist Studies* 16, 1: 115–50.

Deleuze, G. (1968) *Différence et répétition*, Paris: PUF.

Derrida, J. (2000) *Le toucher, Jean-Luc Nancy*, Paris: Galilée.

Desmarais, J. P. (1982) *Révélations d'un survenant du cinéma*, Montréal: Les Editions Lumières.

Dolbec, M. (1995) "Bardot repart en guerre", *Le Devoir*, 21 March: A 2.

Dyer, R. (1993) "Coming out as going in: the image of the homosexual as a sad young man", *The Matter of Images: Essays on Representations*, London: Routledge.

Dyer, R. (1997) *White*, London: Routledge.

Ellman, R. (1988) *Oscar Wilde*, New York: Alfred A. Knopf.

Emberley. J. (1998) *The Cultural Politics of Fur*, Montréal and Kingston: McGill-Queen's University Press.

Ewing, E. (1981) *Fur in Dress*, London: B.T. Batsford.

Farquharson, D.N.G. (1934) "The Beaver Club", *The Beaver* (September): 34, 66.

Fink, M. (1997) "The insider", *People*, 10 November: 55.

Foglia, P. (1995) "L'écologie avec le bâton", *La Presse*, 23 March: A5.

Francis, D. and Morantz, T. *Partners in Furs: A History of the Fur Trade in Eastern James Bay 1600–1870*, Montréal and Kingston: McGill-Queen's University Press.

Francoeur, L.G. (1995), "Le Syndrome de Bambi", *Le Devoir*, 22 March: A1.

"Fur day & night", *Harper's Bazaar* (October 1997): 234–45.

"Fur is hot again, export figures show. And brown is the color of choice, fur show participants say." *Toronto Star*, 12 May 1994: J7.

Fur Trade Associations (1951) *Canadian Fur Review 1950–51* vol. IV

Gagnon, Myriam (1994) "La Fourrure reprend du poil de la bête", *Elle Québec* (November): 85–92.

Gayn, M. (1957) "A song and a dance about Canada", *Star Weekly Magazine*, 10 August: 12–14.

Gingras, S. (1994) *A Century of Sport: Hunting and Fishing in Quebec*, St-Raymond: Les Editions Rapides Blancs, Inc.

Girard, G. (1989), "L'achat d'une fourrure: Une affaire de coeur, mais aussi de raison", *Le Bel Âge* (October) 3,1: 66–9.

Graham, D. (1998) "Let the fur fly: Paula Lishman", *The Toronto Star*, 6 August.

Grenier, L. and J. Guilbault (1997) " 'Créolité' and 'Francophonie' in Music: Socio-Musical Repositioning Where It Matters", *Cultural Studies* 11, 2: 207–34.

Groom, A. (1998) "Fur and feathers fly as Paris catches jungle fever", *The Scotsman*, 20 July: 22.

Gruda, A. (1995) "Le péché d'esthétisme", *La Presse*, 22 March: B2.

Hall, S. (1996) "When was the post-colonial? Thinking at the limit", in I. Chambers and L. Curti (eds), *The Post-Colonial Question: Common Skies, Divided Horizons*, London: Routledge.

Hall, S. (1997) *Representation: Cultural Representations and Signifying Practices*, London: Sage.

Handman, S. (1958) "A College Revue is Breaking All Records", *Weekend Magazine*, 18 January: 16,18.

Haraway, D. (1989) *Primate Visions: Gender, Race, and Nature in the World of Modern Science*, London and New York: Routledge.

Herman, M. (1997) "Nothing's shocking", *Spin* 13, 9: 138–45.

Herscovici, A. (1985) *Second Nature: The Animal Rights Controversy*, CBC Enterprises/Les Enterprises Radio-Canada, Toronto, New York, London.

"Hot for the holidays [the right muff]", *Wallpaper* (November/December 1998).

223

Hutchinson, B. (1997) "Raging rivers? For sure! Park Ave. attack on sable coat", *Daily News*, 17 December: 8.

Innis, H. A. (1956, ©1930) *The Fur Trade in Canada: An Introduction to Canadian Economic History*, Toronto: University of Toronto Press.

Irigaray, L. (1985) "Women on the market", in *This Sex Which Is Not One*, trans. Catherine Porter with Carolyn Burke, Ithaca, NY: Cornell University Press.

Jacobs, J. (1999) "A sexually confused national symbol", *Ottawa Citizen*, 7 July: A1–2.

Jefferies, M. and P. Whealen (1959) "Massey made crown more than symbol in Canada", *The Gazette*, 27 July: 17–18.

Jenson, J. (1999) "From silence to communication? What Innisians might learn by analysing gender relations", in C. R. Acland and W. J. Buxton (eds) *Harold Innis in the New Century: Reflections and Refractions*, Montreal and Kingston: McGill's – Queen's University Press.

Johnson, L. (1952) "Ambassadress of peace", *The Beaver* (December): 42–5.

Kaplan, C. (1995) "A world without boundaries, the Body Shop's trans/national geographics" *Social Text* 43: 45–66.

Kapsalis, T. (1997) *Performing Gynecology from both Ends of the Speculum*. Durham and London: Duke University Press; and Somerville (2000).

Kelcey, B. E. (1994) *Jingo Belles, Jingo Belles, Dashing through the Snow: White Women and Empire on Canada's Arctic Frontier*, unpublished Ph.D. History dissertation, University of Manitoba, Winnipeg.

Kinsman, G. (1996) *The Regulation of Desire: Homo and Hetero Sexualities*, Toronto: Black Rose Books.

Knowles, R. P. (1995) "From nationalist to multinational: The Stratford Festival, free trade, and the discourses of intercultural tourism", *Theatre Journal* 47: 19–41.

Konopnicki, S. (1995) *Eloge de la fourrure: petit traité du poil lustré*, Paris: Seuil.

Krebs, A. (1978) "Notes on people", *The New York Times*, 25 January: 13.

Labelle, C. (1974) *La fourrure*, Montréal: Editions de l'homme.

Lacroix, M. J. (1996) "Pour mieux protéger vos fourrures", *Le Bel Âge* (March), 9: 6: 80–1.

Lacroix, L. (1995). "Bardot repart en guerre: l'ambassadeur de Canada à Paris refuse de la recevoir", *La Presse*, 12 March: A 1–2.

Lamson, C. (1979) *Bloody Decks and a Bumper Crop: The Rhetoric of Sealing Counter-Protest*, Newfoundland: St-John's Memorial University of Newfoundland: Institute of Social and Economic Research, Social and Economic Studies 24.

Lavigne, L. (1993) "Bon chic, pas cher . . . la rage du recyclage", *La Presse*, 11 September: C3.

Leahy, M. and Cohn-Sherbok, D. (eds) (1996) *The Liberation Debate: Rights at Issue*, London and New York: Routledge.

Le Collectif Clio (1992, ©1982) *L'histoire des femmes au Québec depuis quatre siècles*, Montréal: Les Éditions Québec Loisirs.

Le Devoir (1997) "La Marquise et la fourrure", 15 March 1997, C9.

Lender, H. *et al.* (1994) "Gaultier: Eskimo Chic", *Women's Wear Daily*, 4 March: 1, 6–9, 18–19.

Leney, P. (1996) "Annie Mildige, Fur Trader", *The Beaver* (June–July): 37–41.

Lewis, R. (1996) *Gendering Orientalism: Race, Femininity and Representation*, London: Routledge.

Loomba, A. (1998) *Colonialism/Postcolonialism*, London: Routledge.

Luksic, V. (1986) "Cinq soeurs dans la peau" *Châtelaine* 27, 10 (October): 61–3.

Luscombe, B. (1998) "Warming up to fur", *Time*, 19 October: 66–8.

Mackey, D. (1948, ©1936) *The Honourable Company: A History of the Hudson's Bay Company*, Toronto: McClelland and Stewart.

Mackay, E. (1999) *Cultural Politics and National Identity in Canada*, London: Routledge.

Madoui, L. (1993) "Ecologique, la fausse fourrure?" *Science & Vie* 905 (February): 111.

Mahe, P. (1991) "Bardot, la madone des bêtes sacrifiées", *Paris-Match* 2193 (June): 76–83.

Marabout Flash (1964) *Je choisis mon manteau de fourrure: le luxe à la portée de tous*. Paris: Gérard et Co., Verviers.

Maslin, J. (1995) "A madcap maestro of haute couture." Review of *Unzipped*, dir. Douglas Reeve. *New York Times*, 4 August: C1.

Maurois, A. (1964) "BB: the sex kitten grows up", *Playboy* (July): 87.

Mavor, C. (1999) *Becoming: The Photographs of Clementina, Viscountess Hawarden*. Durham and London: Duke University Press.

Mbembe, A. (1992) "The banality of power and the aesthetics of vulgarity in the postcolony", *Public Culture* 4, 2: 1–30.

McClintock, A. (1992) "The angel of progress: pitfalls in the term 'post-colonialism'", *Social Text* 31–32: 84–98.

McClintock, A. (1995) *Imperial Leather: Race, Gender and Sexuality in the Colonial Contest*, London: Routledge.

McDonald, B. *et al.* (1975) "The triumph of *My Fur Lady*", in E. A. Collard (ed.), *The McGill You Knew: An Anthology of Memories 1920–1960*, Don Mills, Ontario: Longman Canada Limited.

McLaughlin, G. (1994) "Fur is hot: high fashion and international demand mean Canada's first industry is making a comeback, *The Financial Post*, 1 February: 20.

McRobbie, A. (1989) "Second-hand dresses and the role of the ragmarket", in *Zoot Suits and Second-Hand Dresses: An Anthology of Fashion and Music*, London: Routledge.

McRobbie, A. (1998) *British Fashion Design: Rag Trade or Image Industry?* London: Routledge.

Merck, M. (1993) *Perversions: Deviant Readings*, New York: Routledge.

Meyer, R. (1991) "Rock Hudson's body", in D. Fuss (ed.) *Inside/Out: Lesbian Theories, Gay Theories*, New York and London: Routledge.

Mills, S. (1995) "Discontinuity and postcolonial discourse", *Ariel: A Review of International English Literature* 26, 3: 73–88.

"Mock mink man-made", *Life* 5 December 1955: 72–8.

Monahan, I. (1994) "Fur crazy: furry, blurry line between the real and the fake as designers mix it up", *The Gazette*, 3 May: D1.

Monahan, I. (1995) "Fur on the fringe", *The Gazette*, 21 November: C1.

Monahan, I. (1996) "For Sauer, shooting was an art", *The Gazette*, 24 September: B3.

Morris, M. (1984) "Identity anecdotes", *Camera Obscura* 12: 41–65.

Morris, M. (1993) "Panorama: the live, the dead and the living", in G. Turner (ed.) *Nation, Culture, Text: Australian Cultural and Media Studies*, London and New York: Routledge.

Mulvagh, J. (1998) *Vivienne Westwood: An Unfashionable Life*, London: HarperCollins Publishers.

Municchi, A. (1988) *Homo in pelliccia*, Modena: Zanfi Editori.

225

Nadeau, C. (1996) "BB and the Beasts: Brigitte Bardot and the Canadian seal controversy", *Screen* 37,3: 240–50.

Neill, M. *et al.* (1994) "Showing her claws", *People Weekly*, 42, 9: 85–7.

Newman, P. (1985) *The Company of Adventurers*, Markham, Ontario: Viking.

Newman, P. (1989) *Ceasars of Wilderness*, Markham, Ontario: Viking.

Newman, P. (1992) *Merchant Princes*, Toronto: Penguin Books.

Newman, P. (1995) "The kingdom of the bay", *Maclean's*, 15 May: 39.

Newman, P.C. (1995) *An Illustrated History of the Hudson's Bay Company*, Toronto: Madison Press Book/Viking Studio Book, 1995.

Newman, P.C. (1998) *Empire of the Bay: The Company of Adventurers that Seized a Continent*, Toronto: Penguin Books.

Olson, K. M. and Goodnight, G. T. (1994) "Entanglements of consumption, cruelty, privacy, and fashion: the social controversy over fur", *The Quarterly Journal of Speech* 80, 3: 249–76.

Parry, B. (1987) "Problems in current theories of colonial discourse", *Oxford Literary Review* 9 (1–2): 27–58.

"Pas si bêtes, l'ex-mari et le fils de BB", *La Presse*, 25 January 1997: D-16.

Picard, G. (1986) *L'enfer des animaux*, (preface by B. Bardot), Paris: Le Carrousel-FN.

Pickles, C. (1996) *Representing Twentieth Century Canadian Colonial Identity: The Imperial Order Daughters of the Empire (IODE)*, unpublished Ph.D. Geography dissertation: McGill University.

Pineau, Y. (1995) "Bardot récolte peu d'appuis au Québec: Greenpeace dit avoir d'autres chats à fouetter", *La Presse*, 22 March: A4.

Plamondon, L. (1977) "Une femme d'affaires en Nouvelle-France: Marie-Anne Barbel, veuve Fornel", *Revue d'Histoire de l'Amérique Française* 31, 2: 165–86.

Pratt, M. L. (1992) *Imperial Eyes. Travel Writing and Transculturation*, London and New York: Routledge.

Probyn, E. (1996) *Sexing the Self*, London and New York: Routledge.

Ray, A. J. (1990) *The Canadian Fur Trade in the Industrial Age*, Toronto: University of Toronto Press.

"Reagan's daughter takes it off for animals", *The Gazette*, 13 December 1994: A-6.

Renan, E. (1990, ©1882) "What is a nation?" in H. K. Bhabha (ed.) *Nation and Narration*, London: Routledge.

Riding, A. (1994) "And God created an animal lover", *The New York Times*, 30 March: C1, 8.

Rioux, C. (1996) "Et Dieu créa B.B.", *La Presse*, 28–29 September: A1.

Robinson, J. (1994) *Bardot: Two Lives*. London, Sydney, New York: Simon & Schuster.

Rogers, P. (1979) *What Becomes a Legend Most? The Blackglama Story*, New York: Simon and Schuster.

Rosaldo, R. (1989) "Imperialist nostalgia", in *Culture and Truth: The Remaking of Social Analysis*, Boston: Beacon Press.

Rowe, K. (1958) "Canada's most popular gal? '*My Fur Lady*' of course!", *Brandon Daily*, 4 June: 5.

Roy, V. (1996) "Rétrospective d'une photographe de mode", *La Presse*, 2 October: C6.

Sacher-Masoch, L. V. (1967) *La Vénus à la fourrure*, Paris: Éditions de Minuit.

Sandoz, M. (1964) *The Beaver Men: Spearheads of Empire*, New York: Hastings House, Publishers.

Sansfaçon, J.R. (1995) "La belle, la bête et la ministre" *Le Devoir*, 24 March: A10.

"Sauvons les bébés-phoques", *Paris-Match* 1033 (February 1969): 1, 70–75, 82.

Scobie, S. (1987) *The Ballad of Isabel Gunn*, Kingston: Quarry Press.

Seidner, D., Harrisson, M. and D. Edkins (1996) *Lisa Fonssagrives: trente ans de classiques de la photo de mode*, Munich, Paris, Londres: Schirmer/Mosel.

Servat, H. J. (1997) "Je ne fait pas de politique, je défends les animaux . . . de droite comme de gauche." *Paris Match* 2514 (31 July): 32–5.

Servat, H.-J. (1989) "BB ouvre la chasse aux chasseurs! La fée des animaux vient à TF1 pour tenter de désarmer les 'prédateurs du dimanche'", *Paris-Match* 2110 (2 November): 86–9.

Shohat, E. (1991) "Gender and culture of Empire: toward a feminist ethnography of cinema", *Quarterly Review of Film & Video*, 13, 1–3: 45–84.

Shohat, E. (1992) "Notes on the postcolonial", *Social Text* 31–2:

Singer, P. (1975) *Animal Liberation*, New York: Avon Books.

Solomon-Godeau, A. (1996) "The other side of Venus: the visual economy of feminine display", in V. de Grazia, with E. Furlough (eds), *The Sex of Things*, Berkeley, University of California Press.

Somerville, S. B. (2000) *Queering the Color Line: Race and the Invention of Homosexuality in American Culture*, Durham and London: Duke University Press.

Sones, M. (1998) "Rag time north of the border", *New York Post*, 13 March: 52.

Spivak, G. C. (1988) "Can the subaltern speak?", in C. Nelson and L. Grossberg (eds) *Marxism and the Interpretation of Culture*, Urbana, IL: University of Illinois Press.

Spivak, G. C. (1996) "Subaltern talk: interview with the editors (1993–94)", in D. Landry and G. Maclean (eds) *The Spivak Reader*, London and New York: Routledge.

Spivak, G. C. (1999) *A Critique of Postcolonial Reason: Toward a History of the Vanishing Present*, Cambridge and London: Harvard University Press.

Stabile, C. (1992) "Shooting the mother: fetal photography and the politics of disappearance", *Camera Obscura*: 28: 179–205.

Stacey, J. (1994) *Star Gazing: Hollywood Cinema and Female Spectatorship*, New York and London: Routledge.

Steele, V. (1997) *Fifty Years of Fashion: New Look to Now*, New Haven and London: Yale University Press.

Stein, Gertrude (1923 ©;1972) "Miss Furr and Miss Skeene", in C. V. Vechten (ed.) *The Selected Writings of Gertrude Stein*, New York: Vintage.

St-Jean, G. (1990) "La concurrence du tiers-monde coûte cher aux ouvriers montréalais", *La Presse*, 5 September: D9.

Stoler, A. L. (1997) "Making empire respectable: the politics of race and sexual morality in twentieth-century colonial cultures", in A. McClintock, A., A. Mufti, and E. Shohat (eds) *Dangerous Liaisons: Gender, Nation and Postcolonial Perspectives*, Minneapolis: University of Minnesota Press.

Stukin, S. (1997) "Animal rites", *US* (August): 88–95.

Taylor, L. (1993) "Paris couture, 1940–44", in J. Ash and E. Wilson (eds) *Chic Thrills: A Fashion Reader*, Berkeley and Los Angeles: University of California Press.

The Imperial Order Daughters of the Empire, Golden Jubilee 1900–1950, Toronto: T.H. Best Printing Co.

"The people's Queen says no to fur", *Evening Standard*, 17 July 1998: 10.

The Softest Touch: What Every Woman Should Know about Fur, New York: The Fur Information and Fashion Council., 196?.

"The thrill is back", *Vogue* (September 1997).

Thibault, D. (1987) "Fourrure: un secret bien au chaud", *Commerce* (April): 117–24.

Tobing Rony, F. (1996) *The Third Eye. Race, Cinema, and Ethnographic Spectacle*, Durham and London: Duke University Press.

Toussaint-Samat, M. (1990) *Histoire Technique & Morale du vêtement*, Paris: Bordas.

Tremblay, M. (1990), "La fourrure à rebrousse-poil", *La Presse*, 15 February: D3.

Triggs, S. G. (1992) *William Notman's Studio: The Canadian Picture*, Montréal: McCord Museum of Canadian History exhibition catalog.

"Trudeau defends sealers" *The Montreal Star*, 17 March 1978: A 12.

Tyrrel, R. (1997) "Why British women will never slip back into fur", *The Evening Standard*, 4 December: 21.

Vadim, R. (1986) *Bardot, Deneuve, Fonda My Life with the Three Most Beautiful Women in the World*, trans. M. C. Porter, New York: Simon and Schuster.

Valverde, M. (1991) *Age of Light Soap and Water: Moral Reform in English Canada, 1885–1925*, Toronto: McClelland & Stewart.

Van Kirk, S. (1980) *Many Tender Ties: Women in Fur-Trade Society, 1670–1870*, Watson & Dwyer Publishing: Winnipeg.

Verne, J. (1985) *Le pays des fourrures*, Montréal: Stanké.

Vidal, G. (1998) *The Smithsonian Institution*, San Diego, New York and London: Harcourt Brace & Company.

Vincendeau, G. (1992) "The old and the new: Brigitte Bardot in the 1950s France", *Paragraph: The Journal of the Modern Critical*, 15, 1: 73–96.

Vincent-Ricard, F. (1989) *Objets de la mode*, Paris: Du May.

Vukov, T. H. (2000) *Imagining Canada, Imagining the Desirable Immigrant: Immigration Spectacle as Settler Postcolonialism*, unpublished M.A. Media Studies thesis, Concordia University, Montreal.

Ware, V. (1992) *Beyond the Pale: White Women, Racism and History*, London: Verso.

White, P. (1999) *Uninvited: Classical Hollywood Cinema and Lesbian Representability*, Bloomington and Indianapolis: Indiana University Press.

Whitlock, G. (1995) "Outlaws of the text", in B. Ashcroft, G. Griffitths, and H. Tiffin (eds) *The Post-colonial Studies Reader*, London: Routledge.

Wilkins Campbell, M. (1954) "Her ladyship, my squaw", *The Beaver* (September): 14–17.

Williams, R. (1983) "The culture of nations", in *The Year 2000*, New York: Pantheon Books.

Wilson, C. P. (1936) "The Beaver Club" *The Beaver* (March 19–24): 64.

Wilson, E. (1993) "Fashion and the postmodern body", in J. Ash and E. Wilson (eds) *Chick Thrills: A Fashion Reader*, Berkeley and Los Angeles: University of California Press.

Wintour, A. (1997) "Letter from the editor: high contrast", *Vogue* (September): 34, 48.

Yourcenar, M. (1995) "À Brigitte Bardot", in M. Sarde and J. Brami (eds) *Lettres à ses amis et quelques autres*, Paris: Gallimard.

Yuval-Davis, N. (1997) *Gender & Nation*, London: Sage.

Yuval-Davis, N. and Anthias F. (1992) *Racialized Boundaries: Race, Nation, Colour and Class and the Anti-racist Struggle*, London: Routledge.

Archives

Notman's Archives, McCord Museum, Montréal
Max and June Sauer Collection, National Archives of Canada, Ottawa
Hudson's Bay Company Archives, Manitoba National Archives, Winnipeg
McGill's Archives, Montréal
Centennial Library, Winnipeg Library Archives

INDEX

Virtuous Vice 12
Vive la fausse fourrure 178
Vogue 87, 91, 177, 179–80

Wallpaper 192
Ware, V. 103, 116,
Watier, L. 61–2
Watson, P. 146
Weaver, S. 146
Webber, G. 120
Weber, F. 138, 149, 153, 155
Weiland, J. 12–3
Wellman, W. 37, 188
Westwood, V. 70, 72, 170
What Becomes a Legend most?
white: anglophone nation 116; colonial
    supremacy 141; femininity 103;
    procreation of the race 19 *see also*
    sexualization

whiteness 111, 114 *see also* white
Whitlock, G.
Wilde, O. 33–4
Wildfur Council 186
William Notman Studios *see* Notman
    Studios
Williams, R. 118, 175
Wilson, C. 41–2, 46, 51, 60
Windsor Local Council of Women 123
Wintour, A. 167, 179
Wolfson Foundation 156
Women's Wear Daily 177, 179, 189

York Factory 44
Young, L. 188
Yourcenar, M. 135–7, 150, 154
Yuval-Davis, N. 21

Zuki 168, 173